W9-BIU-693

NOV 1993

BOUNTIFUL
O·H·I·O

Bountiful Ohio

Good Food and Stories from Where the Heartland Begins

James Hope
Story Author

Susan Failor
Recipe Author

Cover painting by Paul Patton

"Faces of the Land"
Photographed by Barbara Vogel

Designed by Gene Hite and Dean Kette

Consulting Editor for Recipes:
Janet Wood

Gabriel's Horn  Publishing Co.

Bowling Green, Ohio

About the Cover, "Family Reunion on the Farm":

Paul Patton, a folk artist in Maple Heights, and author James Hope reached deep into their memories to produce this view of an American ritual: the family get-together each summer back at the home place. There are games, of course, more food than anyone can eat, and lots of gossip. Through the clang of the horseshoes and the rattle of the dishes you can hear the dialogue: "Hasn't Lottie's boy grown!" and "Do you suppose Evie is expecting *again?*" Of course she is, and a lot of other things have changed since last year, all part of the cycle of birth, life and death that annually rearranges the ranks in the traditional family snapshot. But three things never change at a farm picnic: (1) the men always drift together to talk baseball, cars, and crops; (2) there will be *many* jellied salads; (3) the aroma drifting by from the cow barn won't let you forget where you are. *(Painting photographed by Barbara Vogel)*

About the Frontispiece:

By the Fourth of July or thereabouts, Ohio's ten thousand acres of sweet corn have begun ripening into lusciousness and backyard chefs are rejoicing. If you are very lucky, an Ohio corn princess like Hess Metcalf may help you gather the bounty. Act quickly, though, for childhood is fleeting: enough time has passed so that the young lady in the picture is now a student at Yale, proving that good Ohio corn and Eastern ivy can grow together. *(Photographed by Gregory Thorp)*

Gabriel's Horn Publishing Co., Inc.
P.O. Box 141
Bowling Green, Ohio 43402
Editorial and business office: 419/352-1338
Orders only: 800/235-HORN (that's 4676)

Printed in the United States of America.

00 99 98 97 96 95 94 93   15 14 13 12 11 10 9 8 7 6 5 4 3 2

Softcover: ISBN 0-911861-05-X
Hardcover: ISBN 0-911861-06-8

Acknowledgement of the sources of various illustrations will be found at the end of this book.

Contents

Recipe Finder viii

Preface
Exploring Inner Space xi

Chapter One
In Search of Bountiful 2:
A stranger in a strange land might try filling the vacancy in his soul by eating. But to get the flavor of Ohio, you must taste *the state as well.*
Faces of the Land: Parker's Place 10.

Chapter Two
Green and Yellow Magic 14:
Ohio is where the Corn Belt begins. Corn grows everywhere, giving the state color, shape and texture. And it pops up in your life more than you think.
Faces of the Land: The Good Earth of Tom Carpenter 20.
Corn and Other Recipes 23.

Chapter Three
Peaceable Kingdoms 30:
Three groups of religious seekers came to Ohio to establish their own heavens on earth. The Zoarites and Shakers disappeared long ago, but the Amish keep on growing.
Faces of the Land: Sevilla's World 36.
Amish and Other Recipes 40.

Chapter Four
How Pigs Built a City, and Other Pork Tales 48:
Speaking plainly as always, Harry Truman said, "No man should be allowed to be President who does not understand hogs." Ohioans understand hogs.
Faces of the Land: Mr. Pork 54.
Pork and Other Recipes 57.

Chapter Five

Common Ground 66:
They're not just crossroads of commerce. Old-fashioned public markets are where people *get together. All kinds of people. In Cleveland, you can hear their accents today.*

Faces of the Land: The Haunted Fruit Stand 72.
Ethnic Recipes 75.

Chapter Six

Looking for Johnny Appleseed 86:
One of America's cherished myths turns out to be something more than that. In Ohio you'll find messages from the past that may surprise you.

Faces of the Land: Finding Johnny Ipil-Seed 92.
Apple and Other Recipes 96.

Chapter Seven

Big Ag and Little Ag 106:
Something's happening down on the farm: new farmers are emerging, old ones are changing, and they're all sassing each other. It's getting hot out there.

Faces of the Land: Life Among the Vegetables 115.
Farm Recipes 120.

Chapter Eight

Return of the Vines 132:
Once upon a time, Ohio was America's leading source of wine. Much of the glory has moved elsewhere, but a comeback is possible: there's a ferment in the land.

Faces of the Land: Farmer with a Vision 138.
Recipes Using Wine 142.

Chapter Nine

The Mother of All Food Plants 152:
Ohio doesn't just raise food, it cooks, condenses, freezes, fries, grinds, cans, preserves, jellies, processes and moves it. Lots of it. Look in your pantry.

Faces of the Land: Going for the Glory 160.
Brand-Name Recipes 163.

Chapter Ten

The Two Universes of Tomatoes 172:
Ohio, home of both the backyard tomato and its industrial big brother, is fertile ground for a clash of tomato cultures. Why can't people learn to co-exist?

Faces of the Land: Angel of the Black Swamp 178.
Tomato and Other Recipes 182.

Chapter Eleven

The Fairest State of All 190:
For good old-fashioned country fairs, come to Ohio. But to eat from the landscape, come to its festivals. To understand food in Ohio, go to both.

Faces of the Land: The Man Who Loves Fairs 196.
Fair and Festival Recipes 199.

Afterword

She's a Beauty 204.

Index 207.

We Made This Book 210.

Ordering Information 212.

Recipe Finder

All recipes are also indexed at the back of the book.

HERB ENTHUSIASTS are advised that recipes of special interest to them are marked with an *.

Beverages

Hot Cider Punch 96
Meier's Sparkling Catawba Punch 143
One-Day Root Beer 47
Plain People's Lemonade 47
Shamrock White Sangria 142

Appetizers

Black Forest Sauerkraut Balls 78
* Boursin Cheese 121
Chalet Debonné Famous Shrimp Dip 142
Cheerios Toasted Party Mix 164
Delia's Guacamole 83
Mexican Salsa 182
Montezuma Deluxe Nachos 163
* Stuffed Nasturtiums 120

Soups

Alta's Hearty Vegetable Soup 40
Autumn Harvest Soup 97
* Beside the Point's Split Pea Soup 122
* Chilled Melon Soup 124
Corn Chowder 23
Matzo Balls 84
Matzo Ball Soup 84
* Sausage and Kale Soup 123
* 3 Islands Madeira Cheesy Chowder 144
Tomato Bisque 183

Salads, Dressings and Condiments

Apple Butter 104
* BLT Salad with Creamy Herb Dressing 183
Corn and Pasta Salad 24
Grandma Failor's Cranberry Relish 105
Heinz Super Burger Sauce 164
* Herb Butter 122
* Marinated Tomato Slices 184
* Ohio Apple Maple Chutney 97
* Ohio Field Greens with Sprouts and Orange Segments 121
Old-Fashioned Corn Relish 23
* Tomato & Green Bean Salad with Lemon Vinaigrette 184
Tomato Butter 182
* Waldorf Slaw Salad 164
* Wendy's Pesto 120

Main Dishes

Apple Cashew Pasta 99
Apple-Stuffed Pork Loin with Raspberry Sauce 98
* Beef and Roasted Vegetable Kabobs 62
Bison Stew 126
Bob Evans Farms Hearty Meat Loaf 165
Breaded Pork Chops and Tomato Gravy 59
Chef Tom's Honey Apple Chops 166
Chicken Fricassee with Tomato Dumplings 63
Chikwich Sandwich 63
Christophers Marinara Sauce 187
Cincinnati Chili 80
* Cindy's Fire and Ice Pasta 189

* Firelands Braised Beef Noir 150

Fluffy Rice and Chicken 41

* Freshwater Farms Rainbow Trout with Orange-Basil Sauce 130

George Voinovich's Favorite Pork Chops 96

* Grilled Lamb Markko 146

* Harpersfield Chicken 151

* Heritage Grilled Breast of Chicken and Sauce 64

Honey-Mustard Marinated Pork Tenderloins 57

Janet's Smoked Pork Chops with Apples and Onions 59

Johnny Marzetti 165

Karen's Favorite Chicken Bake 64

Leniwe Pierogi 79

Pastichio 81

Porcupine Meatballs 61

Portage Hills Chinese Chicken and Peanuts 147

Preble County Barbecued Pork Chops 57

Rider's Inn Lake Erie Walleye 127

Rossi Pasta with Peas, Onions and Eggs 167

Rothschild Pork Chops with Raspberry Sauce 58

Salisbury Steak 60

Sara's Amish Dressing 40

Savory Pork Chop Bake 58

Shaker Corned Beef and Cabbage 42

Smucker's Apricot Chicken 166

Southern Peach Pork 60

* Sunnyside Farms Roast Leg of Lamb Dijon 126

Swiss Steak 61

Tomato-Onion Sauce 85

Tony Packo's Hungarian Stuffed Cabbage 85

Turkey Cutlets in Catawba Cream Sauce 143

* Valley Vineyards Pork Ragout 145

* Veal Romano 65

* Vince, Maxine and Judy's Spaghetti Sauce 76

Walleye White Walleye 146

Wm. Graystone Wine Omelet 149

Zesty Barbecue Beef Sandwiches 62

Vegetables and Side Dishes

Caponata 75

Corn Pudding 27

Corn Bread Sausage Stuffing 27

Corn Spoon Bread 24

Fresh Country Fried Corn 29

Fresh Tomato Pasta Sauce 187

Fried Green Tomatoes 188

German Potato Pancakes 78

* Hartmut Handke's Oven-Roasted Tomatoes 186

* Herb-Topped Tomatoes 185

* Homestead Grilled Mushrooms 123

Lennie's Fried Okra 83

Neva's Dilled Green Tomatoes 188

Pareve Noodle Kugel 84

Peerless Mill Inn Corn Fritters 26

Potatoes Supreme 41

Red Cabbage 76

Roasted Corn with Seasoned Butters 29

* Rosemary Scalloped Potatoes 125

Sauteed Zucchini with Walnuts 125

* Scalloped Tomato Casserole 185

Spaghetti Squash with Garlic and Parmesan 124

Spatzle 42

Succotash 28

Summer Vegetable Medley 28

Tomato Pudding 186

Breads and Rolls

Apple-Pumpkin Streusel Muffins 105

Baking Powder Biscuits 131

Cheesy Corn Bread 25

Corn Pone 130

Heartland Corn Bread 25

Marilyn's Yeast Rolls 200

Milan Inn Corn Sticks 26

Moravian Sugar Cake 82

Peach Mountain Muffins 103

Sheila's Banana Bread 201

Strawberry Coffeecake 200

Walnut and Poppy Seed Kuchen 77

Zucchini-Oatmeal Bread 202

Desserts

Apple Pie Bars 128

Aunt Ruth's Concord Grape Pie 151

Biddie's German Apple Cake 100

Buckeyes 203

Campbell's Tomato Soup Cake 171

Celestial Crusts (Bozi Milosti) 80

Chocolate Angel Pie 128

Cookin' with Maudie Ho Ho Cake 45

Cranberry-Apple Crisp 100

Der Dutchman Date Nut Pudding 43

Di's Ohio Sour Cherry Pie 169

Di's Dutch Apple Pie 101

Fresh Peach Cobbler 103

Glazed Raspberry Pie 129

Graham Cracker Pudding 46

Grand Champion Pumpkin Pie 199

Great Grandma Porter's Applesauce Cake 129

Green Tomato Pie 189

* Historical Society Rose Geranium Cake 202

Katie's Peanut Butter Pie 46

Kolaczki 79

Krema Prima Peanut Butter Pie 168

Lazarus-Style Cheesecake 168

Magic Cookie Bars 167

Mike DeWine's Favorite Apple Dumplings 99

Ohio Shaker Lemon Pie 43

Ohio Cream Sherry Pound Cake 148

Peanut Butter Cookies 47

Penuche Icing 129

Rhubarb Crunch Cake 104

Rhubarb Pie 102

Sauerkraut Pie 203

Schmierkase Pie 77

Sevilla's Oatmeal Cake 44

Sevilla's Custard Pie 45

Sister Lizzie's Sugar Cream Pie 44

Snickerdoodles 201

Stouffer's Original Dutch Apple Pie 170

Strawberry Rosé Crepes 148

Dedications

To Joan, who not only made it possible but made it all worthwhile—James Hope.

In loving memory of my parents, who always believed in me —Susan Failor.

Preface

Exploring Inner Space

You don't have to travel far to go a long way in Ohio: the state is so diverse—geographically, economically, ethnically—that the scene outside your window changes constantly. Sometimes that makes it hard for Ohioans to figure out just who they are—what their persona is, so to speak—but it intrigues and delights the authors of this book, and is one of the reasons we decided to write it.

We're glad we did. Being interested in food, we ate our way from border to border and found a lot of it, in a variety ranging from five-star virtuosity (The Maisonette in Cincinnati has held that rare ranking for decades) to the baked beans-and-coffee memorial dinner for veterans that has been held in Rio Grande every year since 1870. The state is one where farm and cookie factory literally exist side by side, too. Ohio is smaller, in land area, than 33 other states, so it packs a surprising amount of agriculture and industry into a small space. Midwesterners that they are, Ohioans don't toot their own horns much. But Ohio ranks among the nation's top ten or twelve states in corn, soybeans, wheat, fresh vegetables, dairy products, chickens, eggs, hogs, and vegetables for processing. It does more than grow food, too: it also processes vast amounts of ketchup, pickles, soup, ice cream, Swiss cheese, cereal and many other things. Most people don't realize what an efficient little cornucopia this state is.

Do as we did: explore inner space, and discover food for the soul as well as the body, all in one state. One of the rewards will be the friendly people you meet...some of whom may have helped us write this book.

We did the book together: Susan Failor and James Hope, the people named on the title page and listed at the end of the book, and all those you'll read about in the following pages. Farmers, grocers, chefs, food processors, homemakers, extension agents, professors, government officials, and dozens of other Ohioans who help, in one way or another, to feed the rest of us every day, also helped us write *Bountiful Ohio* by giving lots of information and friendly access to what they were doing.

Mark Shelton of Athens, a superb writer equally capable of describing the fine points of neurosurgery or a good meal, helped us get started; his research and writing formed the original drafts of parts of the chapters on corn, tomatoes and wine (specifically, pp. 15-19, 133-137 and 173-177). Although they appear here in revised form, much of the work is his.

We appreciate the aid of everyone named in the book, and express our thanks to them now. *In addition* to all those named in the book, we thank the following (and apologize to anyone inadvertently omitted):

Judy Anderson, Jan Antonoplos, Gary Arnold, Linda Ballou, Smokey Lynne Bare, Elaine Bechant, Mary Lou Behrens, Guy Bemis, Robert Bickley, Michael Birchenall, Dan Bissland, Elsie Bissland, Joyce Blake, Naomi Blodgett, Ed and Marlene Boas, LeVern Bock, the Borden cowboys, Sarah, Frank and Matthew Breithaupt, Don Burke, Hudson Catell, Carol Chandler, Lois Clark, Rose Clements, Marlene Collins, Lesley Constable, Margaret Conway, Jama Cumbo, Mary Cusick, Sue Dawson, Chris Dean, Brenda Debolt, Betsy, Mike and Wesley Dockery, Yana Drvota, Harlan and Shirley Failor, Kathleen Fernandez, Ruth Ann Foote, Dan Frobose, Richard Garrett, Roger Gentile, Bob Gottesman, Rachel Graham, Dave Gress, Alcy Haden, Kay Hamilton, David Hampshire, Jo Ellen Helmlinger, Linda Hengst, Melinda Hill, Judy Ho, JoEll Jacobson, Scott and Belinda Jenks, Marsha Johnson, Deb Kerr, Dave Kessler, Cindy Kirkland, Mary Kreinbrink, Lucille Lakatos, Debbie Lautenbach, Marcia Leach, Linda Lee, Anthony Lenhardt, Marilyn Levinson, Bonnie Linck, Jennifer Little, Kaye Loew, Connie Long, Katherine Mantel, Marge McClish, Mary Ann Michaels, Lee Anne Miller, Tim Miller, Mary C. Miller, Jerry Miller, Carol Miller, Norman Moll, Carla Ricketts Moore, Marcia Musgrave, Eric Nicely, Jenny Nickol, Chris Olinsky, Karen Palmer, Linda Pealer, Mary Perencevic, Rhonda Peterson, Veronica Petta, Mary Alice Powell, Mary Powell, Sharon Reardon, Donna Roach, Eleanor Roman, Joyce Rosencrans, Barbara Rothrock, Donna Salvatore, Martha Savage, Margie Schenk, Andrew Schmidt, Gertrude Seybold, Susan Shockey, Ann Sindelar, Melissa Sonksen, Mike Srdjak, Cheryl Stewart-Miller, Debbie Stinner, Marge Stock, Amy Stone, Jim Tarbell, Ann Thomas, Mary Tierney, Lynn Tradoski, Bob Ulas, Laura Ulietti, Mrs. Louis Weiss, Karin Welzel, Bill and Beth Wenner, Vernon Will, Donniella Winchell, Paul Yon, Mary Ann Zepp.

We also thank the following:

Bowling Green State University Center for Archival Collections, Chambers of Commerce across the state, Cleveland Public Library Photograph Collection, Fruit Growers Marketing Association, Gahanna Historical Society, National Agricultural Library, Ohio Wine Producers Association, Ohio Egg and Turkey Marketing Program, Ohio Grape Industries Program, Ohio Lamb Marketing Program, Ohio Beef Council, Ohio Division of Travel and Tourism, Ohio Historical Society, Ohio Magazine, Ohio State University Archives, Ohio State University Extension, Ohioana Library Association, Reynoldsburg Tomato Festival, Inc., Reynoldsburg-Truro Historical Society, tourism bureaus in many places, Western Reserve Historical Society, Worthington Historical Society.

Special thanks to Nancy Lee Nelson and UniGraphics, without whose outstanding work these pages would be blank.

Susan Failor especially thanks her husband, Bill, and son, Brian, for their unwavering support and understanding during the nearly two years she worked on *Bountiful Ohio*.

POSTSCRIPT: *Two voices speak throughout this book. The friendly voice you hear explaining the recipes is that of Susan Failor. The other, telling the stories and pausing now and then for a good Ohio meal, is that of James Hope.*

BOUNTIFUL
O·H·I·O

A nineteenth century vision of prosperity is captured in this view of the peaceable kingdom, near Port Clinton, of Henry J. Miller, farmer and first sheriff of Ottawa County. Appearing in an 1874 county atlas, the neatly arranged abundance was rendered by an artist who knew that subscribers like Mr. Miller were helping pay the bill. Later generations of Millers became prominent in fruit growing, and a photographic view of their efforts appears on page 86.

STOCK FARM AND RESIDENCE OF HENRY J. MILLER, ESQ. SECTION 2, PORTAGE TP, OTTAWA COUNTY, OHIO. SKETCH TAKEN DEC. 6TH 1873. RESIDENT SINCE 1830.

In Search of Bountiful

I took to the road in mid-August, a few days after teaching my last class of summer session. I was a professor at a university in rural Ohio, but now I was free for a year, on leave from classes to do research of the kind that is supposed to add to the world's body of knowledge. I would do that, of course, but I had something else in mind, too.

Like William Least Heat-Moon in *Blue Highways* and Ishmael in *Moby Dick*, I was in search of something. While they were trying to fill gaps in their souls, I was hoping to fill a different kind of vacancy. I was looking for good things to eat.

After years of gulping quick lunches between classes, I was hungry, and I intended to eat leisurely and well. But there was a deeper purpose to this as well. I had a theory (as professors often do) that food, and the search for it, would help me come to know this state, perhaps even become more of an Ohioan.

Culture is all the things a people value: it is how they establish their identity, their sense of who they are, their *uniqueness*. Culture is art, music and literature, of course, but it is also film, furniture, car ornaments, roller coasters and merry-go-rounds. And it is food. Especially food: our foods are among the common statements of who we are; we create and consume them all day long.

Getting to know this place and its culture—to become *part* of it—was important to me. I had lived in Ohio for more than a decade and half, but I still felt like a New Englander, someone from away. I couldn't blame the Ohioans: they seemed friendlier than the taciturn Yankees with whom I was raised. The problem was this: I had never really taken the time to get to know the place, and Ohio still seemed more like an address than a home. Making it harder was that to Easterners like myself, Ohio is just one of those fly-over states that all start with O or I, who can remember which comes first? It isn't really eastern and not western either: just in between. I had learned that even Ohioans have trouble figuring out who they are, what makes them special. "Ohio's claim to fame is the antithesis of uniqueness," one historian wrote, in his solemn historian's way.

New Englanders know exactly who they are, and they have the sights, the sounds, the ancestors and the flavors to prove it to you, whether you ask them or not. They claim a sense of place as birth right and have all the materials for it: I grew up surrounded by mountains and Indian trails, Revolutionary War battlefields, home ports for clipper ships, and brooding houses with small-paned windows that concealed secrets. Legends grew easily in this rocky soil and blended into reality the way they did in Hawthorne's *House of the Seven Gables*, a real place populated by the creatures of his imagination. So the past, real and imagined, was as vivid as the present and always with us in New England, and so were the flavors: Boston baked beans (every Saturday night), the salt cod, cranberries, New England clam chowder (patriots wrote entire treatises comparing it with its hated rival from Manhattan), maple syrup, and country store cheese—most of all, aged Vermont cheddar. Cheese so strong, it was said, that it could be heard pacing the floor at night.

And so, in the sixth decade of my life, I knew where I had been, I did not know where I was now, and I meant to do something about it.

Ohio, in historian Walter Havighurst's memorable phrase, rolls west from the Allegheny Mountains like a flag blowing in the wind. It is a state of 41,000 square miles, about two-thirds the size of all six New England states put together. But Ohio has fewer mountains and straighter highways; looking at a map one day I could see that I could span Ohio in almost any direction, and, with perseverance, return home the same day. Everything began to come together in my mind: I realized I had means, motive and opportunity to explore this state.

And so I did. For much of a year I roamed Ohio, meeting its people, watching them work, trying my hand at what they did, discovering sources of real food produced by real people and bringing home the booty. One day I would return with red raspberries from Delaware County, on the next, with fresh pasta from Marietta, and on another, with cheese and jellies and a homemade cherry pie from Amish and Mennonite country. Near Bryan, I bought sweet corn from an unattended roadside stand. "Self-Service," the sign said, "In God We Trust." These were the flavors of the landscape, and I enjoyed thinking that I was living from the land where I dwelled. These things I bought began to feel like family, too. At Cleveland's West Side Market one day I acquired an enormous, aromatic loaf of Hungarian bread and named it Béla. The West Side is the kind of old-fashioned public market where the vendors call out to you, hustling their fruits and vegetables and meats as you walk by. The place has a personality, and so did Béla: he proved an admirable companion for the long trip home, banking comfortably into the curves and filling the car with his perfume.

I did have help with the book. My partner was Susan Failor of Dublin, a sweet-natured professional foodie who has lived down her Michigan origins by marrying an Ohioan and moving here. For a year and a half Sue harvested and horse-traded recipes across Ohio, bringing them home to try in her own kitchen and test on husband Bill, son Brian, and assorted friends and neighbors. A professional home economist and consultant to the likes of Borden, Sue is the kind of person who remembers names, dates and places by the food served; food is so much on her mind that sometimes she dreams about it.

The reason why the trim Ms. Failor did not long ago turn into a tub of lard is that she *tastes* more than she eats. "There is a difference," she once told me. Never having had that thought myself, I nodded politely and reached for another cookie. After a while, however, I began to realize she was right. I had spent more than 15 years in Ohio, eating but not really tasting.

So I set forth to taste Ohio in as many ways as I could, to meet Ohioans and see what they did, and how and why. In the next few months I reached every corner of the state and most of its 88 counties. I started adjusting to the incongruity of fighting the traffic in downtown Cleveland, one of the nation's biggest cities, and a few hours later crawling along behind a horse and buggy in Amish country. Sometimes, in tall corn country, I felt as if I was navigating a green sea or, in late fall, a wide, brown river: the combines moving deliberately through the fields reminded me of stately river boats. Driving as much as I did meant the part of my face beside the window tanned faster than the other side. I began to fear I would look like a harlequin clown.

But there were benefits to all this: I met dozens of Ohioans who work with food in every way possible: farmers, merchants, cooks, county agents, soup makers, vintners. My fellow New Englanders might have responded with skepticism to the pryings of a stranger, but these Midwesterners seemed glad to see me. Most were patient, if sometimes amused, with my endless questions and pleas to get involved with what

The Ohio Farmer, October 14, 1919

they were doing. I had experiences few people do: I listened in on a meeting of farm labor organizers, workers of Mexican descent who courteously kept most of the discussion in English for my benefit. I dined with the Amish, toured the cavernous storerooms of the West Side Market, walked through the biggest food factory in the world, stumbled through corn fields and around hog pens, met a high-spirited Popcorn Queen, and hugged Elsie the Borden Cow (who ungratefully stepped on my foot). I invaded the kitchen of a toney urban restaurant and quickly got pressed into service, handing plates to a server who was in a hurry. Wherever I went, I tried to go behind the scenes or get into the action, to see what it felt like to be an Ohioan making food.

One day, a friendly farmer named Tom Carpenter invited me into the cab of his combine, an eight-ton harvesting machine about the size of a main battle tank. Sitting in his glass-enclosed cab and driving at a steady 2 to 3 miles per hour, Tom can strip an acre of its corn within minutes, his machine plucking the ears from the stalks, shucking them and stripping the kernels from the cobs all at once. After a while he let me take the wheel, and so I drove up and down his field, demolishing six rows of cornstalks at a time and seeing the golden yellow results pile up in the bin behind me. It wasn't that complicated, although concentrating on the rows of corn rushing into your machine is a bit like staring at the pavement from a speeding car. It gets harder when you realize that you will be doing this hour after hour, but the hardest part of all is when, listening to Tom, you start thinking like a farmer: with prices near $2 a bushel, can I pay to have the corn dried and still make money? Should I have started sooner, when the corn was even wetter, or should I have waited longer? Are all the months I've invested in this corn field even going to pay off?

Later, Tom's corn would be used to make corn starch or corn syrup or animal feed or the gasoline additive ethanol, all examples of the incredible bounty of this native American staff of life. Modern food production is highly technical, but, for the farmer, it still comes down to this: putting seeds in the earth, caring for them, and then seeing results you can hold in your hand and know will feed and fuel the world. It's a spiritual experience. If you can afford it.

I tried my hand at another kind of harvest. On a warm October afternoon I helped Tom Quilter pick grapes in his vineyard, a few miles north of Columbus in the Olentangy River basin. Earlier, on an empty stomach, I had sipped almost every one of the 10 wines Tom and Mary make in their Shamrock Vineyard, located in Waldo; now, slightly heady, I was picking the Vidal grapes used for one of the Quilters' whites. The bunches of small green, brown-flecked grapes felt round and full in my hand; they still had the warmth of the sun in them. Later I took home two bottles of Vidal with plans to toast the Quilters, whose hospitality is legendary in wine circles. A retired physician who works with the precision of a surgeon, Quilter keeps his four-and-a-half acre vineyard as neat as a museum garden. A building the size of a garage houses his crushing and pressing equipment, among which is a device called a bladder press. Quilter takes some kidding on this; his medical specialty was urology.

I wanted to participate in some of the food rituals of Ohioans, too. In Circleville for the 83rd Pumpkin Show, I gazed on a field of pies: 37 in the senior pie division alone. They had been baked by local cooks vying for the title of grand champion pumpkin pie baker, and I was here to sample their wares. It was a daunting prospect, but I was in the company of my co-author, a veteran judge of baking contests and a woman who knows her pumpkin pie. Pie-baking contests are a staple feature of many Ohio agricultural fairs and festivals, and all across the state home ovens are busy from June through October turning out entries. "Taste and appearance are both important, but taste comes first," Sue explained as she bent to her task. Tasting, poking and giving each pie the gimlet eye for color, crust and conformation, Sue and another judge—cleansing their palates with sips of water—narrowed the field to four, and then ranked them. I had a small slice of each of these elite pies. Finishers 4, 3 and 2 tasted equally good to me, but with number 1, I knew I was in the presence of greatness: the new champion had scored a coup by topping her pie with chopped pecans and brown sugar. That added a new texture as well as flavor to an old equation, and the judges were suitably impressed.

To recover from the stresses of judging ("It can burn out your taste buds," Sue told me), we had lunch: a pumpkin burger, which turned out to be a sloppy joe with lots of tomato and a dash of pumpkin ("Not bad," according to Sue's expert palate), followed by pumpkin donuts and pumpkin pretzels. I rolled home that night feeling I had paid as much homage to *Cucurbita pepo* as any native.

I had experiences that had nothing to do with food, too. One cold November afternoon I found myself riding in an Amish buggy, clip-clopping down a Holmes County road with the reins in the experienced hands of 14-year-old Ivan Swartzentruber. A mutual friend had arranged for me to spend the day with an Amish family. After having dinner with them, I was "going around the block" with Ivan, circling the farms in his neighborhood. Riding in an open buggy instead of a hermetically sealed automobile is a sensory experience: you hear the creak of the harness leather and feel the bite of the weather, which is why I was grateful for the Amish buggy robe. We passed blackbonneted women working in their yards and an Amishman plowing with a team of horses; Ivan and his neighbors acknowledged each other with brief flicks of the wrist. Amish children on their way home from school stared wide-eyed at us; for once, I was the object of curiosity instead of them. Then we stopped at the school where only their two teachers remained. They were two Amish girls, 15 and 17; with no formal training—but plenty of confidence—they taught 39 youngsters from first through eighth grade, all in one large room. They faced a formidable task. The Amish ordinarily speak Pennsylvania Dutch in their homes and children come to school having to learn English. Like teachers everywhere, they wanted to show me their students' work: one wall was filled with turkeys colored by pokeberries the students had picked themselves. On my way out I noticed the rope hanging down

The Ohio Farmer, March 12, 1927

from the school's belfry. Bright-eyed, they asked if I would like to hear the bell. As I headed for the buggy, the Amish school bell rang just for me, totally unofficially; I thought of the young teachers back in their school room and hoped they were giggling.

Usually, of course, I traveled by automobile (one that had been made in Ohio, in fact). One day I drove south from Mansfield toward Mount Vernon, retracing, roughly, one of Johnny Appleseed's routes when he lived in this area. That the story of John Chapman—Johnny Appleseed — lives on is due in no small part to Rick Sowash, a native of the region and a story in himself. A former county commissioner, Sowash makes his living as a teller of Ohio stories and humor; he's also a serious musician and composer. Sowash named his son John Chapman Sowash. He calls Johnny "Ohio's greatest contribution to the folklore of the world. He is our only non-violent folk hero. All the others are shooting cannon and killing people and chopping down trees, but he's a nurturer among the destroy-ers, at one with nature." Sowash is working hard to develop a Johnny Appleseed national monument, but in the meantime the very terrain in Richland and Knox counties will serve that purpose in my mind. I was wondering why the low, rolling hills looked familiar when I realized they resembled Johnny's home country in central Massachusetts, not far from where I came from, too. Perhaps that's why he stayed so long in this area.

On another day on a narrow country road in eastern Ohio, I found myself in a growing line of vehicles crawling impatiently behind a farm tractor. The truckers took turns sounding long, angry blasts on their horns, trying to nudge the farmer out of their way. As he continued doggedly on, refusing to budge, I imagined him saying, "You're in my country now, and I paid for this highway." Remembering the stubborn Yankee farmers of my youth, I smiled to myself.

I smiled, too, when I rolled through a northeastern Ohio village called Thompson. The center had a common, with a feed and grain store at each end; just outside of town a farm advertised maple syrup. I was having déjà vu all over again, as the saying goes, and then I realized Thompson bore an uncanny resemblance to Troy, New Hampshire, a town I had traveled through many times but had not seen in years. Northeastern Ohio is like that. The Connecticut Western Reserve was settled by Yankees who believed every town should have a common (which is why Cleveland has Public Square) and who built farmhouses that looked a lot like home. Thompson reminded me that I was beginning to understand Ohio. It isn't just an in-between state, it is an American intersection.

Much of northeastern Ohio looks and feels like New England: industrial cities and rural towns with commons and houses of Federal design. But travel down the Ohio River to southeast Ohio and you enter Appalachia: this is hard-scrabble farm and coal mine country. The terrain is different, the accents are of the Southern hills, and you know you are in the land of Foxfire. Keep traveling along the river and the sense of the South grows stronger: you pass the place where, legend has it, Eliza of *Uncle Tom's Cabin* fled across the ice floes from Kentucky to Ohio. (Ohio is filled with places that were stations on the Underground Railroad.) Eventually you come to Cincinnati, where Stephen Foster lived and wrote many of his Southern songs; you may see riverboats here like those Mark Twain wrote about. A little further north, in Columbus, you can see an elegant old hotel charmingly named the Great Southern; it looks the part. Not far from Columbus is Mount Vernon, whose native son Daniel Decatur Emmett wrote that rallying song of the Confederacy, "Dixie." Then travel west from Columbus and notice how the land levels out, with great fields of corn, wheat and soybeans stretching off to the horizon. The Lake Plains roll west from here to the Mississippi. This is the eastern anchor of America's Corn Belt. This is where the Heartland begins.

Ohio can be hard for the newcomer to understand, just because it has so many intersections. East meets West and North meets South here, but it is even more than that. Ohio is an industrial-agricultural, urbanized-country kind of place, where Amish, who plow their fields with horses, may live only a few miles from laboratories doing breakthrough research on polymers. The state has Rust Belt cities, yes, but they are surrounded by hundreds of towns and small cities with the homey feel of Middle America. This is porch-swing country, too, where the woman who is your neighbor on the porch to the left may be a space scientist, the one to the right, a farmer. It is the kind of place where corn fields come right up to the back door of the local Kmart, as they do in my Bowling Green. These incongruities are part of the everyday life of Ohioans, who move easily from farm country to city, from present to past and back again. The homey diversity, once you get used to it, is one of the glories of Ohio. We're no one thing, we're partly everything here: it's a very American place and quite comfortable, thank you. You'd like it here.

Ohio food is like that, too. It is a mix of flavors and accents, not singular enough to gain a high-profile identity the way some places have for their *cuisine*. If you told Ohioans they had a *cuisine*, they'd look at you doubtfully, and then—being Ohioans—offer you a cup of coffee and a comfortable place to sit down. Ohio food is not pretentious. It is generous. It is comfortable. It is good food from home.

Early one cold, bleak fall day, I crossed the state line and entered Ohio, returning from a visit to family in New England. A little while later I coasted into the first toll gate of the Ohio Turnpike. All day before, New York State toll booth attendants had greeted me with grim visages, guarding their words as carefully as dollar bills. So it was startling when the Ohio toll-taker chirped brightly, "Good morning!" with a smile that seemed to mean it. Then I remembered they often do that.

I was 10 miles down the road before it dawned on me. I was home.

POSTSCRIPT: *A friendly welcome to Ohio is available at any toll booth of the turnpike. Just smile at the attendants, and they'll probably smile back. Do not try this in other states.*

FACES OF THE LAND

Parker's Place

I like Parker Bosley. I like his name, too. A guy gets your attention with a stylish moniker like that. It's a good handle for the hero in one of those 1930s movies who's on a mission to save Civilization As We Know It. But Parker is out to do something far more important: with moustachios flaring and indignation simmering, he wants to serve Ohioans a really good meal.

And to serve it, as much as possible, with food *grown right here in Ohio*. The amazing thing about Parker is that he combines the sophistication of a French chef with the earthiness of an Ohio farmer, firing it all with the zeal of a dedicated teacher. Which he was. And is. But to learn from Parker, you must eat his food.

I met Parker on one of my research trips, which happened that day to take me to a part of Cleveland called Ohio City. One of the state's great treasures, the West Side Market, is located here. Ohio City is a shirt-sleeves kind of neighborhood and here, too, hidden away in what was once a corner tavern on a quiet side street, is one of the state's little treasures. It is called, simply, Parker's.

Parker's is tastefully and subtly decorated, a white-tablecloth place so sophisticated its tablecloths are pink, so *haute* that salt and pepper are kept out of sight, so you can't massacre what the chef hath wrought. The locale itself is not impressive: there are no sweeping lake views, no manicured gardens to hold your attention. When you realize that's the point, you've already begun to learn from Professor Bosley. One is here to dine well on fine food lovingly prepared, not chow down by the light of the setting sun. Parker wants you to concentrate on the culinary wonders he can lay before you, and *learn* what Man can do with the bounty of Ohio. And its environs.

And what wonders they are. While studying the menu, my companion and I were served warm, freshly baked focaccia bread, fragrant with rosemary and thyme and lightly brushed with olive oil. In chorus, all our senses told us we had come to the right place. For reasons of time, we reluctantly bypassed the appetizers (Chicken liver mousse and cream of Ohio mushroom soup were among the home-grown choices) and moved on to the main course. She had grilled salmon fillet with tomato sauce, the tomato being emblematic of Ohio, even if the salmon wasn't. I had

Belgian Blue low-fat beef, raised in nearby Marysville, according to a menu insert giving its family history (another lesson from the professor, I suspect). It was so perfectly flavored that no salt or pepper were necessary, thank you (I think I learned something). Salads of Ohio maiden greens and perfectly prepared plate vegetables—caramelized onions with carrots and leeks—rounded out the main course. The luncheon was sublime, and cost about $8 to $10 per entree—not burger-and-fries prices, of course, but, as our British friends like to say, very good value. Hurrying to another appointment, we left, whining softly at missing desserts like Ohio Apple tart with caramel sauce and chocolate mousse with fresh whipped cream. But we vowed to return, early and often.

These wonders come from a tiny kitchen where Parker presides over one of the best-educated staffs anywhere. Both chefs helping him are college graduates, one in Renaissance literature, the other in chemistry. One of the waiters is a Ph.D. candidate in art history and the bartender is a post-graduate student at Kent State. But the head of this crew has had a few lessons himself. "I always say I'm bilingual," Parker says. "I can go out in the country and talk with farmers about hogs and then I can talk with the Wine Society about a fillet of pork. I know which word to use where."

Raised on a Trumbull County farm, Parker grew up shoveling out cow barns by day and listening to opera by night. He studied voice at Baldwin-Wallace, then spent two years abroad teaching military dependents. Part of the time was in France, where he came to love French country cooking and the connectedness between French menus and the seasons. Parker came back to the States to spend the next twenty years teaching elementary school in Berea (fourth, fifth and sixth grades), but he would return to France every other summer to study travel, eat and study classic French cooking. (Which, by the way, is neither the heavy sauces stereotypically associated with French food, nor the tiny lettuce leaf entrees spoofed by the likes of Dave Thomas in ads for Wendy's. You don't leave Parker's hungry.)

Parker Bosley

Weary of what he saw as the decline of good teaching (one of the subjects on which Parker can wax indignant) and increasingly fascinated by cooking, Parker changed careers at mid-life. First he cooked for others in fine restaurants in Cleveland, then opened his own. After four years it burned down, so he took a year's sabbatical and then re-opened, in November 1992, in a new location. Parker's, now on Cleveland's west side, is a dining place with more than a menu: it has a philosophy.

That philosophy comes from the annual rotation of farm life with which Parker grew up, reinforced by what he learned from the French. It has three axioms. First, use the freshest, most wholesome products available, which means buying locally and regionally, often of organic growers. (Parker gets irate at cooking which ignores local produce. He tells of visiting a country restaurant, next door to a local pork producer, which served "frozen pork chops which probably came from New Jersey.") The second axiom follows from the first: cook and eat according to the seasons. "We're not fanatics about it," says Parker. "If it's coming in season in South Carolina and we need it, we'll buy it. But we try, as much as possible, to be respectful of the seasons and of our own [Ohio] agriculture." The third axiom is: teach people the other two axioms. Parker declares: "I am trying to educate people so that more people will demand that they don't want California strawberries in January, they want Ohio apples in January, and then in June, they want Ohio strawberries."

Parker's does this in several ways. The menus carry insert cards which explain the origins of some menu items, and what diners should expect. Servers are trained to be highly knowledgeable about the cuisine and assist diners in making choices most apt to prove enjoyable. And the salt and pepper, while available on request, are out of sight. Parker believes "you should taste the food. Hopefully the chef has made the dish in such a way that it is complete and ready to eat."

Most of all, though, what Parker does is serve lots of fresh Ohio-grown products and write his menus according to the seasons. To hear him talk about it is to realize what a cornucopia there is in Ohio. Listen:

"Right now [February] we use apples a lot. We get them directly from the grower, out in Chesterland. We never use strawberries out of season, because we won't buy strawberries from some foreign land. In winter, which everyone thinks is a tough time of year, we use mostly native root vegetables [from cold cellars], a lot of carrots, leeks and turnips and cabbage and sweet potatoes.

"The first big thing we'll have in spring is asparagus; we'll have a month or five weeks where we'll have tons of asparagus, and it'll come from organic farmers. We'll use asparagus every way we can: in soup, as an appetizer with sauces, as a vegetable on the plate, cold, with a vinaigrette."

In the latter part of April Parker's will start serving native rhubarb: "Rhubarb tarts, pies, and even a soufflé, which people think is quite spectacular. We make a rhubarb sauce for ice cream. And rhubarb is good when it's combined with meat, such as roast pork.

"During summer we do a lot with poultry. Ohio ducks are excellent. And there are strawberries, raspberries, blueberries.

"By July you're starting to have early apples, and the peaches start in August. I challenge anyone to produce peaches like we have in Huron County. There's a farm out there [from which] we buy peaches, pears, nectarines, sometimes apricots. We have customers who say, We've just never had peaches like those. What's your secret recipe? The recipe is not the secret; the secret is this wonderful peach on the tree, and what some farmer did with it. He's the artist, and he should get as much credit for my dessert as I get. I always try to get people to understand this: when the farmer and the chef get together, that's when you have really wonderful food on your plate."

Parker's makes much more use of fresh sweet corn than most restaurants. "We buy it fresh in the morning, husk it ourselves, take all the kernels off the cob and save the milk, and cook it with butter and salt and pepper. People just can't imagine how it can be so good, but it's the quality of the product. It didn't ride here on a truck from Arizona," Parker says.

"August, September and October are probably the very best time to be a cook in the Midwest, because the gardens are so bountiful. There are all kinds of tomatoes. We use the heirloom varieties, because there's nothing like them for taste and variety. We cut them open, take out pulp and seed, and put chunks, mixed with fresh basil, in a small pie shell with an egg yolk and cream mixture. Bake it and you have a little tart, to serve whole as an appetizer. Tomatoes are one of the great crops of the Midwest."

Parker tells how he served an Ohio dinner to seven people in the middle of February. It began with soup made with heirloom beans, decorated with a purée made from garlic, all grown organically in Ohio. The salad was of greens grown hydroponically in Coshocton or Lorain counties. The main course was roast Ohio duck on red cabbage cooked with apples from Chesterland. Dessert was Ohio apples, layered up with crepes and custard. In the whole dinner, only the olive oil, walnuts and flour came from outside Ohio.

So Parker Bosley, veteran of the elementary school classroom, now teaches the hungry of Ohio about dining well from their own landscape. He also enlists disciples—apprentices and students who carry his philosophy to other restaurants. And he has plans for two cooking schools, one for professionals and the other for amateurs who want to learn "what's cooking at Parker's."

Parker Bosley, the farm boy who went to France, came back to Ohio and discovered a world of food in his own back yard. If you're an Ohioan looking for good food, you're in the right place. In Parker's place. Ohio.

POSTSCRIPT: *Parker's, 2801 Bridge Avenue at West 28th Street, Cleveland, is open for lunch weekdays and for dinner Friday and Saturday evenings. Reservations recommended for lunch, required for dinner; 216/771-7130. While you're there, ask Parker about Ohio wines.*

ANOTHER POSTSCRIPT: *Epicures who find themselves in Ohio but out of reach of Parker's should not despair; there are far more opportunities for fine dining than they might imagine. Ohio is, after all, home to the oldest continuous five-star restaurant in the nation (The Maisonette, 114 East Sixth Street, Cincinnati; 513/721-2260).* Ohio Magazine *publishes a monthly restaurant guide and, annually in late summer, a report in depth on the state's restaurants.*

It's the 1930s and an Ohio farmer and his Percherons are plowing a corn field. Plowing is used less and less by conservation-minded farmers today. While tractors replaced most draft horses in the 1940s, hundreds of Percherons and others are still raised in Ohio for work or show. The Percheron Horse Society of America is located in Fredericktown and has more members from Ohio than any other state.

Green and Yellow Magic

It is fitting that corn—Ohio corn—was chosen to decorate one of the entrances to the huge Ameriflora '92 exhibition in Columbus. Ameriflora was an international flower show celebrating the 500th anniversary of the explorer's arrival in what he called the New World. It was the big event in central Ohio in 1992. There, amongst the Dutch tulips and replicas of the Santa Maria, was good Ohio corn, in the form of dried ears split on a bandsaw and glued up in the shape of an arch.

Corn is like that here, something that surrounds Ohioans, a stolid and unpretentious crop that grows everywhere. It is hard to drive more than 45 minutes in most parts of Ohio without seeing corn. Some visitors marvel that in the same county as a city like Cleveland there is corn, or that on a clear day you can see it from the windows of Columbus's tall buildings. It is out there, around everyone and everything, a part of the state that is at once fundamental and metaphorical.

This makes Ohio sound like a state of farmers, which it is, although it is a state of insurance companies and steel mills as well. And it is a state of tax lawyers and heart surgeons, a state of inventors and Presidents and men in space and film stars and poets. But it is also a place where all of those types grew up near, or lived surrounded by, corn. It's what you see in Ohio most of the year around.

U.S. 33, a highway that cuts diagonally across the state from southeast to northwest, directly through the state capital from Appalachia and on up to the first vestiges of the Great Plains, follows a Corn Belt of its own. About eight miles south of Columbus the contemporary architecture of the city can be seen in the distance, but in summer, the buildings seem to rise from Walter Sears's 633 acres of corn. Stand in his field in July and you can see Columbus glow emerald, like Oz, the shimmer of the green leaves reflecting on the horizon and framing the largest city in the state. When there is a lull in traffic on 33, you can hear the squeaking and groaning of the corn as it grows.

Walter's 600-plus acres are not unusual. It's not even unusual that his acres have been under continuous cultivation by white settlers for nearly two centuries. Just west of his land is a place that was already cleared and under cultivation when the first white settlers arrived. The Indians had been growing corn for hundreds of years when the forbears of the tax lawyers and heart surgeons first stumbled through, when there was no gleaming capital city in sight. Even then corn was the number-one crop in what is now the state of Ohio. It still is. Other states grow more corn of course, but no state grows it so close to so many people. Corn in the same county as Cleveland, corn in Columbus.

And corn grown the hard way, an interesting commentary on the stubbornness of our ancestors. If aerial reconnaissance had been possible in, say, 1805, the smart money would have said that the likely place to grow corn was not Ohio. At the time, the region was mostly dense forest. The likely place to grow corn would have been where it is sensible to grow corn today, the huge, open plains further west, places like Illinois, Indiana and Nebraska. The prairies were difficult in their own way to cultivate, but nothing like the forest of Ohio.

To grow corn—or any crop—in Ohio meant this: follow a river or stream or an Indian trail, through an overshadowing forest of oak and maple and tulip and sycamore and hickory and ash to the intended home place. Build a hut or lean-to for the wife and children. Then begin to clear the land, cutting the huge trees to gain open space and daylight. Turn your hogs loose in the forest and hope they can fend off the bears and wolves. Plant your crops among the stumps, and then, over the years, burn out the stumps and remove the rocks. Care for those crops as if your life depended on it—which it did.

Corn made the settlement of Ohio possible. It was a versatile and hardy crop: early farmers commonly said they had never known a corn crop to fail. Corn provided food for pioneer and livestock in the first winters when simply surviving was the goal, then a crop for trade and barter. It was the first crop planted by the settlers, and for many years their most important. The result can be seen today on a good map of the state. The hundreds of villages and towns and hamlets of modern Ohio mark places that were once clearings and single houses built of hand-hewn logs. One house was a farm, two was a village, a half dozen became a city. By 1849, Ohio was largely settled and long on the way toward being civilized. In that year Ohio was the nation's largest producer of corn as well.

It is no longer. Railroads and steel mills and rubber factories and auto plants came along, turning some of those corn fields into part of the Rust Belt. Even today, however, America's Corn Belt begins in Ohio and the state is a bigger corn producer than you might think: in 1991 it ranked seventh in the nation in overall production, sixth in sweet corn alone. And it does it in a way that is peculiarly Ohioan. Physically, Ohio is smaller than most other states, ranking 34th, but in population, it is among the largest, ranking seventh. If agriculture officials were to compile a statistic called "acres of corn per person," Ohio would probably rank first. The state is remarkable for the numerical relationship between agriculture, land area and population. It has a lot of the first, less of the second than one might think, and more of the third than most other places.

What this means to Ohioans is a physical relationship to corn, all four million acres of it—about one acre, on average, per household in the

The Ohio Farmer, October 23, 1926

state. What a confluence of numbers! For every household in Ohio, one acre of corn. Curiously, this gives certain Ohioans an inferiority complex: all that corn makes it easy to call Columbus a cow town, for example. Of course, there are many towns and cities where they are proud of their farms, their corn. The epitome of this may be Darke County, in western Ohio, a county of more than a third of a million acres of farmland, more than a hundred thousand acres of it in corn. Darke County is Really Big Corn, and its people know it: they like to boast how it ranks number one in the state in corn (and many other farm products). To drive Darke County's roads in late July, when the corn is up over the top of the car, can be disorienting; everything is tinged with green.

When city folk think of corn, they usually think of corn on the cob or popcorn. They may not realize how magical this crop is for its ability to serve many uses. Most of Ohio's corn is harvested for processing— principally oil, grain, and feed, and a smaller fraction for silage. The smallest percentages are for sweet corn, sold for the table, and for pop- corn. Corn can be found in everything from plastic bags to motor fuel (the gasoline additive ethanol is made in Ohio). Even in the early days, corn growers used everything but the squeak: the chopped and fermented stalks as animal feed; the dried husks as mattress and furniture stuffing; the "embryo," or underside of the kernel, for corn oil; the starchy en- dosperm for corn starch, corn meal, corn syrup and ground corn (for grits and corn mush); cracked corn for poultry feed; the cobs for corncob pipes.

Corn syrup is probably the most common corn product today, although only people who read the fine print would know this. Almost everything sweet these days has some corn syrup in it: soft drinks, candy, commercial baked goods, maple-flavored table syrup, ice cream, jellies and jams. Corn syrup is about half as sweet as cane sugar, one of the reasons it shows up so often in commercial products: it adds volume as well as sweetness.

Corn can pop up in other surprising ways. Added to plastic, corn starch is thought to aid in the decomposition of plastics over time. Corn starch is edible and tasty to microbes that won't touch plastic. One of the most glamorous uses of corn can be found in Hollywood. Generations of movie bad guys have been hit over the head with saloon glassware and thrown through saloon windows made from corn syrup; in a drought year, you would think that a single episode of *Gunsmoke* could raise corn prices in the Chicago commodity market. But there is always plenty of corn; indeed, the supply seems inexhaustible. And that is the problem as well as the glory of modern corn.

The acreage of corn harvested in Ohio in 1940 was 3.2 million; in 1991 it was 3.4 million. The number of farms in 1940 was 244,000; in 1991, 80,000. But yield per acre, a result of intensive research and development, about tripled in the same period. Prices, in round numbers, haven't changed much at all, and in real dollars, have dropped in relation to supply. Without government intervention (one of the things that fills all those grain elevators with crop surplus), the situation would be far worse. So fewer farmers grow more corn and sell it for less every year.

This reflects a paradox. Farmers are at once the most important link in the chain while being the weakest. While they are the ones, after all, who actually grow the crops, their only defense against extinction has been to increase production. Constant improvements in seed stock and farming technique have made it possible. In the early 1800s, yields of 45 bushels per acre were common. Today, yields of 120 bushels per acre are typical, and harvests of more than 200 bushels per acre have been reported. But that 120 bushels of corn sells for only $250 to $300.

Nonetheless, there is no dispute that corn is one of the bounties of the New World. Its roots are ancient. Native Americans not only ate it, but planted and cultivated it. As early American history records, they also showed new settlers from Europe how to do both. Ever since, Americans have been busy adapting and reinventing corn as a foodstuff. Note, for example, the rise of tortilla chips from an asterisk in the snack food industry to a major player. Tortillas, of course, were a bread of the ancient Aztecs, much commented upon by the Spanish invaders.

One of the more interesting current food trends is toward so-called "comfort" foods, which might be thought of as the way people cooked before there was such a thing as a food trend. No less an edifice than *Gourmet* magazine has taken to running recipes for old-fashioned corn grits, corn relish and succotash—three recipes that might just as easily come from Estelle Woods Wilcox's *Buckeye Cookery* in 1877. Ms. Wilcox offered a recipe for Corn Oysters—grated corn, eggs and cracker crumbs mixed and fried by spoonfuls in hot fat. Corn oysters, served perhaps with corn relish, sounds very much like a comfort food.

Indeed, corn is perhaps an ideal comfort food: hot corn bread (which will soak up its weight, easily, in melted butter) baked in a round iron frying pan is quite comforting. It's what got a lot of Ohio farmers going in the morning—going out to work their fields of corn. And what more comfortable breakfast can there be than corn flakes?

The mention of grits still has to be explained in many parts of the country. It even needs explaining in parts of Ohio, since the state is sharply divided into two parts: Grits and No Grits. The grits line covers the true Appalachian part of the state, the south and southeast, petering out near Cincinnati. If it weren't for Bob Evans, who started out in southeast Ohio, most Ohioans north of Chillicothe would never have had grits at all. Grits are a mainstay on the Bob Evans menu, though, and still a part of breakfast in the South and places where Southerners have ended up. Grits are a cereal made from ground hulled corn. They also form a perfect, stick-to-the-ribs side dish when one is going out to plow the north forty; with cheddar cheese, they are a nice dinner side dish as well.

In early August, when Ohio sweet corn starts to show up at farm stands, science can be forgotten, worries about the commodities market put aside, and corn can be eaten in the way most desired by lovers of corn. For all the advances in technology and genetics, it is humble old Silver Queen that is Ohio sweet corn personified: firm and sweet and evenly sized ears of Silver Queen are meant to be boiled on the spot (a fair number of farm stands and farmer's markets have kettles on site just for this purpose), drizzled with butter, and devoured.

James Beard, for all of his contributions, should be remembered most for making acceptable what had long been a sort of closet practice for lovers of sweet corn: bringing the kettle right out to the field, pulling down ears of sweet corn, and cooking and eating them on the spot. If one looks closely at farmer's gardens, surrounded though they may be by thousands of acres of corn, one still sees with impressive regularity a couple of rows of Silver Queen (or, lately, the various super-sweet varieties) planted within yards of the house. Right there, next to the picnic table.

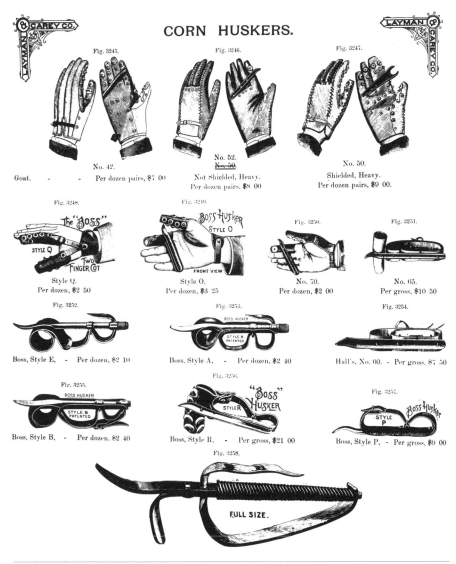

FACES OF THE LAND

The Good Earth of Tom Carpenter

Tom Carpenter leans over his desk and tells a visitor what the numbers dancing on his video display screen mean: he trades on the Chicago commodities market and the screen saves calling a broker for quotations. Nearby are other tools of Carpenter's trade: a two-way radio system with a private frequency and a fleet of 11 vehicles, some housed next to his personal 250-yard golf driving range.

Goodbye, Old MacDonald; hello, modern production agriculture: Tom Carpenter is an Ohio farmer—1990s style.

In fond memory, at least, Farmer Brown (clad in bib overalls, of course) chugged off every morning on his big red Farmall for a long day on the north 40, while Mother baked pies for dinner, using apples from the family orchard, and Bossy made milk for breakfast. There was a charming air of self-sufficiency about all this, and if few farmers got rich, most were fond of saying, "We may go broke, but we'll never starve."

Forget it. Today, farming is both easier and infinitely harder than anything Farmer Brown ever knew. The worst of the backbreaking labor may be gone, but modern agriculture is a high-tech, high-capital, high-risk *business*, and it takes someone with the nerves—and the agility—of Tom Carpenter to stay on top of it. In a typical workday, Carpenter may ponder a $15,000 deal in wheat futures, replace the brakes on his semi-trailer truck with his own tools, and—playing house-husband while wife Diana works as an administrator at a nearby university—put a gentle hand on the brow of his 8-year-old daughter, Amy, home from school with a fever.

Most of all, though, what Tom Carpenter does is what farmers have done since the dawn of time: coax food from the land. Exclusively a grain farmer, he raises corn, soybeans and wheat in endless rotation. His tools are electronic, hydraulic and mechanical; with them he creates food from ancient elements: seeds, heat, light, rain and earth. Especially the earth. "If we are patient," he likes to say, "the land will take care of us."

A trim 42-year-old graduate of a nearby university, where he studied business, Carpenter has the calm courtesy of a well-bred banker. He wears blue jeans, but it's impossible to imagine him in bib overalls. Carpenter farms a thousand acres in Wood County, the heart of northwest Ohio's Black Swamp country. About 12,000 years ago, the glaciers retreated from Ohio, flattening much of the terrain and leaving a 100-mile-long lowland southwest from Lake Erie. This became the Black Swamp: a morass of mosquito-infested marsh covered by vines and forest so dense and forbidding that it was the last area settled in Ohio. By the late 1800s, however, logging and drainage had turned the swamp into some of the richest farmland in America. This table-flat region offers dark, rich sandy loam on top of Hoytville Clay. And Carpenter is twice-blessed: much of his land also has an exceptionally rich black sand loam that accompanies the Portage River.

Asked how successful he's been, Carpenter will only say modestly, "We've been fortunate." Farmers often invoke the plural, as if to acknowledge the many partnerships that shape their lives. Which one is most important depends on the moment. Sometimes it's family: Carpenter started farming on his own by trading labor for use of his father's equipment; start-up costs are so high, he says, that "you just about have to be born into farming." Sometimes it's the weather: Ordinarily Ohio farmers are blessed with one of the nation's most consistent climates, but the late Eighties hammered them with two straight years of drought and then a monsoon-like 1992. Sometimes it's the government: "We're still feeling the effects of Jimmy Carter's grain embargo," says Carpenter. Sometimes it's the commodities market, which is why Carpenter checks his video terminal several times a day: "We play a game of pennies with our marketing," he says. "Just a few cents per bushel can make a significant difference in our profit or loss."

But most of all, Carpenter is in partnership with the earth, coveting the land and caring for it as if it were a living, breathing thing. He owns about 240 acres of his own; another 800 are leased from neighbors, farmers who have retired but who keep their rich land working. "The competition for rental farm land in this area is very keen," Carpenter explains. "If you own a farm and you even think about quitting, you'll have 10 or 15 people at your door almost before you've decided."

A careful, methodical man, Carpenter has good reasons for everything he does, and many of them have to do with preserving the precious earth. The tractors, for instance: although Carpenter works alone most of the year, hiring help only for planting and harvest times, he owns five (plus a combine and four trucks), in sizes ranging from a little red-bellied Ford on up to a green-and-yellow four-wheel-drive behemoth so big it pivots in the middle. Different sizes of tractors are needed to handle jobs as different as plowing and mowing, and Carpenter wants to use the lightest possible piece of machinery for each one. "The soil is a living organism," he explains. "If you take a heavy tractor and keep driving it over and over the farm—we call it tramping the soil—eventually the soil gets so compacted the plants will not grow properly."

To avoid tramping the soil, Carpenter will not work his fields when the ground is wet. Sometimes he'll be asked why he isn't out working when the sun is shining, but it can take two days for a field to drain after a rain. Carpenter will not even rent any of his land to tomato growers, who would pay him several times what he gets from grain alone: he fears they

Tom Carpenter

would tramp down his soil with their heavy vehicles, compacting it beyond redemption.

Carpenter is also making more use of no-till farming, meaning, for example, that last year's cornstalks are left lying in the field instead of being plowed and disked under. Special equipment is used to plant a new crop, right through the debris. It isn't pretty, but no-till saves time and reduces erosion—and compaction. The old way, with its plowing, disking, cultivating, spraying and harvesting, could mean as many as eight trips across a field; no-till can cut that number in half.

All in all, this is not the farming Carpenter's ancestors, or even his father, knew. "The work really isn't physically hard, the way it used to be," he says. But it's a game with much higher stakes: "It doesn't do any good to just go out and work your tail off trying to raise an outstanding crop," Carpenter explains. "You also have to know how to market it and price it. You walk a very fine line, and you really can't afford to have too many mistakes." Some of the old sense of self-sufficiency is gone, too. Once a year Carpenter's father would slaughter a steer, right in the barn, and the family would have meat for months. Now the Carpenters shop at the supermarket like everyone else.

And yet, for all its high technology and global economics, farming has not lost some of its traditional ways. Carpenter rises early, as farmers always have, having his breakfast in time to check his video display terminal by 7 a.m. And farming is always a family affair: occasionally wife Diana, suburban-raised and holder of a master's degree in college student personnel, must drive a tractor. Nor has farming lost its power to charm and beguile. Surrounded on all sides by their crops, the Carpenters live on an immaculate farmstead that looks like something from a picture postcard. And Carpenter treasures the farmer's high-stakes autonomy: "I love it because of the independence—being able to make decisions on my own and then see the results," he says, adding with a laugh: "It's also risky...but I like the risk."

Most of all, though, farming is still a mystical relationship between human beings and the soil—*their* soil. Trying to explain what farming means to him, Carpenter says it's the ability to walk his own land and look at his own crops: "It's that sense of accomplishment: being able to say, this is what I've done; I've worked and I've paid for this, this is mine now...."

Mine—so long as the earth is treated as a living partner.

"If we are patient," says Tom Carpenter, "the land will take care of us."

RECIPES

Corn Chowder

Pioneers coming to Ohio changed their recipes to include ingredients that were plentiful in their new home. Corn chowder is one example: it's just New England clam chowder that moved west. Corn was plentiful in early Ohio. In 1849 the state produced 59,000,000 bushels, making it the largest producer in the nation.

In large saucepan, cook bacon until crisp; remove from skillet. Cook celery and onion in drippings until tender. Add potatoes and water; bring to a boil. Reduce heat; cover and simmer 10 minutes or until potatoes are tender. Add bacon, corn, milk and salt; heat through. Sprinkle each serving with parsley.

Makes about 2 quarts

6 slices bacon, diced
1 cup chopped celery
3/4 cup chopped onion
3 cups diced potatoes
2 cups water
1 (17-ounce) can whole kernel corn, drained
1 (16 1/2-ounce) can cream-style corn
3 cups milk
1/2 teaspoon salt
Chopped fresh parsley

Old-Fashioned Corn Relish

Few dishes are more Midwestern than corn relish. The Amish are particularly fond of it. In almost every traditional community cookbook in Ohio you can find at least one recipe for corn relish. Old cookbooks often call it Corn Piccalilli. This simplified version is a colorful accompaniment to grilled meats. Although it can be eaten year around, it is especially enjoyable during harvest season when made with corn, carrots, green onions and peppers fresh from Ohio fields.

In medium saucepan, combine vinegar, sugar, celery seed, mustard, salt and hot pepper sauce. Bring to a boil; boil 2 minutes. Remove from heat; stir in remaining ingredients. Turn into medium bowl; cover and refrigerate at least 4 hours to blend flavors. Can be made several days in advance, as flavor is better upon standing.

Makes 4 to 6 servings

1/2 cup cider vinegar
1/2 cup sugar
1/2 teaspoon celery seed
1/2 teaspoon dry mustard
1/2 teaspoon salt
1/4 teaspoon hot pepper sauce
2 cups frozen corn, thawed*
1/3 cup each grated carrot, sliced green onions and chopped green pepper

* Corn, freshly cut from the ears, may be used; add to mixture before the 2-minute boiling time.

Corn and Pasta Salad

Makes 6 to 8 servings

2 cups rotini pasta, cooked and
* drained*
1 (17-ounce) can whole kernel corn,
* drained*
1/2 cup each chopped green pepper,
* red onion and sliced radishes*
1/2 cup bottled Italian salad dressing
1/2 cup salsa or picante sauce
1/4 teaspoon salt
1/8 teaspoon pepper

Cleveland is a city of great ethnic diversity. Most Italian immigrants arrived in the early 1900s. Those who came from Sicily, a fruit-growing region, helped make the neighborhood called Big Italy the center of the city's fruit industry. In turn, Italian merchants like Frank Catalano built Cleveland into the state's center of the produce industry. They gave us our taste for oranges, bananas, garlic, olive oil and other delicacies.

Like other Americans, many Italians married members of other ethnic groups. This recipe is a marriage, too: it shows what can happen when Italian pasta meets Midwestern produce.

In large bowl, combine pasta, corn, green pepper, onion and radishes. In small bowl, combine dressing, salsa, salt and pepper. Pour over pasta mixture; toss lightly. Refrigerate at least 2 hours to blend flavors.

Corn Spoon Bread

Makes 6 to 8 servings

1/2 cup butter or margarine
1 (17-ounce) can whole kernel corn,
* drained*
1 (16-1/2 ounce) can cream style
* corn*
1 (8-1/2 ounce) package corn muffin
* mix*
1 cup (8 ounces) sour cream

Ohioans have been enjoying corn spoon bread for years, and there are variations in many Ohio community cookbooks. Ohio's spoon bread may show the influence on Ohio of the South, where it is still a common substitute for mashed potatoes.

The following recipe comes from Susie Bluestone, a registered nurse living in Dublin who likes serving this to her husband, Dave, and children, Jane and Stephen. Susie is always looking for vegetarian ideas for her family.

This is so easy that your children will have fun making it. It is good as a side dish accompanying chicken or pork, but is hearty enough for a vegetarian meal.

Preheat oven to 350 degrees. In 12x7-inch baking pan, melt butter; add remaining ingredients. Mix well. Bake 25 to 30 minutes or until golden brown.

Cheesy Corn Bread

Because cornmeal was so abundant in early Ohio, cooks substituted it for flour in many of their recipes. Dishes such as Indian pudding and corn bread became staples of the settlers' diet.

Even today, recipes for corn bread are many and varied. In this corn bread recipe, cheese and whole kernel corn are added to the batter, providing an interesting combination of taste and texture.

Preheat oven to 400 degrees. In large bowl, combine cornmeal, flour, sugar, baking powder and salt. In medium bowl, combine milk, butter and egg. Add to dry ingredients, stirring just until moistened. Add corn and cheese. Turn into lightly greased 8-inch square baking dish. Bake 20 to 25 minutes or until golden brown. Cool 5 minutes; cut into squares.

Makes 4 to 6 servings

1 cup yellow cornmeal
1 cup flour
1/4 cup sugar
1 tablespoon baking powder
1/2 teaspoon salt
1 cup milk
1/3 cup butter or margarine, melted
1 egg
1 cup whole kernel corn (frozen or fresh)
3/4 cup (3 ounces) shredded Cheddar cheese

Heartland Corn Bread

Be careful where you step in Ohio—there may be an egg there. The state is the fourth largest producer of eggs in the nation, the Ohio Egg Marketing Program tells us. Nearly 20,000,000 birds were at work on the assembly line in 1991. The Ohio Chicken Belt stretches from the vicinity of Columbus westward to the Indiana border.

The use of sausage or ham in this recipe illustrates how hearty variations of corn bread have evolved in the Midwest. Baking the corn bread in a skillet also gives it that unique Heartland touch.

Preheat oven to 400 degrees. In large bowl, combine flour, cornmeal, sugar, baking powder, baking soda and salt. In medium bowl, beat together eggs and buttermilk; add sausage and onions. Add to flour mixture, stirring just until moistened. Turn into lightly greased 10-inch skillet with ovenproof handle.* Bake 40 minutes or until golden brown. Cool 5 minutes; cut into wedges.

Makes 8 to 10 servings

2 cups flour
1-1/2 cups yellow cornmeal
2 tablespoons sugar
1 tablespoon baking powder
1 teaspoon baking soda
1 teaspoon salt, optional
5 eggs
2 cups buttermilk
1/2 cup (2 ounces) smoked sausage or ham, chopped
1/2 cup sliced green onions

* To make skillet handle oven-proof, wrap it completely in aluminum foil.

Milan Inn Corn Sticks

Makes 4 to 6 servings

1 cup yellow cornmeal
1 cup flour
1/4 cup sugar
4 teaspoons baking powder
1 teaspoon salt
1 1/4 cups buttermilk
1/2 teaspoon baking soda
1 egg
1/4 cup solid vegetable shortening,
  melted

Blessed with an abundance of cornmeal, Ohioans found endless ways to use it. Corn sticks, hoecakes (baked on the blade of a hoe), corn pone (the word "pone" is of Algonquian origin and may mean "baked"), johnnycake (perhaps derived from "journey cake"), and hush puppies (sometimes fed to dogs) were among the results. Many of these dishes are still popular in Ohio. Corn sticks are a signature of the Milan Inn, which serves them on a tray with other hot breads.

The Milan Inn is a handsome building set in a New England-style village square. It was built in 1845 and was once a stagecoach stop. The Milan Canal, opened in 1839, connected the town to Lake Erie and made it, briefly, the second-largest wheat shipping port in the world. In 1847 Thomas Alva Edison was born in Milan. All this history and more can be seen in murals at the inn (29 East Church St., 419/499-4604).

Preheat oven to 350 degrees. In large bowl, combine cornmeal, flour, sugar, baking powder and salt. In small bowl, combine 1/4 cup buttermilk and baking soda; add to cornmeal mixture. Add remaining buttermilk, egg and shortening; mix well. Pour into hot, greased cast-iron corn stick pan. Bake 15 to 20 minutes or until golden brown. Remove immediately from pan.

Peerless Mill Inn Corn Fritters

Makes 6 to 8 servings

1-1/2 cups flour
1 (14-1/2-ounce) can cream style
  corn
1 egg
2 tablespoons sugar
1 tablespoon baking powder
Vegetable oil

Early Ohioans were fond of fritters: one old Ohio cookbook had recipes for apple, clam, corn, cream, lemon, jelly, fruit and pork versions. Corn fritters are sometimes called corn oysters or mock oysters because of their shape and flavor. Some recipes, handed down from one generation to the next, call for corn to be minced, allowing release of the milky liquid inside the kernels.

In 1980 Don and Barbara Walsh bought the Peerless Mill Inn in Miamisburg (319 South Second Street, 513/866-5968). The inn is on the site of a flour mill and a saw mill that started operating in the 1820s. Chef Jim Keadey has helped make it a popular restaurant in the Miami Valley. These corn fritters are best enjoyed in front of one of the inn's four huge wood-burning fireplaces.

In medium bowl, combine all ingredients, except oil; mix well. In large skillet, pour oil to a depth of 1/4-inch. Drop batter from rounded tablespoons into hot oil; fry 2 minutes on each side or until golden brown. Remove from skillet and drain on paper towels. Serve warm with maple syrup.

Corn Bread Sausage Stuffing

Like a horse and carriage, hogs and corn often went together in nineteenth-century Ohio. A common way to fatten hogs was to turn them loose in a field of standing corn. Farmers called the practice "hogging down a cornfield." The following recipe combines pork sausage and corn in honor of those pioneer hogs.

It is not necessary to stuff the turkey; stuffing can be made as a side dish. Because the internal temperature of a stuffed turkey is hard to determine, it may even be safer not to stuff the bird. Also, to shorten the cooking time, many cooks choose not to stuff.

In large skillet, cook mushrooms, celery and onion in butter until tender. In large bowl, combine mushroom mixture and remaining ingredients; mix well. Loosely stuff turkey just before roasting or place stuffing in lightly greased baking dish. Bake at 350 degrees for 30 minutes or until hot.

Makes about 1 1/2 quarts

1 cup (4 ounces) sliced fresh mushrooms
1/2 cup chopped celery
1/2 cup chopped onion
1/4 cup butter or margarine
1/2 pound bulk sausage, browned and drained
1/2 cup chopped pecans
4 cups crumbled cornbread
2 cups herb-seasoned stuffing mix
1-1/2 cups turkey or chicken broth
1 egg, slightly beaten
1/2 teaspoon poultry seasoning
1/2 teaspoon rubbed sage

Corn Pudding

Ohioans have various names for this dish: scalloped corn, corn custard and corn au gratin. Corn pudding is a side dish prepared with corn, cream or milk and eggs, baked into a custard-like mixture. For many in Ohio, it is a tradition at Thanksgiving, while others prepare it when fresh corn is most plentiful.

Preheat oven to 350 degrees. In large saucepan, heat milk; remove from heat. Stir in corn, 1 cup crushed crackers, onion, eggs, sugar, salt and pepper. Pour into lightly greased 1 1/2 quart baking dish. In small bowl, combine remaining crushed crackers, butter and nutmeg. Sprinkle on top of corn mixture. Bake 30 to 35 minutes or until set.

Makes 6 to 8 servings

3/4 cup milk
1 (17-ounce) can whole kernel corn, drained
1 (16-1/2-ounce) can cream style corn
1-1/4 cups crushed rich, butter-flavored crackers
2 tablespoons chopped onion
2 eggs, slightly beaten
2 teaspoons sugar
1/2 teaspoon salt
1/8 teaspoon pepper
1 tablespoon butter or margarine, melted
1/8 teaspoon ground nutmeg

Summer Vegetable Medley

Makes 6 to 8 servings

2 cloves garlic, finely chopped
2 tablespoons butter or margarine
3 medium zucchini, thinly sliced
3 medium tomatoes, seeded and
  chopped
1/2 teaspoon Italian seasoning
1/2 teaspoon salt
1/8 teaspoon pepper
3 cups whole kernel corn (fresh or
  frozen)
1/2 cup sliced green onions
1/4 cup Parmesan cheese

In summer, the roadside stands and farmers' markets overflow with the bounty of the state. Ohio has about 1,000 commercial vegetable growers, as well as countless backyard entrepreneurs. In 1991 the state's commercial growers dedicated more than 15,000 acres to sweet corn, celery, tomatoes, onions, potatoes and other fresh vegetables. They produced enough to make the state the nation's twelfth largest producer of fresh vegetables.

Summer or winter, this recipe is a tasty, colorful side dish using several vegetables grown in Ohio.

In large skillet, cook garlic in butter until golden brown. Add zucchini, tomatoes, Italian seasoning, salt and pepper. Cook and stir until softened and some liquid has evaporated. Add corn and onions; cook until heated through. Add cheese; mix well.

Succotash

Makes 4 to 6 servings

4 slices bacon, diced
1/2 cup chopped onion
1 (10-ounce) package frozen whole
  kernel corn, thawed and drained
1 (10-ounce) package frozen lima
  beans, thawed and drained
1/2 cup half-and-half or light coffee
  cream
2 tablespoons butter or margarine
1/8 teaspoon pepper

The Indians taught early settlers to grow beans and corn together, so the cornstalks would support the bean vines. The native Americans also taught settlers to cook the two together, calling the combination *msickquatash*. Succotash may have been served at the first Thanksgiving dinner, in 1621.

Combining beans and corn took on regional differences over the years. Pennsylvania Dutch cooks added green peppers and tomatoes, while southern cooks added okra. Cooks used a variety of beans, but in Ohio the most popular bean for succotash was the lima. The 1880 edition of *Buckeye Cookery and Practical Housekeeping*, one of the nineteenth century's most popular cookbooks, contained summer and winter recipes for making succotash on a wood stove. The following is a modern version of an American classic.

In large skillet, cook bacon until crisp; remove from skillet. Add onion to drippings; cook until tender. Add corn, beans and cream; cook 5 to 10 minutes or until cream has thickened. Stir in bacon, butter and pepper.

Fresh Country Fried Corn

Ohioans love eating sweet corn off the cob, but fried corn is an enjoyable alternative. (It's useful, too, for those who have new dentures or who are temporarily without front teeth!) Ohio community cookbooks provide many different fried corn recipes; this one is outstanding.

In a large skillet, cook all ingredients, except cream, in butter until tender. Add cream. Cook over low heat until thickened, stirring constantly.

Makes 4 to 6 servings

3 cups whole kernel corn (frozen or fresh)
1/2 cup sliced green onions
1/2 teaspoon thyme leaves
1/2 teaspoon salt
1/8 teaspoon pepper
1/4 cup butter or margarine
1/2 cup whipping cream or half-and-half

Roasted Corn with Seasoned Butters

Ohio planted nearly 10,000 acres of sweet corn in 1991 and is the sixth largest producer of sweet corn in the nation. The Sweet Corn Festival in Millersport has been attracting the hungry for nearly half a century; more than 100,000 ears succulent ears are served during the four-day event early in September.

Sweet corn is best if cooked within an hour of picking; after that, 90% of the natural sugar has turned to starch. Corn on the cob, sold commercially, is specially chilled to prevent starch from forming.

Instead of boiling the ears in the usual way, try roasting them in their husks on the barbecue grill. This recipe combines roasting with two seasoned butters to add variety to the summer table.

In small bowl, combine all ingredients for either seasoned butter. Serve on roasted corn.

On each ear of corn, pull the husks back, brush away the silk, then rewrap the husks around the ear. Soak in cold water for 10 minutes; drain. Grill over hot coals, 15 to 20 minutes, turning occasionally; or bake on racks in a conventional oven at 375 degrees for 20 minutes. Ears can also be cooked in a microwave oven; arrange them in oven with space between. Cook on 100% power (high) 10 to 16 minutes, rearranging every 4 minutes. Let stand 5 minutes.

Makes 4 servings

Italian Herb Butter
1/4 cup butter or margarine, melted
1 teaspoon chopped chives
1 tablespoon Parmesan cheese
1/2 teaspoon Italian seasoning
1/8 teaspoon pepper

Spicy Chili Butter
1/4 cup butter or margarine, melted
1 clove garlic, finely chopped
1/2 teaspoon crushed red pepper
1/4 teaspoon chili powder
3-5 drops hot pepper sauce

Roasted Corn
4 ears fresh corn

The Amish do not buy insurance but they don't need to, for they have each other. This 1970 barn raising near Mount Eaton is an example. More than 500 fellow Amishmen of Mose P. Miller built a new barn for him to replace one destroyed by fire three weeks earlier. Nearly 200 Amish women cooked and served them dinner. The barn was built in one day.

Peaceable Kingdoms

On a side street in the northeastern Ohio town of Sugarcreek, across from the railroad station and next to a feed and grain store, is an unpretentious little building. Half the structure was built a few years ago and doesn't quite match the other half, which was probably built a hundred years ago. No matter. This is the crossroads of the Amish universe.

This is not a church headquarters, however: no decrees come down from here, and the Amish do not even own the building. But they pay close attention what comes out of this place, for it is the office of *The Budget*, one of the nation's most unusual newspapers.

Published since 1890, *The Budget* serves the far-flung communities of "plain people," the Amish, as well as some conservative Mennonites. They shun radio and television, and in most cases do not even have telephones, so *The Budget* is the most important medium of mass communication they have. News, mostly handwritten, pours in here from hundreds of Amish and Mennonite correspondents, called scribes. Each week it is formed into the newspaper's national edition and mailed out to more than 17,000 subscribers around the world.

It is fitting that *The Budget* is published in Holmes County, Ohio. People who think all the Amish live in Pennsylvania Dutch Country may be surprised to learn that more Amish live in Ohio than anywhere else, and there are more Amish in Holmes County than any county in America. (Smaller communities of Amish can also be found in other Ohio counties and in states from Delaware to Oregon and even abroad.) Week in and week out, *The Budget* is one way they stay connected.

George R. Smith keeps the paper looking and sounding the way his readers like it: plain and old-fashioned. A Lutheran, Smith has been handling Amish news for over 70 years, and although he sold the paper years ago, continues as editor of its national edition. A typical issue has 24 pages of solid type—no news pictures—divided into community newsletters reporting on local weather, crops, barn raisings and work bees (called frolics), buggy wrecks, births and deaths, and, most of all, the visits the Amish seem to pay each other endlessly.

Readers hooked on news of crime, politics or the Beautiful People should look elsewhere. "Weather hangs on the cold side," reports the scribe in Rebersburg, Pennsylvania. "Farmers have a chance to haul manure. Most of the corn isn't ready to pick yet." From Grove City, Minnesota: "If you happen to talk to my father-in-law...and notice he's not as talkative as usual, it's not because he turned stuck-up at all. He got a new set of dentures recently and they seem to take some getting used to." *The Budget* keeps a constant stream of homey news like this circulating throughout the world of plain people; it is a weekly reassurance that life as they know it goes on.

The Amish need this common medium of communication. "The highest authority in the Amish church is the bishop, and he has charge of just his particular church district [congregation]," explains Smith. Each church district has no more than 40 families or about 200 people in it; the more than 100,000 Amish in Smith's universe are divided into hundreds of such districts. There is no equivalent to Rome for the Amish and the church districts are autonomous. Yet they remain remarkably cohesive. "The newspaper is one of the things that help hold the whole thing together," says Smith.

Also binding the Amish is their shared belief in discipline. "We have our rules," says David Swartzentruber, an Amish harness maker in the Holmes County area. "You've got to stick to the rules—if a group says, 'It doesn't matter,' then things go fast." His own family goes by the "Old Holmes County Rules" or Ordnung, which specify the width of his hat brim, permit him to use stationary engines but not tractors or other vehicles, and allow battery or gasoline lamps in his home, but not electricity from a utility company.

To the "English," as non-Amish are called, the rules may seem strange, but they are designed to preserve life as the Amish know it. Community and family, hard work and humility are highly valued, and they eschew insurance, Social Security and unemployment compensation, preferring to take care of each other instead. If a barn burns, the neighbors rally to build a new one. If a family's hospital bills climb too high, the church district will help pay. If someone needs work, it will be found. If it's time to retire, the elderly will move into their own small house right on the family farm. The Ordnung protect the Amish from the forces of modernism that could rend this fabric of family and community.

Even so, there's room for variations. "A lot of people think the Amish are all alike, but that's far from being the case," says Smith. The biggest differences are between the various orders of Amish. To an outsider they may look alike, but those who know the Amish can tell the differences—by their clothing, their horse-drawn vehicles, their houses, ways of farming, and even hair styles.

"The Swartzentruber Amish are the most conservative of all the Amish," Smith explains, explaining the range of Amish from "low" to "high." "They are the ones who get into trouble with the authorities because they won't use the slow-moving vehicle emblem." The slightly less conservative Old Order Amish are the most numerous. (Despite his name, David Swartzentruber is a member of this group.) They permit the slow-moving vehicle emblem and put lights on their buggies, but do not have telephones. "Then you go on up to into the New Order Amish, which is a fairly recent development," says Smith. Some New Order Amish have telephones and some use tractors instead of horses.

All of these groups use the horse and buggy and are called "house Amish" because church services rotate among their homes. "Then you go up to the Beachy group, the most liberal," says Smith. "They will have cars [plain black ones] and electricity in their homes." Beachy Amish also worship in meetinghouses. There are also a wide variety of Mennonites, who can be harder to distinguish from other Americans; the men usually do not wear distinctive clothing but the women are notable for their white prayer caps and quiet dress styles. The Amish and Mennonites are good friends but prefer not to be confused with each other. They form parallel streams descended from old European Protestants called Anabaptists. Anabaptists believe in adult, rather than infant, baptism.

In one area the plain people not only agree, but are free of Ordnung: their food. It is often rich, but it is not haute cuisine: "It's just good home cooking," says an "English" friend of the Amish. That also means plenty of fats and carbohydrates; it is what one might expect from American country cooking, although it sometimes has a German flavor, with noodles and sauerkraut.

Anyone researching Amish food can learn something at the Mount Hope auction barn, one of several in the Holmes County area. Cattle, horses and horse-drawn farm equipment, produce and other goods are sold regularly at these auctions, and they serve as a regional crossroads of Amish life. Katie Yoder, a Mennonite, runs the food concession and has come to learn something about Amish tastes. "They like their food really simple," she said, adding that she also tries to introduce her Amish customers to new dishes, with mixed success. She has been able to interest them in salads, but not casseroles; baked potatoes have not gone over well with a crowd used to mashed potatoes and gravy. Through experience, the Yoder menu has come to favor hot sandwiches, fried potatoes, and plenty of pies: cherry, peach, elderberry, and raspberry are a typical day's offerings.

"There's good eating here," said an older Amishman, one of many sitting at her restaurant's counter. "I'll tell you my favorite, by a long shot: It's the pork tenderloin. I've got one coming now." He was not alone: deep-fried pork tenderloins on buns poured from the kitchen in a steady stream. Huge apple dumplings with ice cream were also selling well this day, while outside the restaurant other Amish, young and old, were licking ice cream cones: lack of freezers at home makes ice cream a special treat. Indeed, it's generally agreed that the Amish have a sweet tooth and are fond of desserts. "A big thing around here is date pudding," says a friend of the Amish. "It's actually a cake that reminds you of English plum pudding. They like it with caramel sauce and whipped cream."

Elsewhere in the auction barn an Amish youth was getting ready to sell some horses, but paused a minute to talk food. "I like potatoes and meat, like beef and pork, with lots of vegetables," he says. "I guess my favorite

The Ohio Farmer, January 9, 1926

meal is broasted chicken with mashed potatoes and gravy, corn, and pineapple ring with Eagle brand topping," adding, "Amish women are good cooks." Meals aren't always this elaborate, however. When the harvest or other tasks require a quick noon meal, the Amish will sometimes make do with bread soup, which is simply chunks of bread broken up in hot milk.

They may be hearty eaters, but they work it off: to a visitor, the Amish appear no more prone to obesity than anyone else. They are expanding in another way, however: while still a relatively small group, the Amish are a growing denomination. In Ohio, for example, Amish population in the early 1990s was reported near 35,000, about double what it was 30 years ago. The North American total is about 112,000; a century ago it was only 4,000.

Outsiders sometimes confuse Amish with the Shakers or even the Zoarites, both long extinct in Ohio. Then they wonder why the Amish thrive while the others failed. All were devoutly religious Protestants who came to Ohio in the 1800s, establishing agrarian communities which were largely self-sufficient and, in varying degrees, separated from the everyday world. All were hardworking people who preferred plainness and humility to ostentation and materialism. In various ways, all resisted some aspects of government authority, most notably in refusing to serve in the military.

But the Shakers, who founded four communities in Ohio (the first in 1805), were different from the Amish. They welcomed technology, but led stricter lives in other ways: all property was held in common, and they were celibate, relying on converts for their growth. By the late 1800s, however, Shakerism was in decline, attracting fewer members as it was forced to compete with America's booming economy and westward expansion. The last Ohio Shaker communities closed in 1910 and today only a handful of Shakers remain in Maine. In Ohio, Shaker artifacts can still be seen in museums in Shaker Heights and Lebanon.

Another group to have flourished and died in Ohio were the Zoarites. In 1817 about 300 Separatists led by Joseph Bimeler found their way to the fertile Tuscarawas Valley in east central Ohio. Quakers helped them purchase more than 5,500 acres, which they called Zoar, a biblical name meaning "place of refuge." They held property in common and for a while practiced celibacy. By 1850 their thriving community was valued at more than a million dollars. But when Bimeler died in 1853 a visitor remarked that the Zoarites looked like "a flock of sheep who had lost their shepherd." The community gradually came unwound, dissolving in 1898. Listed on the National Register of Historic Places, the Zoar community remains today as a charming museum village.

The Amish also arrived early in Ohio, settling in Holmes County in 1809. Unlike the Shakers and the Zoarites, the Amish believed in private property, and emphatically in marriage. The first Ohio Amish came from Pennsylvania; later settlers came directly from Europe; all heeded the Biblical counsel to be fruitful and multiply, and continue to do so. As each

The Ohio Farmer, January 9, 1926

church district reaches 40 families—the number that can be conveniently accommodated in home or barn worship—it divides and a new district is born; Ohio now has more than 200. In the larger Amish communities at least 75 percent of the young are said to join the church when it comes time to decide at age 18 or 19. With Amish families averaging seven children each, that means a net membership gain every generation. But why are so few young Amish attracted to the material goods, the mobility, and the relative freedom of the outside world?

George Smith explains, "They'd feel like a fish out of water," a homely way of saying that the Amish choose not join the "pursuit of loneliness," as sociologist Philip Slater titled his 1970 dissection of America's social pathology. Our lives are filled with paradoxes, Slater argued: we insist on individualism but yearn for community, are addicted to change while longing for stability, prize self-sufficiency and then feel unsupported. In short, says Slater, "We seek more and more privacy, and feel more and more alienated when we get it."

The Amish may have their own problems, but alienation is not one of them. They are closely involved and interdependent with each other. Their rules are intended to preserve their social values, not to mindlessly deny progress. A few years ago, for example, certain Amish agreed to permit motor-powered hay balers, so long as they were towed into place by horses; it was reasoned that haying was a family activity that machines would not disrupt. On the other hand, grain combines remain forbidden; it is thought they would displace community threshing. In short, the Amish prefer to control technology, and not be controlled by it.

The Amish have considered the plain and the fancy and made their choice. "We try to hold back as much as we can," says David Swartzentruber. "It's hard in this modern world, change creeps in, but we have rules. We try to keep things as plain as possible.

"We like the pace a little slower."

FACES OF THE LAND

Sevilla's World

You drive over a rise and then drop gently into a valley, your automobile slowing to the pace of another world. A horse and buggy are ahead; a team of horses is plowing the field beside the road. Corn stands in hand-built shocks on a nearby hillside. With its rounded hills and small farms, the landscape looks like someone's dream of rural life a century ago. Finally, you come to a stop at a neat white house and a small barn; nearby is a shop with a sign saying that horse and pony harness is made here.

This is the world of Sevilla Swartzentruber, an Amish wife and mother. In many ways her life is very different from that of the fast-track businesswoman or suburban mother. And in some ways it is not.

"We've been canning turkey all morning," says Sevilla as she meets the visitor her husband, David, has brought in from the harness shop. Amish speech is like that: unadorned, unemotive, sometimes disconcertingly matter-of-fact. They are not given to our flowery thank-yous or gushy greetings. "I bet you think we talk very flat," jokes David, and a visitor thinks, They don't sound quite like us, something's missing: there's none of the snappy argot that comes from watching television. They probably don't know who the Simpsons are or what a New York minute is.

Or care. For most of the year the Swartzentrubers' world is bounded, not by electronics or interstate highways, but by how far their horse and buggy can carry them. Within that 15-mile radius, however, is a rich world of human relationships, a tightly woven community with its own rules, hierarchies, economy. Within it lie the Swartzentrubers' church district, schools, most of their family and friends, the dry goods store where Sevilla buys the cloth to make the family clothes, the Amish food store where she travels once a week by horse and buggy for the foods she cannot make.

Sevilla, 41, was born about five miles from where she lives now; David, 38, grew up on a farm only a half-mile distant. Married 18 years, the Swartzentrubers have five children: daughters Iva, 16, and Mary, 15; sons Leroy, 14, Ivan, 11, and Levi, 8. Like their parents, Amish teenagers appear calm and plain-spoken to visitors, with none of the squirminess and Ohmygods of their non-Amish peers. Amish children usually go to school until they finish eighth grade or are 14. So Iva works at home, learning the domestic arts helping her mother, while Leroy learns harness-making by working with his father. Fifteen-year-old Mary serves as one of two teachers (the other is 17) in the nearby one-room schoolhouse. (Teachers in the Amish parochial schools have no formal training beyond their own eighth-grade educations.)

Sevilla, whose long straight hair is pinned up under the traditional white prayer cap, wears a plain, solid-colored dress and apron. Her black knee socks and comfortable black walking shoes are Amish women's everyday garb. Most of what she and her husband wear—her dresses, his shirts and trousers—she makes herself. But making clothes and three meals a day for seven people take only part of her time: "If I didn't have a garden, I wouldn't know what to do," she says. Like most Amish women, Sevilla keeps boredom at bay as she provides for the family by "putting food by," raising lots of garden produce and canning the harvest.

"We don't live out of the store," explains Sevilla, who limits her shopping to staples such as flour, sugar, milk, butter and cheese, much of it bought at a bulk food store run by her sister. Just outside Sevilla's back door are two gardens, neatly enclosed by white wooden fences: the little garden, about 18 by 45 feet, is used for produce for the table, especially lettuce, peas, onions and carrots; the big garden, about 75 by 90 feet, for canning corn, strawberries, non-acid tomatoes, cabbage, celery, parsley, broccoli. Sevilla cares for the garden, with some help from her family, from early spring through early November. Its produce, as well as some bought elsewhere—the turkeys, beef and pork—is canned in glass jars cold-packed in a gasoline cooker. Lining a room in the Swartzentruber cellar are shelves groaning with the results: row on row of glass jars filled with fruits, vegetables, meats, preserves, even prepared pizza sauce.

Working together, Sevilla and Iva have used their gasoline-fired stove this late November day to prepare the noon meal, which the Amish call dinner. "This is the same as usual, nothing different," Sevilla explains: the bread is homemade, the corn home-canned. The main dish today is turkey breast, cut into small pieces, rolled in flour and fried in butter and lard, then simmered on the stove with water and gravy. Other dinners feature steak, fried hamburgers, chicken. Mashed potatoes and gravy, an Amish staple, accompany this meal. On other occasions Sevilla may serve home fries, or less often, french fries, scalloped potatoes or even baked potatoes. There is always plenty of butter and jam to spread on the bread. And there is applesauce. Everyone, including 14-year-old Ivan, drinks coffee with their meal. Dessert is a freshly made custard pie, darkly rich and wickedly delicious. Puddings, tapioca or fruit may also serve as dessert.

Sevilla makes sure her family does not go hungry. Rising at 5 or 5:30 a.m. the Swartzentrubers may have pancakes, fried eggs, or french toast, and cereal—hot in the winter, cornflakes in summer. Sometimes they'll have coffee soup: Saltines broken up with brown sugar and mixed with coffee and cream. The evening meal, called supper, may offer soup, such as chili, chicken noodle or vegetable; sandwiches, spaghetti and meatballs, an apple dumpling or shortcake for dessert. Pizza is a Swartzentruber favorite, but, says Sevilla, "I like the homemade best. I'm not so fond of those strong seasonings."

Homemade cookies, such as chocolate chip, butterscotch, or whoopee pies (two cookies with a cream filling), are favorites for after school. After supper the Swartzentrubers may work in their garden during the summer; snacks of chips, cookies, or melon will follow. "Amish bedtime" is 9 or 9:30 p.m.

The Swartzentruber home, built in 1977, is a two-story white farmhouse, simple and solidly built, sparkling clean inside and out. The shining hardwood floors are mostly bare, except for an occasional small rug, and the plain white walls have only a few decorations: clocks, a calendar or two, a set of gift plates brightly hand-painted with the names and birth dates of family members. The bathroom is modern. In the living room an air-tight wood stove keeps the house pleasantly warm (the Ordnung prohibit a furnace), but the center of family life appears to be the huge kitchen, where a rocking chair and small couch, as well as another stove, add comfort. Though plain, the overall effect is not stark. A visitor notes with amusement that even the family pets—Boots, the cat, and Mickey the Dalmatian dog—wear good, modest Amish black and white. That, of course, is only a coincidence.

Like many Amish, the Swartzentrubers get around more than you might expect, using taxis or sharing hired vans to go out of state occasionally. Even though this can get expensive, David still thinks owning a horse and buggy is a better deal in the long run: "For $3,000 or $3,500, you can get a pretty good outfit," he says.

It also helps preserve the community and family life which is so important to the Amish. Although they own their own land and equipment, they practice communal responsibility, meaning they take care of each other instead of relying on Social Security or insurance. In the Swartzentrubers' case, however, they have a special anxiety: two of the children are "bleeders"—hemophiliacs who pose more than a financial risk: like non-Amish, they must rely on the public blood supply in the age of AIDS. "They tell us the blood is screened, but you can't help worrying," says Sevilla. "There's an Amish boy who got HIV, from the blood supply."

The outside world can push in on the Swartzentrubers in other ways. A car raced down their country road one afternoon a few years ago and nine shots were fired at their house, while the family was in it. No one was injured and there was never any explanation for the shooting, but the Swartzentrubers left the bullet holes in their kitchen walls untouched for a long time, a silent reminder of another, more violent world that is never very far away.

Most of the time, however, family life goes on in traditional ways, with modern touches here and there. David, whose dust allergy forced him from farming into harness making, ships custom-made leather gear all over the country; about half his customers are non-Amish. Sevilla quilts when she's not busy otherwise; she also writes her "circle pals," eight other Amish women, each of whom adds her own letter to a common envelope and sends it on to the next member. And though the Amish are hardworking, they also take time for fun. One Wednesday evening, for example, they were getting ready to go to a neighbor's for a birthday party: seven families were getting together for cake and ice cream, the children to play games like basketball and Pictionary, the adults "just to visit," the quintessential Amish amusement. At home, games are also popular among the Amish; a Swartzentruber family favorite is Monopoly. An image of the plain people, prayer caps and all, battling with bundles of money for control of Boardwalk and Park Place may not rise naturally to the non-Amish mind, but it is reality: such games take the place of radio, television and riding around.

The Amish are different from you and me. As F. Scott Fitzgerald once said of another kind of people, they are strong where we are weak, and vulnerable where we may be tougher. Their strength lies in the ties that bind their families and communities into peaceable kingdoms where there are no homeless, no hungry, no one who is not cared for. But their rules cannot protect them against everything and sometimes they have an innocence exploited by hucksters from a more cynical world. "It's Amish this and Amish that," says David of the region's commercial fringe. There are even Amish, seemingly caught in a time warp, who still worry about Communists as a clear and present danger in this country. And always, the modern keeps pressing around the edges.

Overhead, the jets leave their white trails in the Amish sky. The trailer trucks roll down the country roads of Holmes County, rocking the buggies as they swoosh by. The Swartzentruber family think about the bullet holes in their kitchen wall, wondering why anyone would want to shoot at them. And Sevilla gazes at her boys and worries about the blood supply.

And then she goes back to work, putting food by, making her clothes, teaching her children. And Amish life goes on in Holmes County...almost the way it has for 200 years.

RECIPES

Alta's Hearty Vegetable Soup

Makes about 2 quarts

1 pound lean ground beef
1 cup chopped onion
2 cups tomato juice
1 cup sliced carrots
1 cup diced potatoes
1/2 cup chopped green pepper
  (optional)
1/2 teaspoon salt (regular or seasoned)
Dash of pepper
4 cups milk
1/3 cup flour

Alta Mullet, mother of five, lives on a Mennonite family farm in Sugarcreek. She has some modern conveniences (a van, refrigerator, freezer and phone), but cooks the old-fashioned way, from scratch, rather than with prepared convenience foods. Like her Amish neighbors, Alta has a large garden and her family raises beef and hogs and has dairy cattle for milk. She frequently makes this soup, a family favorite. The creamy texture provided by the milk sets it apart.

In large saucepan, cook ground beef until no longer pink; drain. Add onions, cook until tender. Add remaining ingredients except flour and milk; bring to a boil. Reduce heat; simmer, covered 1 hour or until vegetables are tender. In small bowl, combine 1 cup milk and flour; stir into soup. Bring to a boil; reduce heat. Add remaining 3 cups milk; heat through (do not boil).

Sara's Amish Dressing

Makes 6 to 8 servings

8 cups (2 quarts) bread cubes
2 cups chopped cooked chicken
1 cup diced cooked potatoes
1/2 cup chopped cooked carrots
1/2 cup sliced celery
1/4 cup chopped fresh parsley
2 cups milk or chicken broth
3 eggs, slightly beaten

Sara Yoder and her family are Amish and live in Mount Hope. One of ten children, Sara has seven children of her own. She and her family own and run three businesses: The Mount Hope Harness and Shoe Shop, the Lone Star Quilt Shop, and the Homestead Furniture Store. This is Sara's recipe for a classic Amish dish often served with noodles and chicken gravy.

Preheat oven to 350 degrees. On a 10x15-inch jelly roll pan, place bread cubes; bake 15 minutes or until golden brown. In large bowl, combine chicken, potatoes, carrots, celery and parsley; add bread cubes, mix well. In medium bowl, combine milk and eggs; beat well. Add milk mixture to bread mixture; mix well. Turn into lightly greased 3-quart baking dish. Bake 1 hour or until golden brown.

Potatoes Supreme

Potatoes are a favorite Amish dish. And this is one of my all-time favorite ways to serve potatoes. Whenever we are having a special dinner, my husband, Bill, requests this side dish.

Preheat oven to 350 degrees. In large bowl, combine all ingredients except hashed browns and potato chips; mix well. Stir in hashed browns. Turn into lightly greased 9x13-inch baking dish. Top with potato chips. Bake 1 hour or until golden brown.

Makes 6 to 8 servings

2 cups (8 ounces) shredded cheddar
   cheese
1-1/2 cups sour cream
1 (10 3/4-ounce) can cream of
   chicken soup
1 cup chopped onion
1/2 cup butter or margarine, melted
1/4 teaspoon pepper
1 (2-pound) package frozen hashed
   brown potatoes, thawed
1 cup crushed potato chips

Fluffy Rice and Chicken

Another of Alta Mullet's favorite recipes is this delicious rice and chicken dish. It is easy to make because the rice and chicken cook together in a creamy sauce. Amish and Mennonite families enjoy chicken and prepare it often, either fried, baked or served in a combination dish like this one.

Preheat oven to 350 degrees. In medium bowl, combine cream of mushroom soup and milk; reserve 1/2 cup mixture. To remaining soup mixture add rice and half the onion soup mix. Pour into ungreased 12x7-inch baking dish; top with chicken. Pour reserved soup mixture over chicken; sprinkle with remaining onion soup mix. Cover; bake 1 hour. Uncover; bake an additional 15 minutes.

Makes 4 servings

1 (10-3/4-ounce) can cream of
   mushroom soup
1 soup can milk
3/4 cup uncooked regular rice
1 (about 1-1/2 counces) envelope
   onion soup and dip mix
1 (2-1/2- to 3- pound) broiler-fryer
   chicken, cut up or 2 whole chicken
   breasts, halved

Spatzle

Makes 4 to 6 servings

4 cups flour
1/2 teaspoon salt
3 eggs, slightly beaten
1/2 cup milk (approximately)
1/2 cup water (approximately)
2 tablespoons butter or margarine

Zoar, south of Canton, is a charmingly restored museum village where people still live. The Zoarites who founded the village as a religious community are no longer there, of course, but many of their buildings are.

From Field To Table, A Collection of Original Zoar Recipes, published in 1985, features a recipe for "Spetzla" very similar to this one. The thrifty Zoarites usually made spatzles on Monday, which was also wash day. Starch was added to the water in which the spatzles had been cooked and then used to starch the clothing later hung on the backyard clothesline.

Spatzles are small dumplings, eaten as an everyday pasta dish in Germany. They are considered authentic only if made by hand.

In large bowl, combine flour and salt; add eggs, mix well. Gradually add enough milk and water to form a soft dough; beat until dough pulls away from the side of the bowl. Turn dough out onto floured surface. In large kettle, bring salted water to a boil. With the broad side of a large knife, scrape thin strips of dough directly into boiling water. Cook in gently boiling water for 3 minutes or until swollen. Remove with slotted spoon; rinse in hot water, drain. Toss with butter or brown lightly in butter before serving.

Shaker Corned Beef and Cabbage

Makes 6 to 8 servings

1 (about 4-pound) corned beef brisket
6 each medium carrots, onions, potatoes, and turnips, peeled and cut into serving size pieces
1 small cabbage, cut into wedges

Striving to be self-sufficient in the production of meat as in other things, the Shakers usually did their own butchering. Late each fall, butcher knives were sharpened, meat grinders and sausage makers were brought out, and earthen crocks were filled with brine, for converting the surplus stock of the farm into hams, sausages and corned beef. The Shakers abhorred waste of any kind.

The recipe comes from the Shakers' North Union community. The Cleveland suburb is known today as Shaker Heights.

In large kettle, place brisket; cover with cold water, let stand 1 hour. Drain; cover with fresh cold water, bring to a boil. With large spoon, remove fat from surface of water. Cover; simmer 3 to 4 hours or until meat is tender. Thirty minutes before brisket is done, remove 2 cups of cooking liquid. In separate large kettle, combine liquid with carrots, onions, potatoes and turnips. Bring to a boil. Cover; reduce heat, simmer 15 minutes. Add cabbage; cook 15 minutes longer. Remove brisket from cooking liquid; place on serving platter; surround with drained vegetables.

Der Dutchman Date Nut Pudding

Der Dutchman Restaurant and Gift Barn in Plain City (as well as Sugarcreek, Walnut Creek and Bolivar) serves Amish and Mennonite cooking in appropriate surroundings. There is even an Amish-style buggy in the dining room. Der Dutchman offers family-style dinners, with bountiful salad bar, broasted chicken, roast beef, ham, mashed potatoes, vegetable, freshly baked breads AND dessert. If you visit during the summer, you may even get a ride around the grounds in a horse-drawn buggy. Elsie Gingerich, assistant manager at Plain City, listened to our pleas and gave us the recipe for this popular Amish dessert.

Preheat oven to 350 degrees. In large bowl, combine dates, shortening and baking soda. Pour water over date mixture; stir. Let stand 10 minutes. In medium bowl, combine sugar, eggs, vanilla and salt; add to date mixture. Mix well. Add flour and walnuts; beat well. Turn into greased 9x13-inch baking pan. Bake 25 to 30 minutes or until golden brown; cool. Cut into 1-inch cubes. In serving dishes, layer pudding, whipped cream and bananas.

Makes 8 to 10 servings

1 (1-pound) package pitted dates, chopped
2 tablespoons solid vegetable shortening
1 teaspoon baking soda
1 cup boiling water
1 cup sugar
2 eggs
1 teaspoon vanilla extract
1/2 teaspoon salt
2 cups flour
1 cup chopped walnuts
Sweetened whipped cream
Bananas

Ohio Shaker Lemon Pie

This is a very old lemon pie recipe, and a good example of Shaker simplicity and good taste. It is spectacularly different because it includes slices of lemon with the rind on.

In large bowl, combine lemons and sugar; mix well. Let stand for at least 2 hours. Preheat oven to 450 degrees. Divide pastry dough in half; on lightly floured surface, roll each half out to 1/8-inch thickness. Line pie plate; trim edges even with plate. Add eggs to lemon mixture; mix well. Turn lemon mixture into pastry lined plate. Moisten edges of pastry in pie plate; lift second pastry circle onto filling. Trim 1/2-inch beyond edge of pie plate; fold top edge under bottom crust, flute edges. With sharp knife, slit top pastry in several spots for steam vents. Bake 15 minutes. Reduce oven temperature to 400 degrees; bake 10 to 15 minutes or until knife inserted near center comes out clean.

Makes one 9-inch pie

2 lemons (rind on, ends cut off) sliced very thin
2 cups sugar
Pastry for 2-crust pie
4 eggs, slightly beaten

Sister Lizzie's Sugar Cream Pie

Makes one 9-inch pie

1 cup firmly packed light brown
   sugar
1/3 cup flour
1 (9-inch) unbaked pastry shell
2 cups light coffee cream or half-
   and-half
1 teaspoon vanilla extract
Nutmeg

The Golden Lamb, 27-31 Broadway, in Lebanon (513 / 932-5065), is Ohio's oldest inn. In 1803 Jonas Seaman was issued a license to operate "a house of public entertainment." Among the inn's visitors over the years would be Mark Twain, Charles Dickens, William Henry Harrison, Ulysses S. Grant and Henry Clay. All the rooms are furnished in antiques and many artifacts are displayed in the dining rooms. A Shaker community existed nearby; just across the street is the Warren County Historical Museum with seven rooms of Shaker exhibits. The Golden Lamb serves typical American fare; Shaker Sugar Cream Pie is an example.

Preheat oven to 350 degrees. In small bowl, combine sugar and flour; mix well. Spread evenly in pastry shell. Pour cream and vanilla over sugar mixture. Dot with butter; sprinkle with nutmeg. Bake 40 to 45 minutes or until firm to the touch and golden brown.

Sevilla's Oatmeal Cake

Makes one 13x9-inch cake

1-1/2 cups boiling water
1 cup oats (quick)
1-1/2 cups flour
1 teaspoon ground cinnamon
1 teaspoon baking powder
1 teaspoon baking soda
1 teaspoon salt
2 cups firmly packed light brown
   sugar
1/2 cup butter or margarine
2 eggs
1 teaspoon vanilla extract

Topping:
1/3 cup butter or margarine
2/3 cup firmly packed light brown
   sugar
1/3 cup milk
1 cup flaked coconut
1 cup chopped pecans
1 teaspoon vanilla extract

This recipe is from the kitchen of Sevilla Swartzentruber, Amish housewife. We copied it from her handwritten notebook of recipes. Sevilla's mother often baked it. This cake is tender and moist; the broiled topping is an optional extra that we added.

Preheat oven to 350 degrees. In small bowl, pour boiling water over oats; let stand 10 minutes In large bowl, sift together flour, cinnamon, baking powder, baking soda and salt. In large mixer bowl, combine sugar and butter; beat until creamy. Add eggs and extract; beat until fluffy. Add oatmeal mixture, then flour mixture; mix well. Turn into greased and floured 13x9-inch baking pan. Bake for 30 to 35 minutes or until cake springs back when touched lightly with finger. Serve as is, or prepare topping and frost immediately.

In large saucepan, melt butter; add sugar, cook until mixture boils. Add milk; return to a boil. Remove from heat; add remaining ingredients, stir well. Spread hot topping on cake immediately after it is removed from oven. Turn oven to broil; broil cake about 6 inches from heat for 2 minutes or until frosting bubbles over entire surface of cake. Let cool before cutting.

Sevilla's Custard Pie

Creamy custard pie, rich and dark from the addition of brown sugar, is a favorite of the Swartzentrubers, an Ohio Amish family. It was served at dinner—traditionally the Amish noon meal—when we visited them. Here's our recipe for Sevilla's Custard Pie.

Preheat oven to 350 degree. In small saucepan, bring milk to a boil; remove from heat. In large bowl, combine eggs, sugar, flour, extract and salt; mix well. Beating slowly, add 1 cup hot milk to egg mixture; mix well. Add remaining milk. Pour mixture into pastry shell; sprinkle with nutmeg. Bake 35 to 40 minutes or until knife inserted near center comes out clean. Cool completely before cutting.

Makes one 9-inch pie

3 cups milk
3 eggs
3/4 cup firmly packed light brown
  sugar
2 teaspoons flour
1 teaspoon vanilla extract
1/4 teaspoon salt
1 (9-inch) unbaked pastry shell
Ground nutmeg

Cookin' With Maudie Ho Ho Cake

The Budget is a weekly newspaper, published in Sugarcreek, that serves Amish and Mennonite communities everywhere. One of the favorite sections of the paper is the Cookin' with Maudie column. A recipe exchange, the column prints contributions from throughout the world of "plain people." The recipes are many and varied, and most Amish and Mennonite cooks will confess to using many of "Maudie's" recipes over the years. This recipe is from Volume I of the *Cookin' with Maudie* cookbooks. Ho Ho cake is vastly richer than the commercial confection it is named after, and a must for any confessed chocaholic.

Prepare cake mix according to package directions; bake in greased 15x10-inch jelly roll pan for 20 to 25 minutes or until cake bounces back when touched lightly with finger. Cool. In medium saucepan, combine milk and flour; cook until thickened; cool. In large mixer bowl, beat sugar, butter and shortening; beat until fluffy. Add milk mixture; beat well. Spread over cooled cake.

In medium bowl, combine topping ingredients; beat well. Spread over second layer. Refrigerate at least one hour.

Makes one 15x10-inch cake

First layer:
1 (18-1/4-ounce) package dark
  chocolate or devil's food cake mix

Second layer:
1-1/4 cups milk
5 tablespoons flour
1 cup sugar
1/2 cup butter or margarine
1/2 cup solid vegetable shortening

Topping:
3 cups confectioners' sugar
1/2 cup butter or margarine, melted
3 (1-ounce) squares unsweetened
  chocolate, melted
1 egg, slightly beaten
2 tablespoons hot water
1 teaspoon vanilla extract

Katie's Peanut Butter Pie

Makes one 9-inch pie

Bottom layer:
3/4 cup confectioners' sugar
1/3 cup creamy peanut butter
1 (9-inch) baked pastry shell

Filling:
2 cups milk
1/2 cup sugar
1/3 cup flour
3 egg yolks, slightly beaten
2 tablespoons butter or margarine
1 teaspoon vanilla extract
1/8 teaspoon salt

Topping:
1 cup (1/2-pint) whipping cream,
*   whipped, or 1 (8-ounce) container*
*   frozen non-dairy whipped topping,*
*   thawed*

Katie Yoder has been feeding the Amish in the Mount Hope area for almost 14 years. She runs the cafeteria at the Mount Hope Sale Barn where almost 75% of her customers are Amish. She finds that most Amish enjoy the sweet flavor of peanut butter and especially love it in pie. This peanut butter pie is her top seller.

Katie and her husband, Mennonites who live in nearby Millersburg, raised 9 children, so finding someone to cook for has never been a problem.

In medium bowl, combine sugar and peanut butter; mix until crumbly. Reserving small amount for topping, sprinkle remainder in bottom of pastry shell. In medium saucepan, combine all filling ingredients; cook over medium heat until thickened, stirring frequently. Cool slightly; pour over crumb mixture in pastry shell. Chill. Before serving, top with whipped cream; sprinkle with reserved crumb mixture.

Graham Cracker Pudding

Makes 4 to 6 servings

Crust:
16 whole graham crackers, crushed
1/4 cup sugar
1/4 cup butter or margarine, melted

Filling:
1/2 cup sugar
2 tablespoons cornstarch
1/4 teaspoon salt
2 cups milk
3 eggs, separated
1 teaspoon vanilla extract
2 tablespoons sugar

Graham crackers have been popular since 1882 and they appear in many old recipes. This Amish and Mennonite pudding is a particular favorite in Holmes County.

In medium bowl, combine crust ingredients; mix well. Reserving 1/4 cup mixture, press remainder into bottom and halfway up sides of 2-quart baking dish. In large saucepan, combine 1/2 cup sugar, cornstarch, salt.

In small bowl, slightly beat egg yolks; add to saucepan along with milk; mix well. Cook over medium heat until bubbly, stirring constantly with rubber scraper. Remove from heat; add vanilla. Pour into crust. Preheat oven to 350 degrees. In small mixer bowl, beat egg whites until foamy; gradually add 2 tablespoons sugar. Beat until stiff peaks form.

Top pudding with beaten egg whites, making certain mixture touches sides of baking dish; sprinkle with reserved crumb mixture. Bake 5 to 8 minutes or until lightly browned. Cool; refrigerate before serving.

Peanut Butter Cookies

This recipe is similar to many seen in Amish cookbooks. We've made these cookies for close to twenty years using a small scoop to place the dough on the cookie sheets, instead of rolling each ball by hand. The traditional crossed forks decorate the top of our cookies as they do most of those made by the Amish.

Preheat oven to 350 degrees. In large mixer bowl, combine butter and sugars; beat well. Add eggs; beat well. Add extract and peanut butter; mix well. In medium bowl, combine flour, baking soda and salt; add gradually to sugar mixture, stirring well by hand. Shape into 1-inch balls. Place 2 inches apart on ungreased cookie sheets; flatten with fork dipped in flour to prevent sticking. Bake 10 to 12 minutes or until golden brown. Cool. Store tightly covered.

Makes about 6 dozen

1 cup butter or margarine
1 cup sugar
1 cup firmly packed light brown
  sugar
2 eggs
1 teaspoon vanilla extract
1 cup peanut butter, creamy or
  crunchy
3-1/4 cups flour
2 teaspoons baking soda
1/2 teaspoon salt

Plain People's Lemonade

Lemonade is a favorite beverage among Amish and Mennonite families. The Amish traditionally prepare lemonade by pressing sliced lemons to release the flavorful oils. However, this easy recipe with grated lemon rind seems to impart a similar flavor.

In jar with tight-fitting lid, combine sugar, rind and boiling water; shake until sugar dissolves. Add lemon juice; shake well. Chill. Before serving, add water and ice cubes.

Makes 2 quarts

1-1/2 cups sugar
1 tablespoon grated lemon rind
1/2 cup boiling water
1-1/2 cups freshly squeezed lemon
  juice (from about 6 large lemons)
6 cups cold water
Ice cubes

One-Day Root Beer

Katie Yoder remembers making this root beer for her nine children when they were small. Root beer was a favorite concoction in the nineteenth century, but much less convenient to make than today: roots, bark and leaves were needed to do the job.

In one gallon glass container, combine all ingredients except water. Add water; shake well. Cover; set in sunshine or warm place for one day. Chill; ready to serve next day.

Makes 1 gallon

2 cups sugar
4 teaspoons root beer extract
1 teaspoon active dry yeast
1 gallon lukewarm water

When nineteenth-century Ohio farmers dreamed of hogs, this is what they saw: hippopotamic porkers for whom "fat" is too small a word. The five in the engraving show the ideal that pork producers were aiming for in 1896, when this view was published. Times change and so have hogs. The bottom picture shows what a lean machine the modern hog has become.

How Pigs Built a City, and Other Pork Tales

Let's get this straight: devotees of the hog are not claiming pigs discovered America. At least, they aren't yet. On the other hand, they do assert that swine have left their cloven hoofprints all over the pages of American history. Pigs, they say, have been at right hand of Americans at almost every turn: opening the continent, making medical breakthroughs, and of course, giving the last full measure of devotion at the family dinner table. Talking with pork people, one has a vision of stouthearted porkers, shoulder to shoulder with snouts high, marching to make America a better place in which to live.

Certainly, Ohio's landscape would be markedly different were it not for the Other White Meat. Without pork, the Bob Evans chain of bright-red family restaurants—landmarks in much of the Midwest—might not have been born, leaving Ohioans with no place to go for sausage gravy at dawn. Without pork, there would be no Preble County Pork Festival (the Olympics of pork-eating, as it were), no Ohio pork queens, and no Porkettes (the former name of the pork producers' women's group, a sobriquet long gone but fondly remembered by some of us). And Cincinnati—well, without pork, Cincinnati today might be no more than a suburb of Covington, Kentucky, instead of the Queen City of the West.

In Cincinnati's Sawyer Point Park there are four tall columns, each with a curious figure at the top. Looking closely, you can see the figures are pigs with wings. The flying porkers—each poised to take off like Superman—are reminders that pigs helped make Cincinnati what it is today. The bronze creatures symbolize the rising hopes of the city.

The Cincinnati pigs' lightfooted posture is symbolic of something else, as well: from a food that had a public relations problem, pork has danced its way into the front rank of the modern American commodity scene. In a turnaround as impressive as the Three Little Pigs' face-off with the Big Bad Wolf, pork stared disaster square in the eye and didn't blink.

But back to our story. Hogs were the most important livestock of Ohio's earliest settlers. Pioneer hogs often roamed the forests unfenced, fending for themselves and living on roots and nuts. These free-range razorbacks were fast, wily and tough; nicknamed "landsharks" or "rail splitters," a herd of them, with the boars sporting six- to eight-inch tusks, could successfully fight off bears and wolves. Even when penned they required little care, eating almost anything, from swill to offal. They fattened faster than cattle and produced two litters a year, just like clockwork. And when fattened on corn, they became, in effect, a useful way of getting that crop to market.

As early as 1793, a Cincinnati merchant was advertising cash for pork that had been corn-fed. Thousands of fat Ohio hogs were driven over the mountains to markets in New York and other cities, but it was Cincinnati that beckoned most of all to hog raisers. Strategically located on the Ohio River where it could serve as a crossroads for the North, South and Midwest, the place boomed as farmers, packers, merchants, flatboats and steamboats converged on it. Most of all came the hogs: from throughout southwestern Ohio and nearby Kentucky and Indiana during the first half of the 1800s great herds were driven down rural roads leading to Cincinnati, tens of thousands each year. Typically, one herdsman would drive about 100 animals, but one herd passing through Hamilton in 1830 was said to number 1,800 head.

Propelled by pork, Cincinnati blossomed into the nation's sixth largest city by 1830. By 1841 the city had 62 beef and pork slaughterhouses and 48 pork-packing establishments, producing (as civic boosters liked to point out) enough sausages to girdle the globe. A "pork aristocracy" of wealthy packers and merchants arose. Pigs and pork became so emblematic of Cincinnati that it gained a nickname it has never quite shaken: "Porkopolis."

Of course, not everyone was charmed. Frances Trollope, an acerbic Englishwoman who lived in the United States from 1827 to 1830, later wrote, "I am sure I should have liked Cincinnati much better if the people had not dealt so very largely in hogs. The immense quantity of business done in this line would hardly be believed by those who had not witnessed it." Not only were convoys of hogs constantly moving through the streets on their way to the slaughterhouses, up to 6,000 of the animals roamed the city at will, serving as scavengers. Her nose wrinkling in disgust, Mrs. Trollope complained that she and her companions could not walk the street without "brushing by a snout fresh from dripping from the kennel [gutter]" nor being "greeted by odors that I will not describe, and I heartily hope my readers cannot imagine."

Working in this paradise of pork but competing with each other for the byproducts were two brothers-in-law: candle-maker William Procter and soapmaker James Gamble. They married the Norris sisters, whose father urged them to stop competing and join forces. In 1837 they did, creating the soap and candlemaking firm of Procter & Gamble, with Procter tending the office while Gamble went out to collect fats and scraps from packing plants. A century and a half later, P&G was the largest soap company in the world, one of the nation's largest corporations and biggest advertisers (and parent of the "soap opera"). It had also become a legendary creator of new consumer products ranging from Ivory Soap ("It floats") to Crisco (a vegetable shortening revolutionary in its time), Tide (the first multi-duty laundry detergent), Crest (the first anti-cavity

The Ohio Farmer, March 19, 1921

toothpaste), and Pampers (the first disposable diapers).

Not only is this marketing gorilla a source of pride for Cincinnatians, it is also one of their biggest employers, a shaper of the landscape (P&G's twin, 17-story octagonal office towers are downtown landmarks), and a major contributor to civic and cultural events. Thus, pigs helped build this city, directly in the early days and more indirectly up to the present. Not all Cincinnatians care to remember this. Still smarting, perhaps, from Mrs. Trollope's acid tongue, some opposed erecting the Winged Pigs, for example. They thought the flying porkers detracted from the city's image. A decent regard for history prevailed, however, and that is how pigs grew wings in Ohio.

Hogs loomed large in the lives of nineteenth-century rural Ohioans as well—in their personal economy, work practices and legends. Not a fussy critter to raise, the hog appealed to farmers of limited means, giving it an early reputation as a poor man's animal. But any farmer could appreciate the ease of adding a few porkers to the farm when hard times set in: their value as a cash crop earned the animals a reputation as "mortgage lifters." Drovers circulated in rural areas buying animals for market. Their appearance in the farmyard meant welcome cash for families who saw precious little of it during the year.

In southwestern Ohio, the early pork industry exhibited remarkably efficient divisions of labor. In the Miami Valley, two classes of farmers arose. The "growers," usually small farmers, raised a few animals at a time, while the "fatters" were bigger operators who bought young pigs from the growers and then fattened large herds for market. In Cincinnati, meanwhile, pork processing achieved an efficiency that would impress a modern auto maker. Massive systems of conveyor belts were used before they were common in other industries; Henry Ford learned something about the modern assembly line from visiting Cincinnati. Slaughterhouses and packing plants worked so fast that one visitor observed that, not counting transit time between the two facilities, "from the time moment piggy gets his first blow till his carcass is curing and his fat boiling into lard, not more than five minutes elapse."

Bursting with regional pride, early Ohioans boasted how they had developed an important new breed, the Poland China, a variety still with us today. Early Ohioans liked tell to stories about their pigs, too. The Coitsville homing pigs became well known. A new settler in that northeastern Ohio town told how his sow and piglets vanished one day, only to turn up hale and hearty months later at his former farm in Pennsylvania. Mother Pig had even added eight or ten new piglets to the family.

Ohioans have always been close to their hogs, if not living cheek to jowl with them, nonetheless sharing a certain neighborliness. In the 1840s, Ohio's hog inventory of 2,000,000 animals was the third largest in the United States. In modern times just about as many hogs live here today as did 150 years ago, although the state's rank has slipped to ninth. Ohio's human population, meanwhile, has multiplied to nearly 11,000,000, meaning that—on the average—every square mile of Ohio has about 266 people and 48 hogs. (In some of Ohio's biggest pork-producing counties, such as Darke, Mercer and Clinton, hogs outnumber humans by better than 2 to 1.) Unlike Cincinnatians of Mrs. Trollope's day, however, modern Ohioans and their hogs have found ways to avoid running into each other most of the time: city folk no longer keep a pig or two in the backyard the way they once did, modern hog farms are clean, well-lit operations located outside town, and Ohio State University extension agents roam the land, advising pork producers (a term they prefer to "pig farmers") on such things as porcine bathroom manners.

More amazing to moderns is how many products come from the hog. Even in Trollope's day, Cincinnati bustled with industries producing such hog byproducts as soap, candles, lard, glue, bristles, dyestuffs. Today the hog's blood, brains, bones, fatty acids and glycerine go into products ranging from porcelain enamel to floor waxes. Even the pig's gallstones are used (for ornaments). Pork people are especially proud that nearly 40 drugs and pharmaceuticals come from the hog, partly because physiologically the hog resembles the human in many ways. Insulin made from with the hog's pancreas is the best known lifesaver; 60,000 hogs can supply enough of it to keep a thousand diabetic humans alive for a year. The hog's skin is so similar to human skin that it is used in healing massive burns. And tens of thousands of hog heart valves have been transplanted in humans.

Another remarkable story is that of how an entire industry, facing disaster, could slim down and turn itself around. For years, pigs had been bred for fatness: their lard was an American staple for cooking. After World War II, however, demand for lard dropped and health consciousness rose as consumers began to worry about fat and cholesterol. Porky Pig was starting to get the fishy eye from Americans when pork producers went to work in the 1950s to slim down their animals, through breeding and feeding practices. In effect, they strove to reverse generations of breeding for fatness; now they were striving for lean. They have had notable success: between 1963 and 1990 the fat in a three-ounce broiled pork loin was cut 77% (to 6.9 grams); calories were cut 53% (to 165 calories). Three-ounce roasted center loins or tenderloins even have slightly less cholesterol than some equivalent cuts of chicken or beef. And cured pork products are now cured with 50% less salt than years ago.

Pork people are fond of showing comparative pictures of the old and the new hog. The effect is not unlike those before-and-after photos seen in ads for diet schemes. One picture, labeled "Today's leaner hog," shows a svelte animal; on the other hand, "the 1940s hog" is, well, rather piggy looking. Exhibits like this are one way the pork people have cannily let their light shine forth in recent years. Under the banner of the "The Other White Meat," an advertising campaign launched in 1986, the National Pork Producers Council and its affiliates, including the Ohio Pork Producers Council, have produced a veritable barrage of advertising, publicity, and special events to boost pork.

Their favorite critter has the look of a winner: in the modern hog, farmers, scientists and extension agents have developed a lean, mean Other-White-Meat-producing machine of awesome speed and efficiency. For example, a hog can be prepared for market in just 150 days, when it will yield about 105 lbs. of lean pork. That means it gained an average 3/4 of a pound of usable meat every day of its life. What's more, it only took about 3.5 lbs. of grain for every pound of that gain; cattle need 7 to 10 lbs. to do the same.

To pork people, of course, the hog is not just a mighty fine animal, it's downright incredible. They can tell you, for example, how hogs beat the Pilgrims to these shores by nearly 100 years: Hernando de Soto brought them to Florida in 1539. They'll tell you how hogs helped America win the war: pork was the basis for "C" and "K" rations during World Wars I and II (and let us not forget Spam on the home front). Not only that, fat from the pig went into making nitroglycerine for explosives. They'll even tell you that the hog is the second most commonly domesticated animal around the globe—exceeded only by the dog.

But perhaps most amazing of all is the goal pork producers have set for themselves: to make pork America's "meat of choice" in the 21st century. In other words, they predict that someday you'll more likely slice a pork roast for Sunday than roast of beef, grill pork loins instead of steaks on the backyard barbecue, and call for a MacRib sandwich instead of a Big Mac at the Golden Arches.

In plain language, they're out to turn red-meat-addicted Americans onto...the Other White Meat.

You may not think they can do it. But, then, you probably didn't think pigs could have wings, either.

Breed The Best
THE WORLD NEEDS LARGE
FAT HOGS
Why lose money breeding
and feeding scrub hogs?
Two of our O. I. C. Hogs
Weighed 2806 Pounds.

FOR FREE BOOK
"The Hog from Birth to Sale"
THE L. B. SILVER CO.
R. 195, SALEM, OHIO

The Ohio Farmer, October 4, 1919

FACES OF THE LAND

Mr. Pork

Slim as a whippet and just as swift in mind, tongue and body, Dave Gerber roams Hog Country like a circuit rider, bringing wit and wisdom to man and animal alike. "Gerber's my name; people AND pigs are my game," he'll tell you.

Gerber is a district swine specialist with the Ohio State University Extension, covering 35 counties in the state's southwest and south. Godfather to a million or more hogs, he is concerned about everything affecting them, from the roofs over their heads and the air they breath to their sex lives and bathroom habits.

"The Legend That is Dave Gerber," as a friend calls him, is famed the length and breadth of Hog County as a wisecracking, fast-talking professional who knows more about hogs and cares more about people than anyone they know. "At one time I used to say, 'Pigs are my game,' but really, people come first," says Gerber. "Pigs are a way that you work with people."

One way Gerber works with people is to amuse them. "I'm from the Government, and I'm here to help you," he'll tell an audience. Gerber can unloose a rapid-fire barrage of facts and quips on the unwary: "Did you know pork is high in B-12?" he may demand. "Don't take vitamins! Take pork!" But the chuckles Gerber evoke don't detract from the widespread respect he has earned: a spokeswoman for the Ohio Pork Producers Council calls him "Mr. Pork."

As an extension agent, Gerber is part of a uniquely American educational venture: the partnership between counties, land-grant universities like Ohio State, and the U.S. Department of Agriculture. Extension services like Ohio's serve both producers and consumers, bringing education to farmers in the field and to homemakers and youth in their communities. Thus, Gerber is a professor in the OSU College of Agriculture, but he usually teaches people where they work instead of in classrooms. Extension agents have various tasks: some run 4-H programs, others focus on home economics, and others are concerned with natural resources. Gerber is an agricultural agent, specializing in swine. Most agents are assigned to one or two counties, but as a specialist Gerber works a larger territory, backing up other agents as well as working directly with farmers.

In southwest Ohio—"Hog Country"—Gerber is custodian of hallowed ground, for this is the storied land of "Porkopolis" (Cincinnati), where hogs once roamed the streets. The region is the birthplace of the Poland China hog, and it was the site of the big hog drives from the nineteenth-century farms of the Miami and Scioto valleys. Even now about half of Ohio's nearly 2,000,000 hogs live in Gerber's territory alone. This is also where Ohio celebrates the glory of it all in the Preble County Pork Festival, held every September.

Gerber crisscrosses this 17,000-square-mile territory constantly, spending no more than a day and a half a week in his office in Springfield. "Every day is a little bit different," says Gerber. "Today I'm consulting with someone who wants to build a new hog barn. Tomorrow I have to check out a firm that wants to buy hogs for a medical training of doctors, and work out a place to buy them and what a fair price is."

Gerber knows hogs, respects hogs, even esteems hogs—but he does not romanticize them. City folk can get misty-eyed about life on the farm and the charm of its animals, but farmers have to be more practical. "We've got to think about net income," Gerber says. "It has to be a business—we've got to make it so it pays off."

"Whatever the topic, our job is education," Gerber says of his work as an extension agent. He spends a lot of time advising farmers on the best designs for hog buildings, and has become something of an expert on gas levels; he has written and lectured on the problems—sometimes life-threatening to both hogs and humans—that can arise if hog facilities are not adequately ventilated.

Dave Gerber

Gerber carries out his job various ways: sometimes he consults one-on-one with farmers, sometimes he addresses workshops or conferences, and sometimes he takes Ohio pork producers on tours to other states. Gerber especially likes to work with youth: he is an advisor to OSU students interested in animal science, and has made several instructional videos to help 4-H youngsters with their pig-raising projects.

In fact, there's isn't a great deal of Gerber's life that doesn't have something to do with hogs. A farm boy from Findlay who began showing pigs at fairs at about age 10, Gerber later wrote a master's thesis on pork production. He wears a big belt buckle that says "PORK PRODUCER" on it, and likes to cheer on pork producers by handing out cards that urge, "GO WHOLE HOG." At home, he has built up a collection of more than 50 figures of pigs—glass, metal, ceramic, cloth—and he keeps a wardrobe of what he calls "pig hats" (but denies wearing pig shorts of the kind sold at the state fair). From time to time he puts on a pork barbecue, using a portable cooker that can be towed behind his car while it is roasting a whole hog at once. Naturally, Gerber is a dedicated pork eater: "There have been times we've had it three times a day for three days," he'll say, adding that about once a day is more typical. Gerber will eat pork in most any form, but pork chops on the grill are his favorite.

And so, dedicating everything but his underwear to the cause, Mr. Pork roams Hog Country, preaching the gospel of modern agricultural methods and singing the praises of the incredible pig. The hog, according to Gerber, is a remarkable animal: It is clean ("If you give it a chance, it's cleaner than a dog"), protective of its young ("You better not be in a pen with a sow if she hears a piglet squeal"), and smart ("You can train a pig to a leash, you can toilet train it"). The hog has made numerous contributions to medical science. And it has helped people get ahead: "The hog has paid for more farms over the year than any other animal," Gerber says.

But for all his fondness for hogs, Gerber will never lose sight of just what they are for, anyway.

Some people look at them and see swill machines. Some see pets, shaped in the image of cartoon characters like Porky Pig. Some see a handy metaphor for slobs, gluttons or boors.

But Dave Gerber sees none of these. When Dave Gerber looks at a pig, he sees...

Pork chops.

RECIPES

Preble County Barbecued Pork Chops

The Preble County Pork Festival is held the third weekend of September at the county fairgrounds in Eaton. Over 50,000 pork chops and 42,000 pounds of pork loin are served. Industrial paint sprayers are used to apply this sauce to the chops.

In medium saucepan, combine all ingredients except chops; bring to a boil. Remove from heat. Grill or broil chops as desired, brushing frequently with mixture.

Makes 6 to 8 servings

1 cup cider vinegar
1 cup water
1/4 cup butter or margarine
1 tablespoon Worcestershire sauce
1 teaspoon salt
6 to 8 loin pork chops

Honey-Mustard Marinated Pork Tenderloins

Every August, Hamilton hosts the Ohio Honey Festival. Visitors enjoy honey in ice cream, Greek pastries, hard candy and honey butter. Entertainment includes the Little Miss Honey Bee contest This savory marinated pork tenderloin, cooked on a barbecue grill, was inspired by what the Festival people do with honey.

Partially slit tenderloins lengthwise, being careful not to cut all the way through; arrange in shallow glass dish or resealable plastic bag. In small bowl, combine remaining ingredients; pour over meat. Refrigerate 6 hours or overnight Remove meat from marinade; grill or broil as desired, basting frequently with marinade. Slice crosswise, in 1/2-inch slices.

Makes 4 to 6 servings

2 pork tenderloins (about 1-1/2 pounds)
1/3 cup vegetable oil
1/4 cup red wine vinegar
3 tablespoons brown sugar
3 tablespoons honey
5 teaspoons Dijon-style mustard

Rothschild Pork Chops with Raspberry Sauce

Makes 4 servings

1/4 cup flour
1/4 teaspoon salt
4 boneless center loin pork chops
2 tablespoons vegetable oil
1 clove garlic, finely chopped
3/4 cup chicken broth or stock
1/2 cup dry white wine
1/4 cup Rothschild Red Raspberry
  Vinegar
1 tablespoon pink and green whole
  peppercorns
Fresh raspberries

In 1976, Bob and Sara Rothschild moved their family from San Francisco to Urbana and bought a 176-acre farm. After trying corn, soybeans and broccoli, they decided to grow Heritage Red Raspberries. Since 1984, when they produced 400 cases of raspberry preserves, the Rothschilds have producing gourmet delicacies such as sauces, mustards, extra virgin olive oil, chutney, vinaigrette and fruit-based liqueurs. At the International Fancy Food Show in New York, Rothschild was named as Outstanding Product Line of 1991.

In shallow dish, combine flour and salt; coat both sides of chops with mixture. In large skillet, brown chops in oil; remove from pan. Add garlic, broth and wine, stirring well to remove any brown bits from skillet. Return chops to skillet. Reduce heat; cover and simmer 25 to 30 minutes or until tender. Remove chops from skillet; keep warm. Add vinegar and peppercorns; cook and stir until thickened. Pour sauce over chops; garnish with raspberries.

Savory Pork Chop Bake

Makes 4 to 6 servings

1/4 cup flour
1/4 teaspoon salt
1/8 teaspoon pepper
6 loin pork chops
2 tablespoons vegetable oil
1 (10-3/4-ounce) can cream of
  mushroom soup
3/4 cup water
1/2 teaspoon ground ginger
1/4 teaspoon crushed rosemary
  leaves
1 (2.8-ounce) can french fried
  onions

Although Eleanor Hart, the co-author's mother, did not really enjoy cooking (there were too many other things she'd rather have done), she did like to make this pork chop dish. It is the kind of meal families across Ohio and the Midwest sit down to nightly.

In shallow dish, combine flour, salt and pepper. Coat both sides of chops with mixture. In medium skillet, brown chops in oil; drain. Arrange in lightly greased 12" x 7" baking dish. In same skillet, combine remaining ingredients except onions; heat. Pour over chops; top with half can onions. Cover; bake 50 minutes. Uncover; top with remaining onions, bake 10 minutes longer.

Janet's Smoked Pork Chops with Apples and Onions

Janet Wood owns what is may be the largest private cookbook collection in Ohio. Her collection of nearly 3,000 titles ranges from the most recent to books published in the 1800s. Her husband, Don, helps her find the historical editions. You'll be glad you found this recipe: the sherry adds a rich nutty flavor to the mellow flavors of caramelized apples and onions.

In large skillet, brown chops in oil. Reduce heat; add sherry. Cover; cook 25 to 30 minutes or until sherry has reduced to a rich brown juice. In another skillet, cook apples and onion slices in butter, stirring frequently until almost tender. Add pepper to taste. Increase heat; cook until lightly browned and caramelized. Serve apple and onion mixture over chops.

Makes 4 to 6 servings

6 smoked loin pork chops
2 tablespoons olive oil
1 cup dry sherry
4 tart apples, cored and thinly sliced (Janet uses Granny Smith)
2 medium onions, thinly sliced
2 tablespoons butter or margarine
1/8 teaspoon pepper

Breaded Pork Chops and Tomato Gravy

Shirley Failor of Toledo (mother-in-law of the co-author) makes the best breaded pork chops in the world. The recipe for tomato gravy (how Ohio can you get!) was inspired by a Mennonite cook, and goes well with the chops.

Preheat oven to 350 degrees. In shallow dish, combine egg and water. In another shallow dish, combine crumbs, cheese and parsley. Coat both sides of chops with crumb mixture, dip in egg mixture, then coat again with crumb mixture, pressing firmly so mixture adheres evenly. Place chops on lightly greased 10" x 15" jelly roll pan. Bake 30 minutes; turn chops over. Bake additional 30 minutes or until golden brown.

In medium saucepan, bring tomato juice to a boil. In small bowl combine half-and-half, flour, salt and pepper. Add half-and-half mixture to tomato juice, stirring constantly until thickened. Serve with pork chops.

Makes 4 to 6 serving

1 egg, slightly beaten
2 tablespoons water
1-1/2 cups dry bread or cracker crumbs
2 tablespoons Parmesan cheese
1 tablespoon chopped fresh parsley
4 to 6 loin pork chops
1 cup tomato juice
1 cup half-and-half or milk
2 tablespoons flour
1/2 teaspoon salt
1/8 teaspoon pepper

Southern Peach Pork

Makes 4 servings

1/2 cup flour
1 teaspoon salt
1/2 teaspoon white pepper
8 (3-ounce) boneless pork loin slices
2 tablespoons butter or margarine
2 cups peach slices (fresh or frozen)
1/4 cup peach brandy
1/2 cup whipping cream
Chopped fresh parsley

At age 15 he was washing restaurant dishes; by 16 he was cooking. Charles Langstaff's talent has been apparent ever since. Chef of Hoster Brewing Company in Columbus, Langstaff has been honored by the National Pork Producers Council as Chef Par Excellence and Chef of the Year by the American Culinary Federation,Columbus chapter. The Hoster Brewing Co., opened in 1836, serves a variety of beers brewed on the premises. Part of the brewing process visible in the front of the restaurant. This recipe won first prize in the 1988 Ohio Pork Producers Taste of Elegance Contest.

In shallow dish, combine flour, salt and pepper; coat both sides of pork slices with mixture. In large skillet, brown pork slices in butter; continue cooking 5 minutes or until pork is slightly pink inside. Remove pork slices from skillet; keep warm. Add 1 cup peach slices; cook 1 minute. Remove skillet from heat. In blender or food processor, puree remaining 1 cup peach slices; add to skillet along with peach brandy. Return skillet to heat; bring to a boil. Add cream; continue cooking at low heat until sauce thickens. Serve peach sauce over pork; sprinkle with parsley.

Salisbury Steak

Makes 4 servings

2 medium onions, sliced
2 tablespoons butter or margarine
1 pound lean ground beef
1 cup fresh bread crumbs (2 slices)*
1 egg, slightly beaten
1/2 teaspoon salt
1/8 teaspoon pepper
1 cup water
2 tablespoons catsup
1 tablespoon dry sherry
1 teaspoon soy sauce

* To make fresh bread crumbs easily, place bread in food
  processor, process until fine crumbs; or crumble by
  hand.

Dr. James H. Salisbury, who moved to Cleveland in 1864 to help start a hospital, became famous for arguing that diet could help cure disease. Chopped lean beef that had been patted into cubes was one of his dietary measures. It didn't hurt Salisbury, who lived to 81.

In large skillet, cook onions in butter until tender; remove from skillet. In medium bowl, combine ground beef, crumbs, egg, salt and pepper; mix well. Shape into 4 to 6 oval patties. Brown patties in skillet; remove. Add remaining ingredients to skillet; cook, stirring constantly until thickened. Return onions and patties to skillet; cover and simmer 15 minutes or until patties are done.

Porcupine Meatballs

Gone are the days when Ohio brides received pressure cookers as wedding gifts. However, there are still many pressure cookers in use in our kitchens. Pressure cookers were an economical way to cook less tender cuts of meat; they also saved time and fuel because they cooked in a relatively short period of time. Because only a small amount of water used in most recipes, foods— especially vegetables—retained most of their vitamins and minerals.

In large bowl, combine all ingredients except soup and water. Mix well. Form into 2-inch meatballs. In pressure cooker, combine soup and water; drop meatballs into soup mixture. Close cover securely. Place pressure regulator on vent pipe; cook 10 minutes with pressure regulator rocking slowly. Let stand until automatic air vent plunger drops and no steam escapes when pressure regulator is tilted. The cooker may be cooled more rapidly by running cold water over the lid.*

(Do not EVER open pressure cooker until pressure is completely reduced. Remember, the hot food inside is under pressure. Many a cook who made this error has found herself scraping food off the ceiling and perhaps burned by the contents.)

* If you do not own a pressure cooker, this dish may be prepared by cooking meatballs in a large, covered saucepan. Simmer until meat is done and rice is tender.

Makes 4 to 6 servings

1-1/2 pounds lean ground beef
1/2 cup uncooked rice
1/4 cup chopped onion
1/2 teaspoon salt
1/8 teaspoon pepper
1 (10-3/4-ounce) can tomato soup
1 cup water

Swiss Steak

Any Ohio community cookbook you look in is sure to have a recipe for Swiss Steak. It is a stick-to-the-ribs dish that's especially good during winter months. Many variations exist, but basically Swiss Steak is round steak cooked until tender in a tomato-vegetable gravy.

If your schedule permits, the meat can be browned and then put in your crock pot with other ingredients and cooked on low for 8 to 10 hours.

In shallow dish, combine flour, salt and pepper: coat both sides of steak pieces with mixture. In large skillet, brown steak in oil; remove from pan. Drain excess fat; return steak to skillet. Add remaining ingredients: bring to a boil. Reduce heat; cover and simmer 1-1/2 to 2 hours or until tender. If desired, thicken gravy with additional flour dissolved in a small amount of water.

Makes 4 to 6 servings

1/4 cup flour
1/2 teaspoon salt
1/8 teaspoon pepper
1 (1-1/2- to 2-pound) round steak,
  cut into serving-size pieces
2 tablespoons vegetable oil
1 (28-ounce) can tomatoes,
  undrained and broken up
1 rib celery, chopped
1 medium onion, peeled and sliced
1 tablespoon bottled steak sauce

Zesty Barbecue Beef Sandwiches

Makes 10 to 12 servings

1 (4-pound) boneless beef chuck
  roast, cut into cubes
2 tablespoons vegetable oil
1-1/2 cups chopped onion
1 cup chopped celery
1 (28-ounce) can tomatoes,
  undrained and broken up
2/3 cup cider vinegar
1/2 cup catsup
1/3 cup Worcestershire sauce
1/4 cup sugar
Sandwich buns or hard rolls

This barbecue beef sandwich is a variation of the ever-popular Sloppy Joe. It uses beef chuck roast, that after cooking for a long period of time, falls apart into tender shreds. It makes a large amount and is a great make-ahead meal for a crowd.

In large kettle, brown beef in oil; drain. Add onion and celery; cook until vegetables are tender. Add remaining ingredients; bring to a boil. Reduce heat; cover and simmer 2-1/2 to 3 hours or until tender; stirring occasionally. Using 2 forks, pull meat apart into shreds. Serve on buns.

Beef and Roasted Vegetable Kabobs

Makes 4 servings

1/2 cup vegetable oil
1/4 cup red wine vinegar
1 clove garlic, finely chopped
1-1/2 teaspoons rosemary leaves,
  crushed
1/8 teaspoon pepper
1 (1-1/2 pound) sirloin steak (about
  1-inch thick), cut into cubes
8 cherry tomatoes
2 ears corn, cut into 2-inch pieces
2 medium onions, quartered and
  separated into bite-size pieces
1 green pepper, cut into bite-size
  pieces
Hot cooked rice

Every summer, Ohioans head for their backyards and fire up their barbecue grills. Some of the beef they cook comes from their own state, which in 1991 counted 43,000 cattle farms and 1,600,000 head of cattle and calves. Believe it or not, the Ohio Beef Council says the Buckeye State has more cattle (when you count in dairy animals) than some western ones, such as Wyoming, Utah or Nevada.

In the following recipe, meat and vegetables are cooked together, so all you need do is prepare a quick salad and rice and your meal is complete. That leaves plenty of time to get back on your horse and round up those little dogies roaming the Buckeye range.

In small bowl or jar with tight-fitting lid, combine oil, vinegar, garlic, rosemary and pepper; shake well. In large shallow baking dish, pour marinade over meat. Cover; refrigerate 6 hours or overnight, stirring occasionally. Drain meat, reserving marinade. Skewer meat and vegetables.* Grill or broil as desired, basting frequently with marinade. Serve on rice.

* Metal or wooden skewers may be used. If using wooden, soak in water for 30 minutes before meat and vegetables are put on. Use a sharp metal utensil to put holes through corn pieces.

Chikwich Sandwich

The Chikwich chicken sandwich is the creation of Alice Walters, director of marketing for the Ohio Poultry Association. It was designed for sale on the midway at the Ohio State Fair in 1993.

The last time Ohio Department of Agriculture counted beaks, there were nearly 20,000,000 chickens in the state. That's a lot of Chikwiches.

In large kettle, combine all ingredients; bring to a boil. Reduce heat; cover and simmer 1 hour or until chicken is tender, stirring occasionally. Using two forks, pull chicken apart into shreds. (If mixture still has a lot of liquid, simmer, uncovered, until liquid reduce is reduced.) If desired, add few drops hot pepper sauce. Serve on buns.

Makes 8 to 10 servings

6 whole skinless, boneless chicken breasts
3 cups chicken broth or stock
1 all-purpose apple, peeled, cored and chopped
1 medium onion, chopped
1/4 cup cider vinegar
1-1/2 teaspoons pepper
4 cloves garlic, finely chopped
Hot pepper sauce (optional)
Sandwich buns or hard rolls

Chicken Fricassee with Tomato Dumplings

Pat Bruns shares this recipe with us. It is a favorite of her family and friends (whose names were scribbled on the recipe). A typical midwestern dish, it hearty and delicious on a cold winter night. Pat adds a unique touch to the dumplings, adding tomato juice, which gives them a unique taste and golden color. (Pat raises golden tomatoes and makes juice from them. Commercial tomato juice will work as well, but imparts a deeper color.)

In large kettle, combine all fricassee ingredients except water and flour; bring to a boil. Reduce heat; cover and simmer 2 hours or until chicken is tender. In small bowl, combine water and flour; mix well. Add to chicken mixture; stir. In large bowl, combine all dumpling ingredients except tomato juice; mix well. Gradually stir in tomato juice, forming soft dough. Drop dumpling mixture, in rounded tablespoons, over chicken mixture. Cover; cook 15 to 20 minutes or until dumplings are done. (Do not lift cover during cooking time.)

Makes 6 to 8 servings

Fricassee:
2 (2-1/2- to 3-pound) broiler fryer chickens, cut up
3 cups water
2 ribs celery, chopped
2 medium carrots, thinly sliced
1 medium onion, chopped
1/2 teaspoon salt
1/4 teaspoon pepper
1/4 teaspoon ground allspice
1/2 cup cold water
2 tablespoons flour

Dumplings:
1-1/2 cups flour
2 teaspoons baking powder
3/4 teaspoon dry mustard
1/2 teaspoon salt
3/4 cup tomato juice

The Heritage Grilled Breast of Chicken and Sauce

Makes 8 servings

Chicken:
8 skinless, boneless chicken breast
  halves
3 cloves garlic, finely chopped
16 large fresh basil leaves

Marinade:
1/2 cup white wine
5 tablespoons olive oil
3 cloves garlic, finely chopped
1/2 teaspoon salt
1/4 teaspoon pepper

Fresh Basil Tomato Sauce:
Makes about 2 cups
1/4 cup chopped green pepper
1/4 cup chopped onion
1 clove garlic, finely chopped
2 tablespoons butter or margarine
2 (8-ounce) cans tomato sauce
1/2 teaspoon salt
1/4 teaspoon pepper
1/2 cup chopped fresh basil leaves

This historic 1827 Cincinnati farmhouse has been a restaurant since the turn of the century. Howard and Jan Melvin, restaurant's owners, opened The Heritage in 1959. They restored the building to its early appearance and created a menu that ranges from simple American cooking to the latest in innovative cuisine. Jan grows her own herbs and has developed recipes to use them. Profits from the sale of their cookbook, *The Heritage Tradition Cookbook, A Quarter Century of Innovative Dining*, benefit the Cincinnati Zoo. ($15.95, plus shipping and handling, from The Heritage Restaurant, 7664 Wooster Pike, Cincinnati, OH 45227, 513/561-9300.)

Insert 1/8 of the garlic and basil leaves under the skin of each chicken breast; place in shallow, non-metallic baking dish. In small bowl, combine marinade ingredients; pour over chicken. Cover; refrigerate 4 to 6 hours or overnight. Remove chicken from marinade; grill over hot coals, 8 to 10 minutes per side. Serve with Fresh Basil Tomato Sauce.

In medium skillet, cook onion, green pepper and garlic in butter until tender. Add tomato sauce, salt and pepper; bring to a boil. Reduce heat; simmer uncovered for 10 minutes. Add the basil and serve immediately.

Karen's Favorite Chicken Bake

Makes 4 servings

4 skinless, boneless chicken breast
  halves
4 slices (about 4 ounces) Swiss
  cheese
1 (10-3/4 ounce) can cream of
  mushroom soup
1/2 cup dry white wine
2 cups herb-seasoned stuffing mix
1/2 cup melted butter or margarine

Veda Rose is the manager of product services for Borden Foodservice. The wonder of this recipe is that it is easy to put together, yet elegant enough to impress. Veda got the recipe from her sister, Kay Anne Day, who was born and raised in Ohio, but now lives in Philadelphia. The dish is named for Kay's daughter.

Preheat oven to 350 degrees. In 8-inch square baking dish, place chicken breasts; top with cheese slices. In medium saucepan, combine soup and wine; heat. Pour soup mixture over chicken. In medium bowl, combine stuffing mix and butter. Sprinkle evenly over soup mixture. Bake uncovered, 1 hour or until golden brown.

Veal Romano

Makes 6 servings

Breading:
1 cup flour
1 teaspoon basil leaves
1 teaspoon oregano leaves
1/2 teaspoon garlic powder
1/2 teaspoon onion powder
1/2 teaspoon white pepper

Coating:
5 eggs
1/4 cup milk
1/4 cup freshly grated Romano cheese
1 tablespoon Worcestershire sauce

Remaining ingredients:
6 (4-ounce) veal cutlets, cut into medallions
1/2 cup olive oil
18 sun-dried tomatoes
1/2 cup balsamic vinegar
1/2 cup olive oil
2 tablespoons chopped scallions
1 tablespoon chopped red pepper
3 cloves garlic, finely chopped
1/2 teaspoon basil leaves
1/2 teaspoon oregano leaves
1/8 teaspoon white pepper
Dash Worcestershire sauce
1 pound capellini (Angel Hair pasta), cooked and drained

The Lafayette Hotel in Marietta is one of the last Riverboat Era hotels. The Gun Room, the hotel's main dining room, houses a fine collection of antique muskets and firearms. Other highlights of the property are Victorian decor and steamboat instruments, particularly an 11-foot pilot wheel from the steamboat J.D. Ayres. The Lafayette is an official stop of the Delta Queen and Mississippi Queen river boats, and is a charter member of Historic Hotels of America, an honor shared with only two other hotels in the state. Executive Chef Kevin Caskey updated this favorite recipe with the addition of sun-dried tomatoes.

In shallow dish, combine flour, basil, oregano, garlic powder, onion powder, and pepper. In another shallow dish, combine eggs, milk, cheese, Worcestershire and garlic powder. Coat both sides of meat with seasoned flour; dip in egg mixture. In large skillet, brown meat in hot oil; remove from pan. Reduce heat to low, add tomatoes; stirring constantly, cook 3 minutes. In large bowl, combine vinegar, oil, scallions, red pepper, garlic, basil, oregano, white pepper and Worcestershire; add hot pasta and toss.

Divide pasta, veal and tomatoes evenly among serving plates. Serve with additional Romano cheese.

On the west wall of the West Side Market there is a balcony, and from it you can look out over the great food hall, smell the aroma of the food, hear the babel of accents from the shoppers, and view the nearly 100 indoor stands (more than 80 others are just outside). This picture was taken in the early 1970s and it all looked, sounded and smelled pretty much the way it did when the West Side Market opened in 1912. It still is like that today.

Common Ground

Here's how *you* shop for groceries. You race down aisles that stretch away to the horizon. On your left are eighteen brands of potato chips; on the right, eight brands of pantyhose. These shelves were filled by unseen forces that move only by night. Working swiftly and silently, you collect the products of their invisible hands: sealed, standardized, *prix fixe*, and Lite! Lite! Lite! Then comes checkout: the beep-beep-beep of the scanner in rhythm with the cashier's chewing gum. From start to finish, few words are spoken, but then, in the 19 minutes, 46 seconds you typically spend whipping through the place, who has time?

Now here's how your ancestors shopped. Making a family adventure of it, they gathered up the kids and meandered through a cluster of small shops: the Hungarian butcher, the German baker, the Italian fruit-and-vegetable man, the Jewish fishmonger. Often the owners themselves waited on folks and greeted them by name. Fresh cuts of meat, unwrapped loaves of bread, big blocks of cheese surrounded your ancestors; their nostrils were filled with the aromas of coffee, fish, fruits and vegetables from nearby fields. They didn't just grab items off shelves, either: they talked, they tasted, they compared, they bantered and haggled with the shopkeepers. And if they played their cards right, your ancestors could strike a bargain or two and go home exulting, Such a deal! Such a deal!

Guess what? There are still places in Ohio where you can shop that way. They aren't fake-front yuppie traps with names like Ye Olde Festival Marketplace, either: they're the real thing, right down to the smell of the fish. The modern supermarket where you shop now is a great place for a hurried suburbanite to buy *products*, but here, you buy *food*...slowly.

These are the old-fashioned public market houses, where small vendors still gather under one roof to sell food at retail the way their forebears did: up close and personal. These centers of food commerce—the malls of their time—were built long ago to replace outdoor farmers' markets; they usually stand on sites where food had been sold since before the Civil War. In Ohio the oldest such building is Findlay Market, a 1902 cast-iron structure in the neighborhood Cincinnatians call Over-the-Rhine. The newest, physically, is North Market in Columbus; it's simply a Quonset hut (although new quarters are planned). But the biggest and best known is West Side Market in Cleveland, a place that isn't just a market, but an ethnic crossroads.

Opened in 1912, the West Side Market is a huge temple to food commerce about the size of the Roman Colosseum. The market fills a block on Cleveland's west side in an old, hardworking neighborhood called Ohio City. It's about a mile from Public Square, the heart of downtown Cleveland. From the market's parking lot you can even see the square's Terminal Tower, long an emblem of the city.

"This is one of the jewels of Cleveland," declares Nate Anselmo, one of West Side's fruit and vegetable merchants and an inveterate booster: "The orchestra's a jewel, the museum is a jewel, and so is the West Side Market." With its bounty of fresh produce and exotic atmosphere, the place has stunned out-of-town visitors, among them that all-time great authority on American food, the late James Beard. "Nothing like this in New York," exclaimed Mr. Beard, who seemed especially impressed by the market's ethnic diversity.

It is that cultural potpourri which makes the West Side Market a better symbol of Cleveland than Terminal Tower. The 52-story tower may be a lofty monument to railroad tycoons, but the West Side Market is a living testimonial to the everyday people who make Cleveland one of America's most ethnically diverse cities. At one time 48 different nationalities were said to live in the city and more than 40 languages were spoken here; the number may well be larger today. It didn't start out that way, of course. Laid out in 1796 by Connecticut Yankees, the city was dominated at first by Americans of British and German origin. The Civil War changed all that: an explosive growth of industry demanded laborers for the steel mills and oil refineries.

The Czechs and Slovaks came first, and then Poles, Italians, more Germans, Slavs, Irish and Hungarians. Russians, Greeks, Jews and others joined the influx. They settled in immigrant ghettoes where their own languages ruled the streets: Little Italy, Warszawa, the Haymarket, the Cabbage Patch. The Poles, Czechs and Slovaks dominated the South Side, Slavs and Lithuanians the East Side, Germans, Irish and Roumanians the West Side. And Ohio City was where the Hungarians settled. Many of the ethnic neighborhoods have dissolved as newer generations have melted away to the suburbs, but at the West Side Market they come back together again. On market days the place is like an international bazaar, a mix of races, a babel of tongues, and everywhere there are the heaps of food: huge loaves of Hungarian bread, gefulte fish, Gruyère cheese, Polish hams, links of sausage hanging down.

Even the market's architects were ethnically diverse: they were a Kansan named Charles Hubbell and an immigrant from Prague named W. Dominick Benes. Their job, from 1909 to 1912, was to replace the city's decrepit old Pearl Street Market, a wooden structure that had been built on a site on the Cuyahoga's west bank where food had been sold since the city's earliest days. Hubbell and Benes knew they were building a great public meeting place as well as an economical, fireproof, hygienic food hall; their inspirations included the railroad stations and assembly halls of

Europe. The result was a huge yellow brick building of vaguely classical design, with a 137-foot-high clock tower at the southwest corner. The interior of the building features a main concourse 241 feet long, 124 feet wide and 44 feet high. The original tiles still cover all of the building's surfaces: a splendid blue pattern for the vaulted ceiling; white for the walls; reddish brown for the floors.

The city of Cleveland owns the market house and rents the stands to vendors. The main building houses 99 food stands, operated by 65 vendors (some operate more than one stand). In an arcade outside there are 82 more, operated by 40 vendors. Each stand has its specialties lovingly displayed in old-fashioned glass cases or on wooden racks; over them are the names of the owners, reflecting a veritable United Nations of origins: Wendt, Spanos, Ehrnfelt, Dohar, Walker. The market management says stand operators reflect 22 different nationalities, from Croatian to Scottish.

Many of the stands compete directly with each other, meaning customers can easily compare quality, price and service, all within a few steps. Inside the main food hall, about 19 stands offer luncheon and smoked meats, while 18 specialize in beef, 13 are dairy stands, 10 handle pork, 10 bakery, 6 chicken, 5 lamb, 3 veal, and 2 fish. The rest run a gamut of specialties, from spices to candy. A hot dog stand, which may be the nation's oldest, is just one of the places where you can eat something on the spot. Outside the main building there's even more: long, open-sided arcades along the market's northern and eastern sides house the specialists in fruits and vegetables, who stack up their glistening produce in pyramids and promote it with handwritten signs. You can also buy flowers here. Side curtains and heaters permit the outside merchants to operate year-round.

The Ohio Farmer, October 4, 1919

"One of the older tenants always says, these are families serving families," says George Bradac, supervisor of markets for the city of Cleveland, and a symbol of ethnic diversity himself: his grandparents were Italian and Slovenian. The stands are all small family-owned businesses; some merchants are the fourth generation to work here, and a few even have roots back as far as the old Pearl Street Market. Families have been shopping here for generations, too, and they come from all walks of life: in the aisles of the West Side Market on a typical day you can see Polish grandmothers in plain black coat and babushka, retired men talking Hungarian with each other, people from the nearby projects paying with food stamps, smartly dressed suburbanites and business people from nearby offices, even—it is said—wealthy matrons brought here in chauffeur-driven limousines. They compare, they bargain, they haggle. For Clevelanders of all kinds, this is truly...common ground.

The market is open Mondays, Wednesdays, Fridays and Saturdays. Saturdays are so busy that it can be hard work pushing through the crowd, but if you go on a Monday vendors may call out to you as you pass, competing for your attention and offering special bargains. They may even give you a tour of the market house, as Bob Leu did for a visitor one recent Monday. Leu and his brother Charlie, whose roots are in Switzer-

land, have spent their lives at the West Side Market. The Leu brothers'
grandmother ran a butter, egg and cheese stand in the old Pearl Street
Market, their own stand has been in the family since 1912, and now Bob's
two sons have their own stands.

Bob, who remembers sleeping under the counter when he was a child,
has a perpetual twinkle in his eye. He delivers a rapid-fire narration as he
trots though the market. "Around the market we have predominantly
German, Polish, Italian people," he says, warming up. "There's different
kinds of sausages, very ethnic oriented—we get head cheese and souse
which the Germans like. Sauerkraut is a big item, they like all their food
with sauerkraut. We have Polish sausages—we've got three different
kinds—garlic, hot, mild.

"Gentleman in the back over there—he's got all kinds of lentils for lentil
soup. He's got probably about eight or nine different kinds of noodles, pasta.
The fish people over there, they've got fish from all over the world, any kind
you want—and he will even show you while he skins 'em up and fillet 'em up
for you. We have cheeses from France and all over the world. The chicken, of
course, is all fresh—they cut it right before your eyes. And we probably sell
more ribs in this place than any place else in the country. On fourth of July
every one of these stands is just piled high with pork ribs. We have Chinese
and Taiwanese, they all come here and they buy and they bargain very hard,
yeah, they're hard buyers."

Do West Side Market vendors actually bargain with customers?

"Yeah," says Bob Leu with a grin, "Especially this week, this is near the
end of the month. It's called the E-O-M, you take your pick—it's end of
the money or end of the month, whichever comes first. I go this way: A
pound of bacon is for $1.99, I'm going to sell you three of them for $5.75
today. It's give and take, it depends on what they got. If you can't make a
dime, you can always make a nickel, right?"

Such old-fashioned flexibility in dealing with individual customers, unheard of in the supermarket, may be just one reason why the old institution
survives. Since opening, the market has seen the rise of chain supermarkets
and the flow of population to the suburbs, but it carries on pretty much as it
has for nearly a century. In fact, that may just be *why* it survives.

"The West Side Market has flourished because we've tried to keep it as
pure food market," George Bradac argues. "We've been successful keeping
the market the way the original intent was."

And, says Bradac, West Side Market is "competitive with most of chain
stores in the area, and there are things you can find here you can't find in
chain stores. In fact, prices can be lower here, especially in the fruit and
vegetable arcade. And there is the personal touch that you can get here."

He laughs as he recalls operators of so-called "festival marketplaces"—
glitzy concentrations of trendy shops and fast-food operations—who've
visited West Side, called it hopelessly out of date, then gone away only to
fail. "We're not interested in that kind of business," Bradac explains; the
tenants' association resists proposals to add new kinds of stores, to go up-
scale, to let go of tradition.

And so the rest of the food world modernizes: standardizing, glamorizing, and impersonal-izing. But the West Side Market goes stubbornly on with no pretensions, as comfortable and familiar as an old shoe, looking pretty much the way it did a century ago—and sounding, smelling and tasting that way, too.

Says Bradac, "People come here to do their food shopping, and we try to keep it that way"...a common ground for the people.

POSTSCRIPT: *The **West Side Market**, West 25th Street and Lorain Avenue on Cleveland's West Side, is open Mondays and Wednesdays 7 a.m. to 4 p.m. and Fridays and Saturdays, 7 a.m. to 6 p.m. In Columbus, **North Market** is located at 29 Spruce Street, with some shops open seven days a week. "Prime market days" (when all 29 shops are open) are Thursday and Friday 9 a.m. to 6 p.m. and Saturday 7 a.m. to 5 p.m. A major expansion is scheduled to open by 1995. In **Cincinnati**, Findlay Market, on Elder Street between Race and Elm in the city's Over-the-Rhine district, is open Monday and Wednesday 7 a.m. to 1:30 p.m.; Friday 7 a.m. to 6 p.m. and Saturday 6 a.m. to 6 p.m.*

FACES OF THE LAND

The Haunted Fruit Stand

Every market day, as Nate Anselmo arranges his display of tomatoes from Cleveland hothouses, sweet corn from Amish fields, and pineapple from distant lands, he is surrounded by ghostly figures: the Hungarian steel worker on his way home from the mill...the Sicilian widow in black...the Chinese student...the Polish mother carrying a string bag. There are Latinos, too. And Finns. Koreans. Arabs. Jews. Czechs. Slovaks. African-Americans. Slovenians. Serbs.

And every time Nate Anselmo looks into the eyes of his customers, he sees his ancestors and people like them. New Americans all, filled with hope but struggling with their fears as they try to learn the language and strange ways of a new land. Anselmo sees the people his grandmother knew, and talked with, and sold produce to....80 years ago.

For this is the West Side Market in Cleveland, a place where past and present are seamlessly woven together. Ever since the city's founding, the immigrants have been coming here, making it one of America's great melting pots: first it was the English and Germans, then the southern and eastern Europeans; more recently, Hispanics and Asians and Russians. As you watch the people and listen to their accents, it can be hard to tell if this is 1993 or 1913, who is real—and who is only an image from the past. This place is haunted by memories of the way things were for almost everyone in this land of immigrants—and still are for many of the people you see here.

Most of all, Anselmo notices the newcomers to America. "They are what we used to be," Nate says of many of his customers. "They are the families still sitting down to eat together. They enjoy the meal the way we used to." They make their meals from scratch, instead of picking it up in sacks at a fast-food drive-through, and they serve them on the dining room table, along with the day's news: Maria earned an A in math, Sandor got the job at the convenience store, the Delgados' baby is getting better, Aunt Kyoo is coming to visit next month. They count their pennies, because they have to, and they want to shop the way they did in the Old Country. So they come to the West Side Market, along with Cleveland's Yuppies and Old Money, wanting to buy fresh food directly from the hands of someone they know, someone who can find that special fruit or vegetable for a traditional recipe, someone who doesn't mind a little haggling and may give them a bargain now and then.

And that is how it has always been at the West Side Market. Nate Anselmo does not literally see ghosts, of course, but he does see his memories come to life every day. His family has been at the market since its opening in 1912, and he grew up there, sleeping under the counters as a child, giving up his beloved baseball games to work in the family business as a teenager. In his nearly six decades of life he has seen the grocery world change, with big, impersonal mall and supermarkets and wholesale clubs and fast-food chains driving out the family food merchants. Just about everywhere except the West Side Market.

"Somebody might come up to me and say, 'Nate, we have a bar mitzvah coming up and we'd like to have the pineapples a certain way.' We work personally with the people in a way the chain store can't," says Anselmo. "If you're looking for something special and you're familiar with the person running the stand, he'll get it for you, because he feels that by satisfying a customer, you'll come back and bring somebody else. And that's how it's continued through all these 80 years."

"You sort of get personal with the customers out here. My son knows them, my wife knows them—it's a family serving families."

The family, the family. A sign over his stand says, "Nate Anselmo & Family," and the Anselmo truck, decorated with colorful fruit baskets, proclaims, "Four Generations of Quality Produce." Anselmo explains, "That's the old way of putting things—in the old days, they would never forget the family. The family was always involved. We're proud to display our name, because if we give people a good product and treat them nicely, that keeps our family going, from generation to generation, in the same business."

Nate Anselmo

Today, Nate's 22-year-old son, Tony, works with him on the stand (another son is a lawyer in Florida and the Anselmos' daughter is a teacher). Mary Ann, Nate's wife, works part of each week at the Anselmos' second business at the West Side Market: a luncheonette, which is basically a hot dog stand with a pedigree. Anselmo says the stand dates back to shortly after the market's opening in 1912, making it the oldest in the country—older, even than the famous Nathan's of Coney Island. "We have customers who have been coming here for four generations," says Anselmo. "They bring in their grandchildren and set them up on the counter and say, 'My father used to put me up there.'"

It isn't all gentle nostalgia, however: running a market stand is a lot of hard work. "You're talking about fourteen-hour days," says Anselmo. He gets up at 3 or 3:30 every morning the market is open (Mondays, Wednesdays, Fridays and Saturdays). First, he sets up the hot dog stand for the day, then he goes to the city's food terminals to buy his produce. Returning in time to open at 7 a.m., he stays on the job until the market closes, which is 4 p.m. Mondays and Wednesdays and 6 p.m. Fridays and Saturdays. On Tuesdays the Anselmos may work on bookkeeping, on Thursdays he's buying product.

Working long hours on their two businesses at the West Side Market, the Anselmos are living out one of the great American dreams: to go it alone as a family, spurning the corporate life to be their own bosses, making their own profit instead of depending on a weekly paycheck. "That's what's great about the market," says Nate Anselmo. "It gives the small guy—the butcher, the baker, whoever—a chance to make it on his own. The way people are being laid off today [from corporations], I'd rather take a chance on myself, anyway."

And so Nate Anselmo goes on, selling produce the way his mother and grandmother did before him. He offers customers tastes of his merchandise, believing, "Your eyes may deceive you, but your taste buds can't." Even with customers who don't speak English he can bargain, playing a game of fingers: "They'll hold up three fingers, meaning three dollars, I'll hold up four." He banters and teases: to onlookers he'll say, "This isn't the art museum—you're allowed to take something home." He moralizes: "Never deceive a customer to make a dollar." Always, he is thinking about the long-term relationships with the customer, not just the immediate sale; to succeed, he needs customers who keep coming back.

"It's really an old-fashioned way of serving people," muses Anselmo. "I had a woman come back years ago, her husband was a politician and they moved down to Washington," he recalls. "She hadn't been back to Cleveland for forty years. She came to visit and she said to me, 'I haven't been here since I was a young girl, and the only thing that hasn't changed [in Cleveland] is the West Side Market.'"

And that is why you may want to visit the West Side Market the next time you're in Cleveland. It isn't just a place to buy food. It's a place where the past lives on. It's a place to see people like Nate Anselmo bringing an American dream to life. It's a place to see and hear new Americans who are in pursuit of their dreams, too.

And, if you look closely, you may see the ghosts.

RECIPES

Caponata

"If you can't eat well, then why eat?" Those are the words of Duke Ianucci, father of Mike Yannacey, owner/chef/manager of Ianucci's Italian Ristorante in Dublin. They appear on the menu, as do Duke's Sauce and Mama Scarpaci's Meatballs. Mike's family has a great influence on what he eats and cooks; he was born and raised in Warren, where tables laden with Italian foods are a family tradition.

Caponata is an Italian relish, named because it was a traditional accompaniment to roast capon. In most Italian households it ends up on the table all the time. Mike serves Caponata on trays of antipasto with homemade Italian and pepperoni breads. It should be made ahead of time and brought to room temperature before serving.

In large colander, generously salt eggplant; drain for 30 minutes. In large skillet, cook celery, onion and garlic in 1/4 cup olive oil until tender. Remove vegetables from skillet. Add remaining olive oil and eggplant; cook 6 to 8 minutes or until eggplant is tender. Return vegetables to skillet. Add tomatoes, red peppers, vinegar and sugar; bring to a boil. Reduce heat; simmer, uncovered, 8 to 10 minutes, stirring occasionally. Stir in olives and capers; add salt and pepper to taste. Refrigerate 6 hours or overnight. Remove from refrigerator one hour before serving. Serve on pieces of Italian bread.

Makes 8 to 10 servings

1 medium eggplant (about 2 pounds), peeled, cut into 3/4-inch pieces
Salt
1-1/2 cups chopped celery
1-1/2 cups chopped onion
2 cloves garlic, finely chopped
1/2 cup olive oil
1 (28-ounce) can tomatoes, undrained and broken up
1 (7-ounce) can roasted red peppers, drained and chopped
1/4 cup red wine vinegar
1/4 cup sugar
1 (4.25-ounce) can chopped ripe olives
2 tablespoons capers, drained
Salt
Pepper

Vince, Maxine and Judy's Spaghetti Sauce

Makes about four quarts

Extra Virgin Olive Oil
3 medium onions, chopped
1 pound sweet Italian sausage
  (about 3 links), cut in 1-inch pieces
1 cup beef broth or stock
1/2 cup red wine
3 quarts Fratelli Spaghetti Sauce
1/2 cup grated imported Romano
  cheese
3/4 teaspoon garlic powder
1 teaspoon ground cinnamon
1/2 teaspoon basil leaves
1/2 teaspoon oregano leaves
Cooked and drained pasta*

* Vince advises using imported pasta with a high semolina
  content for best flavor and texture.

Our friend Vince Pettinelli gave us this recipe. Vince was its creative mastermind, Maxine (Judy's mother), had the task of writing down what Vince did, and Judy felt that, although she was napping during the actual sauce production, she was certainly there in spirit. Hence the name.

This delicious Italian sauce is made with Fratelli Spaghetti Sauce, which Tony Cappadonna and his partner, Alfons Marra, have been producing since 1984. (The word "Fratelli" means "brothers" in Italian.) It is available at their store, Fratelli Imported Foods, 1627 Golden Gate Plaza, Mayfield Heights, 216/ 473-0848, and 150 other stores around the state. About 600 cases a month are gobbled up by Fratelli's loyal following.

In large kettle, pour enough olive oil to cover bottom of pan, cook onions until almost tender. Add sausage; cook until gray in color, adding more oil if necessary. Add broth and wine, scraping bottom to remove brown bits. Bring to a boil; boil 2 minutes. Add remaining ingredients, except pasta; bring to a boil.

Reduce heat; cover and simmer at least 2 hours, stirring occasionally. Serve over pasta.

Red Cabbage

Makes 4 to 6 servings

1 medium red cabbage, thinly sliced
1/4 cup sugar
1 teaspoon salt
1/4 cup butter or margarine
1/2 cup red currant jelly
1 large apple, chopped
2 tablespoons red wine vinegar

Sandra Carpenter is a senior home economist with Borden, Inc., in Columbus. She develops recipes, using Borden products, for use with cookbooks, recipe samplers, packages and newspapers. Every now and then she prepares a traditional German meal for her family, complete with red cabbage, Sauerbraten and potato stuffing.

No traditional German meal would be complete without this side dish. It can be served hot with a main meat dish or cold with a selection of cold meats.

In large saucepan, cook cabbage, sugar and salt in butter for 15 minutes. Add remaining ingredients; cover and simmer 1-1/2 to 2 hours, or until tender, stirring occasionally.

Schmierkase Pie

Jack and Ruth Youngquist established the Red Door Tavern, 1736 West Fifth Avenue, Columbus, in 1964. In 1988 they sold it to John and Pat Parsons, but Ruth continues to bake the pies. Ruth gets up at 3:30 a.m., six days a week to bake 15 to 20 pies each day. Schmierkase pie, with its unusual custard-like filling, is popular in German households.

Preheat oven to 425 degrees. In large bowl, combine cottage cheese, sugar, flour and salt; mix well. Stir in half-and-half, eggs and vanilla; add raisins. Pour filling into unbaked pastry shell; sprinkle cinnamon evenly over filling. Bake 10 minutes. Reduce oven temperature to 350 degrees; bake 35 to 40 minutes or until knife inserted near center comes out clean. Cool.

Makes one 9-inch pie

1-1/2 cups small curd cottage cheese
1/2 cup sugar
4 teaspoons flour
Dash salt
1-1/2 cups half-and-half or milk
2 eggs, well beaten
1-1/2 teaspoons vanilla extract
1/2 cup golden raisins
1 (9-inch) unbaked pastry shell
Ground cinnamon

Walnut and Poppy Seed Kuchen

Elizabeth Neidert, born and raised in Akron, retired with her husband, Andrew, to Florida. But each Christmas they return to visit family in Ohio, where Elizabeth always makes traditional family Christmas treats.

This recipe, for walnut and poppy seed kuchen (pronounced KOO-ken), is everyone's favorite. The recipe makes two each, walnut and poppy seed, so your family can decide which is their favorite.

In medium bowl, combine ingredients for walnut filling. Repeat for poppy seed filling. Set aside.

In small bowl, sprinkle yeast over water; add sugar, stir to dissolve. In large bowl, combine flour and butter; mix until crumbly. Add egg yolks and salt; mix well. Add yeast mixture, whiskey and lemon juice; beat until smooth. Divide into four portions.

On lightly floured surface, roll out each portion to a 12x14-inch rectangle. Spread two rectangles with walnut filling; spread two with poppy seed filling, spreading filling close to edges. Starting at a 12-inch side, roll up each, jelly roll-fashion. Place rolls side by side on two lightly greased 10x15-inch jelly roll pans, allowing room for expansion. Set pans in warm place; allow to rise one to two hours or until doubled in size. Preheat oven to 350 degrees. Brush rolls with slightly beaten egg whites. Bake 30 to 40 minutes or until golden brown, rotating pans halfway through baking time. Remove from oven. Cover rolls with a dampened towel for 10 minutes. Cool completely; store tightly wrapped in refrigerator.

Makes four 12-inch rolls

Walnut filling:
1-1/2 cups (6 ounces) ground
   walnuts
1/4 cup hot milk
1/4 cup sugar
1/2 teaspoon maple extract
1/2 teaspoon vanilla extract

Poppy seed filling:
1/2 cup poppy seeds
1/2 cup sugar
1/4 cup hot milk
2 tablespoons honey

Dough:
2 packages active dry yeast
1 cup warm water (105-115 degrees)
1/4 cup sugar
4-1/2 cups flour
1/2 cup butter or margarine
3 eggs, separated
1 teaspoon salt
2 tablespoons whiskey (optional)
1/2 teaspoon lemon juice

German Potato Pancakes

Makes 4 to 6 servings

4 medium potatoes, grated
1 medium onion, grated
2 eggs, slightly beaten
2 tablespoons flour
1/2 teaspoon baking powder
1/2 teaspoon salt
1/8 teaspoon pepper
Vegetable oil
Applesauce
Sour cream

Potato pancakes are a favorite part of any German meal. They are delicious served with Sauerbraten, but hearty enough to be a main dish. Serve immediately after frying, or keep warm on a baking sheet lined with paper towels at a low oven setting.

In medium bowl, cover potatoes with cold water; let stand for 10 minutes. Drain well; return to bowl. Add onion, eggs, flour, baking powder, salt and pepper; mix well. In large skillet, pour oil to a depth of about 1/4-inch; drop 2 to 3 tablespoons of mixture from spoon into hot oil, flatten with back of spoon. Fry 3 minutes on each side or until golden brown. Remove from skillet and drain on paper towels. Serve with applesauce and/or sour cream.

Black Forest Sauerkraut Balls

Makes 8 to 10 appetizer servings

1 pound bulk pork sausage
2 tablespoons chopped onion
1 cup (4 ounces) sauerkraut,
  drained and cut
4 ounces cream cheese
1 egg, slightly beaten
1 tablespoon flour
1 teaspoon dry mustard
Salt
Pepper
2 cups milk
3 eggs, slightly beaten
2 cups dry bread crumbs
Vegetable oil for frying

The Black Forest Restaurant is said to be the only authentic German-owned restaurant in the Cincinnati area. George Fraundorfer, a fifth-generation restauranteur has created a little piece of the Bavarian Alps in the Queen City.

The Black Forest (8675 Cincinnati-Columbus Road, Westchester, 513/777-7600) serves authentic Bavarian dishes or recipes Fraundorfer has developed over the years. German bands entertain every Friday and Saturday evening. The restaurant is decorated with German memorabilia, including a stuffed Walperdinger (a must see!). On May 1 a Maypole is set up and a Bavarianfest held. A "Fest Platter" that includes sauerkraut, red cabbage, hosenfeffer, weisswurst and Oktoberfest chicken is served.

These Sauerkraut Balls took first place in the 1987 "Taste of Cincinnati" contest.

In medium skillet, cook sausage and onions until sausage is gray in color; remove from heat. Add sauerkraut, cream cheese, egg, flour, mustard, salt and pepper to taste; mix well. Roll into 1-inch balls; place in freezer until partially frozen.

In medium bowl, combine milk and eggs. Drop each ball in egg mixture, then roll in bread crumbs. In large skillet, pour oil to a depth of about 1/2-inch; fry balls in hot oil about 5 minutes or until golden brown. Remove from skillet; drain on paper towels. Serve with seafood cocktail sauce.

Leniwe (Lazy) Pierogi

Carol and Jim Orzech grew up just four doors apart in the Polish neighborhood just south of downtown Cleveland. In the neighborhood where church steeples tower over bungalows and storefronts, they were raised celebrating Wigilia, the Polish vigil feast celebrated on Christmas Eve. Their children are now growing up in the same neighborhood and learning the same traditions.

As the feasting begins, so does the celebrating. The Christmas tree is lit, gifts are exchanged and toasts are given. Although the traditional pierogi are served, also served is *leniwe (lazy) pierogi,* a refinement by the immigrant women who often worked in Cleveland's factories and mills and had less time to spend in the kitchen. The feast of Wigilia would not be complete without a compote of apricots, prunes and cinnamon, followed by cakes, poppy seed kuchen and *kolaczki,* tender pastry horns filled with fruit preserves or nuts.

In medium skillet, cook onions in butter until tender; keep warm. In large kettle, bring lightly salted water to a boil. In large bowl, combine cottage cheese and eggs; add flour and salt, mix well. (Carol says it may work best to mix with hands; dough is sticky.) On a lightly floured surface, working with 1/4 of dough at a time, knead gently; roll out to 1/4-inch thickness. Using a fluted cutter, cut into diamond shapes. Drop immediately into boiling water, cooking entire 1/4 batch at once. After pierogi rise to surface, cook an additional 3 to 5 minutes. Remove with slotted spoon; drain (do not rinse). Repeat with remaining dough.

In large serving dish, layer pierogi and onions. Serve with sour cream.

Makes about 25 servings

2 medium onions, chopped
1-1/2 cups butter or margarine
1 (24-ounce) carton small curd creamed cottage cheese
6 eggs
5 cups flour
1 teaspoon salt

Kolaczki

In large bowl, combine ice cream, butter, flour and sugar; mix well. Cover dough; refrigerate overnight.

Preheat oven to 400 degrees. On a lightly floured surface, using a small amount of dough at a time, roll out to 1/8-inch thickness. Using a pastry wheel, cut into 2-inch squares. Spoon a small amount of filling into center of each; fold two opposite corners over center. Bake for 10 minutes or until lightly brown. Cool; sprinkle with confectioners' sugar. Store loosely covered. (Kolaczki can be made ahead of time as they freeze well.)

Makes about 200

1 pint (2 cups) vanilla ice cream, melted
2 cups butter or margarine, softened
4 cups flour
2 teaspoons sugar
2 (12-ounce) cans almond, apricot, cherry, pineapple, prune, or raspberry filling and topping
Confectioners' sugar

Celestial Crusts (Bozi Milosti)

Makes about three dozen

3 eggs
1/4 cup milk
1 tablespoon butter or margarine,
  melted
1 tablespoon sugar
1/8 teaspoon salt
3 cups flour (approximately)
Vegetable oil
Confectioners' sugar

The Rev. Carol Weiss lives in Sunburg. Her maiden name of Polivka means "soup" in Czechoslovakian.

Carol's mother makes these irresistible Celestial Crusts on Shrove Tuesday and also on the first snowy day of winter.

In large bowl, combine eggs, milk, butter, sugar and salt; beat well. Add flour, beating well until dough is no longer sticky and stiff enough to roll. On lightly floured surface, roll out to 1/4-inch thickness; cut into diamond shapes. With a fork, make several holes through each piece. In large skillet, pour oil to a depth of about 1 inch; add pieces to hot oil, a few at a time; fry until lightly browned. Remove from skillet; drain on paper towels. Sprinkle with confectioners' sugar or cinnamon and sugar mixture.

Cincinnati Chili

Makes 1-1/2 quarts

2 pounds lean ground beef
2 medium onions, chopped
4 cups water
1 (16-ounce) can whole tomatoes,
  undrained and broken up
1 tablespoon chili powder
2 bay leaves
2 teaspoons ground cumin
1-1/2 teaspoons ground allspice
1-1/2 teaspoons salt
1-1/2 teaspoons vinegar
1 teaspoon cayenne pepper
1 teaspoon ground cinnamon
1 teaspoon Worcestershire sauce
1/2 teaspoon garlic powder

Optional:
8 ounces spaghetti, cooked and
  drained
1-1/2 cups shredded Cheddar cheese
Oyster crackers
1 cup chopped onion
1 (16-ounce) can kidney beans,
  heated

Chili is as much a part of Cincinnati culture as the Reds and the Bengals; it almost seems as if there is a chili parlor on every corner. Many recipes for chili are called Empress Chili after a local chili parlor begun by a Greek family. That chain and its many competitors add cinnamon and make the beef fine-textured by simmering it in water. The real recipe is a secret, so versions abound.

In a Cincinnati chili parlor, you must know the lingo. For basic "three-way chili," chili is ladled on spaghetti and topped with cheese. Pass the oyster crackers. For "four-way chili," add chopped onion. For "five-way chili," spoon kidney beans on top.

This is the favorite Cincinnati chili recipe of Joyce Rosencrans, food editor for the Cincinnati Post. Over the years, Joyce has become well acquainted with what Cincinnatians love to eat.

In large kettle, combine ground beef, onions and water; simmer until beef browns. Add tomatoes, chili powder, bay leaves, cumin, allspice, salt, vinegar, cayenne, cinnamon, Worcestershire and garlic powder; bring to a boil. Cover; reduce heat and simmer 3 hours, stirring frequently. (If possible, make ahead of time; refrigerate, skim fat off top.)

Pastichio

Anastasia Antonoplos (maiden name Langas) is proud of her Greek ancestry. Her father came to America in 1895 and Sassa (her nickname since childhood) was born in Pittsburgh, but Sassa has visited Greece many times. She and her husband, Anthony, have lived in Sidney, where Anthony has served as mayor.

Pastichio, one of her favorite dishes, is served regularly in Greek households. Sassa often uses regular spaghetti instead of elbow macaroni. In Greece, a long, hollow spaghetti is used. This is a great dish to make ahead of time and freeze. Defrost in refrigerator, and bake until cheese sauce is brown and bubbly.

In medium saucepan, melt butter; add flour, cook until mixture is golden brown, stirring constantly. Gradually stir in hot milk; continue stirring, cook until sauce is smooth and thickened. Add salt; set aside. When partially cool, add eggs.

Preheat oven to 350 degrees. In large kettle, cook onions in butter until tender; add meat, cook until browned. Add water, tomato paste, cinnamon, salt and pepper to taste; bring to a boil. Reduce heat; simmer, uncovered, 45 minutes. In large bowl, combine macaroni and eggs; mix well. Add half of the cheese. Turn half of the macaroni mixture into lightly greased 13x9-inch baking dish; top with meat mixture, then half of remaining cheese. Top wtih remaining macaroni; bake 10 minutes. Pour cream sauce over top; sprinkle with remaining cheese. Dot with butter; bake an additional 30 minutes or until bubbly and well browned.

Makes 8 to 10 servings

Cream Sauce:
6 tablespoons butter or margarine
3/4 cup flour
4 cups (1 quart) hot milk
2 teaspoons salt (optional)
3 eggs, slightly beaten

Meat mixture:
2 medium onions, chopped
1/4 cup butter or margarine
2 pounds lean ground beef (preferably ground round)
3/4 cup water
2 tablespoons tomato paste
Dash of cinnamon
Salt
Pepper
1 pound elbow macaroni, cooked and drained
3 eggs, slightly beaten
3 cups (12 ounces) freshly grated Parmesan cheese
2 tablespoons butter or margarine

Moravian Sugar Cake

Makes five 9-inch cakes, or two 13x9-inch cakes

Cake:
1 tablespoon plus 1 teaspoon active dry yeast
1 teaspoon sugar
1/2 cup warm water (105-115 degrees)
2 cups milk
1 cup butter or margarine
1 cup sugar
1 teaspoon salt
3 eggs, slightly beaten
5-1/2 to 6-1/2 cups flour

Topping 1:
1/2 cup sugar
1 tablespoon ground cinnamon

Topping 2:
2-1/4 cups firmly packed light brown sugar
1/2 cup butter or margarine, softened

The Moravians, followers of the fifteenth-century Bohemian reformer John Hus, were the among the first white settlers in Ohio. The first white children born in eastern Ohio were Moravians. The group established a settlement called Schönbrunn, near present New Philadelphia, which has been rebuilt on its original site. It is operated as a state memorial by the Ohio Historical Society.

Moravians have many unique worship customs. Large white advent stars are displayed through the seasons of Advent and Christmas. Lovefeasts, after the pattern of the early Christian community, are held throughout the year. Members of the congregation receive a beverage and bun, made with dough similar to the cake dough, in an informal service emphasizing the oneness of Christians and the fellowship of the gathered family.

Carrie Wherley, home economics program assistant at Tuscarawas County Extension, sent us this recipe. It has been made in her congregation at Dover First Moravian Church for many years. The women of the church make over 300 cakes a month and sell them for their building fund.

The recipe makes five cakes. The idea is to give one cake away, freeze two, eat one warm from the oven, and have the fifth for breakfast. If a thicker cake is desired, the recipe will fit into four 9-inch pans or two 13x9-inch pans.

In large bowl, combine yeast and 1 teaspoon sugar; add water, stir to dissolve. Let stand 10 minutes. (The mixture should bubble and expand in the bowl. This is called "proofing" the yeast, and assures you that the yeast is fresh and will provide sufficient raising of the dough.) In medium saucepan, heat milk, butter, 1 cup sugar and salt; cool to lukewarm. Add milk mixture to yeast mixture, along with eggs; mix well. Add 5 cups flour; beat well. Add remainder of flour in 1/2-cup increments until a soft dough is formed. (Dough will be sticky.) In large, greased bowl, place dough. Set bowl in warm place; let rise until doubled in bulk.

Punch down dough. Divide evenly between five greased 9-inch square baking pans. In small bowl, combine Topping 1 ingredients; sprinkle evenly over top of cakes. Set pans in warm place; let rise until doubled.

Preheat oven to 350 degrees. With finger tip, make indentations in dough, about 1-inch apart and 1-inch deep all over top of cake. In small bowl, combine Topping 2 ingredients; sprinkle over top of cakes, allowing topping to fill holes. Bake 15 to 20 minutes (rotate pans midway through the baking time or bake 2 cakes at a time) or until golden brown. Cool in pan 5 to 10 minutes. Remove from pans, cool on wire rack.

Delia's Guacamole

This recipe for the classic dip, Guacamole, is from Delia Vargas, of Bowling Green. Born in Mexico, Delia grew up picking cotton in Texas. She remembers weighing 99 pounds and dragging bags of cotton weighing more than 100. At 18, she and her family came to northwest Ohio to harvest pickles and tomatoes. Now Delia is a popular hairdresser in Bowling Green and has four children. She loves to make the traditional recipes of her family in Mexico, of which this is one. Among others are Tamales, Enchiladas, Mexican Rice, Beef Tacos, Flour Tortillas, Eggs in Salsa, Mexican Sausage, Pinto Beans, and Refried Beans.

In medium bowl, combine all ingredients; mix well. Chill at least 2 hours to blend flavors. Serve with tortilla chips or fresh vegetables.

Makes about 1-1/2 cups

*2 medium avocados, peeled and
    mashed*
*2 jalapeno peppers, seeded and
    finely chopped*
1 medium tomato, finely chopped
1 small onion, chopped
2 tablespoons lemon juice
1 teaspoon salt
1/4 teaspoon garlic powder

Lennie's Fried Okra

Okra seems to be one of the most maligned vegetables in the western world. However, in African and African-inspired cooking, okra is valued as a fresh vegetable and also for its thickening properties in stews, gumbos, sauces, etc. The trick is to cut and cook okra as little as possible so it does not become slimy. The term "okra" comes from "okruma", the term for the vegetable in the Twi language of Ghana.

This recipe for fried okra is a favorite of Lennie V. Nix, of Toledo, who calls it, "Very good!" Donna Sharper of Toledo, who is Mrs. Nix's granddaughter and one of the most outstanding journalism students at Bowling Green State University, helped us obtain it. Donna is proud of the culinary versatility of her family. The recipes of her Aunt Ruth (Ruth A. Smith of Toledo) range from Sweet Potato Pie to Fried Chicken to Hummingbird Cake (pineapple, walnuts and bananas are among the ingredients). And Mrs. Nix can offer you recipes for Greens, Biscuits, Rabbit and Squirrel!

Place flour in plastic bag; add okra. Toss lightly until okra is coated with flour. In large skillet, pour oil to a depth of about 1/8-inch; add okra to hot oil. Fry until golden brown, turning carefully. (Do not overcook, okra will become too soft.) Drain on paper towels. Salt and pepper to taste.

Makes 4 to 6 servings

1 cup flour
*1 pound okra, caps removed and cut
    into 1/2-inch slices**
Vegetable oil
Salt
Pepper

* Small okra may be fried whole.

Matzo Ball Soup

Makes 1-1/2 quarts

5 pounds assorted chicken parts
1 bay leaf
5 cups water
2 ribs celery with leaves, cut in
  pieces
1 large carrot, peeled and sliced
1 large onion, chopped
Salt
Pepper

These recipes come from Paula Weinstein in Columbus. Paula and her partner, Julie Komerofsky, run a catering company that prepares many kosher menus for Jewish celebrations.

In kosher cooking, meat and dairy products are separated. Two sets of dishes are kept, one for serving dairy, the other for meats. This menu is a meat meal, so it includes no dairy products. Pareve margarine is used instead of butter and non-dairy creamer is used instead of milk. The word pareve (pronounced parv) is used to describe food items that contain neither milk nor meat products.

In large kettle, place chicken parts and bay leaf; cover with water. Bring to a boil; reduce heat, cover and simmer 30 minutes. Skim fat off surface of water. Add vegetables; cook until chicken is tender and falls off the bones. Season to taste with salt and pepper. Remove chicken and vegetables from broth; strain broth to obtain clear mixture.* Drop uncooked matzo balls, one at a time into boiling broth; boil for 20 minutes.

* Chicken, carrot and onion can remain in soup, if desired; remove bones, bay leaf and celery.

Matzo Balls

4 eggs, separated
1 cup matzo meal
1 teaspoon salt

Slightly beat egg yolks and whites separately. Combine beaten yolks and whites; add matzo meal and salt gradually, mix well. Refrigerate mixture for 30 minutes. Using lightly oiled hands, form small balls. They will puff up when cooked in broth.

Pareve Noodle Kugel

Makes 12 servings

1 (1-pound) package wide egg
  noodles, cooked and drained
1 dozen eggs
3/4 pound onions (3 medium),
  chopped
1/2 cup pareve margarine, melted
3 tablespoons pareve chicken soup
  mix

Preheat oven to 350 degrees. Place noodles in lightly greased 13x9-inch baking dish. In large bowl, combine remaining ingredients; beat well. Pour over noodles. Bake uncovered 40 to 45 minutes or until golden brown and knife inserted in center comes out clean. Cut in squares to serve.

Tony Packo's Hungarian Stuffed Cabbage Rolls

Corporal Max Klinger, on the popular television show M*A*S*H*, was known for his allegiance to Toledo, and often mentioned Tony Packo's eatery, known for its Hungarian hot dogs (a spicy sausage covered with chili beef sauce) and other specialities. The restaurant, opened in 1932 on Toledo's East Side (1902 Front Street, 419/691-6054), has been voted the city's favorite ethnic restaurant. Many celebrities have visited over the years and have signed their names on hot dog bun; the petrified buns remain on diplay at the restaurant.

(My husband's aunt, Lucille Lakatos, also sent me a delicious recipe for a stuffed cabbage dish she calls "piggies.")

Core the cabbage. Fill large kettle with water; bring to a boil. Immerse cabbage in boiling water: cook, uncovered for 10 minutes or until leaves wilt. Using a slotted spoon, remove cabbage from water; cool. Remove about 12 large outer leaves from cabbage; trim large vein even with edge of leaf.

In large bowl, combine eggs, 1/2 cup onion, garlic, 1 teaspoon salt, 1 teaspoon paprika and 1/2 teaspoon pepper. Add meat and rice: mix well. Place about 1/3 cup meat mixture on each cabbage leaf; fold in sides. Starting at unfolded side, carefully roll up each leaf. Chop remaining cabbage. In large bowl, combine chopped cabbage, sauerkraut, tomatoes, soup, sugar, and remaining onion, salt, paprika and pepper.
In a 6- or 8-quart kettle, spoon half of the sauerkraut mixture. Arrange cabbage rolls, seam side down, over sauerkraut mixture. Spoon remaining sauerkraut mixture over the rolls. Fill kettle with enough water to cover. Bring mixture to a boil; reduce heat, cover and simmer for 2 hours, adding water as needed to keep rolls covered. Place rolls on serving dish; spoon Tomato-Onion Sauce over top. Serve with sour cream.

Makes 8 servings

1 head cabbage (about 3 pounds)
2 eggs, slightly beaten
2 medium onions, chopped
1 clove garlic, finely chopped
2 teaspoons salt
1-1/4 teaspoons paprika
1/2 teaspoon pepper
2 pounds lean ground beef (or 1 pound each ground beef and ground pork)
1 cup uncooked long grain rice
1 (16-ounce) can sauerkraut, drained
1 (16-ounce) can whole tomatoes, undrained and broken up
1 (10-3/4-ounce) can condensed tomato soup
2 tablespoons sugar
Sour cream

Tomato-Onion Sauce

In small saucepan, cook onion in butter until tender. Add tomatoes; heat through. (If desired, add 1/2 cup sour cream to sauce instead of serving it separately.)

Makes about 2 cups

2 small onions, chopped
1 tablespoon butter or margarine
1 (16-ounce) can whole tomatoes, undrained and broken up

It is apple-picking time in 1899, and on a hot, sunny day a photographer lugs his glass-plate camera into the orchard of William Miller (son of Henry, whose farm appears on page 2), near Port Clinton. It is agreed that including a dog in the picture would be amusing. The photographer laboriously sets up his equipment, Towser is coaxed onto a barrel, crew members pause on their ladders and beside their barrels. Everyone holds perfectly still in the blazing sun. Everyone, that is, except....

Looking for Johnny Appleseed

My father, who loved to grow things, died unexpectedly one May, so the big perennial garden he had started that year was never finished. After his funeral I went out to look at the garden and saw the footprints he had left the evening before he died. Gradually, the wind and the rain washed the footprints away, but the garden remained, even though there was no one to take care of it any more. For years I was haunted by the image of those footprints, fading while the plants kept on growing.

—James Hope

He was too good to be true. His story is one of those you enjoy but don't believe. It makes a great yarn, and, best of all, it's inspiring.

That's why Johnny Appleseed is right up there in the pantheon of American mythological heroes, along with Paul Bunyan and John Henry. In fact, most would agree he leads the pack. For Johnny wasn't just extraordinary, he was extraordinarily *good*, so good some call him a latter-day St. Francis. (Johnny Appleseed scholar Rick Sowash likens him to John the Baptist.) Wearing shabby clothes and a mush pot for a hat, he travelled barefoot through the snow, sleeping outdoors in all kinds of weather. Indians, feared by the settlers, were friendly to him. Johnny could commune with the animals (at least he acted as if he could), sleeping at the other end of a hollow log from a bear and putting out a campfire that was drawing mosquitoes to their deaths. And he devoted his life to planting trees in the wilderness—apples trees, because they helped the settlers feel at home. Asking little, giving much, he roamed the Old Northwest frontier like an angel leading the pioneers to the promised land.

But Johnny Appleseed was no myth. He was a real person, with a real name: John Chapman. And for much of his adult life—from around 1801 to 1840 or so—Johnny lived in Ohio. If you go looking for apples in Ohio, you just might catch a glimpse of him.

There are plenty of places to look, too. Not many farmers grow apples as a sideline anymore, but Ohio does have hundreds of full-time commercial orchards, large and small. While Ohio isn't the nation's biggest apple producer, it's still pretty big: 120,000,000 pounds of fruit in 1991, ranking it tenth among the states. Yes, Ohio growers will concede, if a bit wearily, you hear a lot more about the apples of Washington State. But our apples can be just as good, they'll tell you, and lot closer to home. And there probably isn't any place in America where every apple comes with such a sense of history. Ohio apples aren't just fruit; they're messages from the past.

Why needs to be explained here. More, perhaps, than other producers, apple growers stand poised on the cusp of time. The nature of apple trees forces them to look further into the future than your average corn farmer, for example. Mitch Lynd, who (with lots of family) grows apples in five townships in western Licking County, began trying out a new kind of Russian root stock in the mid-1980s. Because it takes years for an apple tree to bear results and prove itself, it wasn't until December 1991 that Lynd knew he wanted more. His order went to a nursery in Belgium, which shipped the roots to California for grafting and two years of quarantine. That meant Lynd would have to wait until 1996 for his first fruits, and until around 2000 for a really good commercial crop that would pay back his investment. Elapsed time from idea to payoff: about 15 years.

"They're very long-term thinking people, apple growers," Lynd says. "You're focusing your mind on events that are way off in the future all the time. It's just the way it is. You plant a tree and you wait a long time." Perhaps that's why Johnny Appleseed spent so much time working just ahead of the frontier. He liked to move into the wilderness, set up a nursery in a remote spot, and have seedlings ready for transplanting when the first settlers arrived. Johnny understood the concept of lead time.

Always forced to think far, far ahead, apple growers get some recreational relief by...thinking backward. Lynd is not unusual among orchardists in keeping so-called antique varieties growing beside his work-horse commercial ones. He grows 18 varieties of apples commercially and 130 more just for fun. Among his recreational trees is one said to descend from the very tree that dropped an apple on Isaac Newton's head. Lynd insists English horticultural records support his claim to the tree's ancestry, but the point here is not the authenticity of story or tree. It is, rather, that apple trees let us see, feel, and taste the past with astonishing precision.

This is because of the botanical facts of life for apple trees. Ordinarily, orchardists don't grow their trees from seed: promiscuous cross-pollination between trees means that seeds yield unpredictable results. Instead, growers start new trees by taking buds or twigs ("scions") from successful adults and grafting them onto young root stock. Nurseries can supply growers like Lynd with thousands of these little bionic wonders, with the fruit-growing top some hot new variety like Fuji and the root stock down below something else. (Useful new *varieties*, by the way, pop up from seed only by chance or the most tedious experimentation.) Grafting preserves the genetic integrity of the original tree, so the same variety can remain virtually unchanged over centuries. Hogs, humans and many other living creatures evolve over the years, every generation different from its parents, but apples—when propagated by grafting—do not change.

And so Mitch Lynd can offer you a Roxbury Russet, the first important variety of apple to originate in the New World. It looks and tastes the way

A HANDY APPLE PEELER

The Ohio Farmer, January 15, 1927

it did when somebody discovered it in Massachusetts in the early 1600s. Or you can try a Westfield Seek-No-Further, another Massachusetts discovery, from the 1700s, and Lynd will say, "You can taste the same apple Benjamin Franklin might have known." It's all due to the grafting.

Most authorities believe John Chapman did no grafting—opposed it, in fact, saying it hurt trees—and instead planted his orchards from seeds gathered at Pennsylvania cider mills. As a result, apples from most of his trees were apt to be something less than great, by our standards: they were the product of random mating instead of careful selection. Only rarely are such apples much good, at least as eating apples. But that doesn't mean Johnny's trees weren't important: apple trees were regarded as a sign of civilization in frontier society and one of the first things a pioneer farmer did was plant an orchard. Having to do so, in fact, was written into the law in some areas. Moreover, cider was an important apple product then, and vinegar was widely used as a preservative. John Chapman's apples were just fine for that.

Like many Ohio orchardists, Mitch Lynd orients himself in time and space by Johnny Appleseed. In Mitch's case, his great great great grandfather, John Lynd, was a pioneer who came to the Ohio wilderness in 1793—about a decade before John Chapman. Mitch Lynd enjoys thinking how his ancestor, like other general farmers of the time, was probably already growing apple trees in Ohio when Johnny Appleseed arrived on the scene. About seventy or eighty years later the Lynd family switched to raising apples exclusively. Still later—in 1919—Mitch Lynd's grandfather moved from the Ohio River Valley to Licking County. By coincidence, his new county was one Johnny had visited frequently. There are still farmers there who claim to have a Johnny Appleseed tree.

Lynd himself doubts any verifiable trees remain in Licking County, but the county does form one corner of what some call "Johnny Appleseed Country." This is not the only part of the Midwest that Johnny frequented: the footloose Chapman left traces, tangible or spiritual, in various corners of Ohio and nearby states. But the territory lying between Columbus and Cleveland—particularly Licking, Muskingum, Knox, Coshocton, Richland and Ashland counties—is where John Chapman had many of his wilderness nurseries and did much of his traveling. So Johnny Appleseed just may have traveled over the 700 acres Lynd owns today and, although there is no evidence of it, could even have had an orchard here.

The Lynd Fruit Farm has 80,000 trees and, in 1992, produced 180,000 bushels of apples. That made it Ohio's number-one producer. Lynd sells most of his huge crop to the likes of the Kroger, Big Bear and Meijer chains, but, in season, he also invites the public to pick their own or buy at the roadside (S.R. 310 & Morse Road, 614/927-1333).

Clearly an industrial-strength operation, the Lynd orchard anchors the southwest corner of Johnny Appleseed Country. A hundred miles to the northeast is another orchard which may, with poetic license, be said to mark the northern end. A different kind of operation, it is Mapleside Farms, 294 Pearl Rd., Brunswick (216/225-5577), not far from Cleveland.

This is where, the Eyssen family likes to say, apples are grown to music.

It doesn't take long for a visitor chatting with the family Eyssen to begin wondering when Julie Andrews will come prancing across the meadow to the strains of "Edelweiss." The thought arises first because of the setting: while Medina, Ohio, does not offer the Alps, of course, it does have hills and Mapleside Farms just happens to be on their highest point. It is a place of lovely views, especially from the second floor of the Mapleside farms restaurant during apple-blossom time.

The restaurant is part of a complex that started with a rundown farm in 1927 and evolved into a 50-acre orchard and much more. There is also a gift shop, a fruit salesroom with a "cider bar" and a bakery offering both pies and cheese (because "apple pie without cheese is like a kiss without a squeeze"). Presiding over all this is the 66-year-old patriarch of an apple-growing-and-selling clan, William "Apple Bill" Eyssen Sr.

Eyssen grew up on the farm, which his father had bought for relief from the strain of selling hardware in Cleveland. Gradually Bill turned it into an orchard with a retail sales front on Pearl Road—at first, only a table with an umbrella. Apple Bill didn't just raise children, however: he also raised children, six of them, all with apple juice in their veins. The result is Medina County's answer to *The Sound of Music*. All six children still work at Mapleside Farms: Son Dave and wife Sue manage the shop and bakery; son Bill Jr. runs the orchard and his wife Joannie is office manager; daughter Janelle, with her husband, Mark, manage the restaurant. Three other children—Tim, Jon and Linda—have other careers, but help out on special occasions, such as the restaurant's Thanksgiving Dinner. Several even have their homes on farm property.

The Eyssens work together harmoniously, apparently avoiding the intramural quarrels to which family businesses are prone. Perhaps it is the music. On special occasions, like the orchard's annual Johnny Apple-seed festival, the Eyssen Family Singers of seven youngsters are among the performers. But the musical leadership comes from Apple Bill. Blessed with a fine baritone voice, he sang in church choirs for many years and then developed a half-hour program about apples in which he alternately sings and tells the story of Johnny Appleseed. He has given it hundreds of times—at civic clubs, in schools, in schools and to the 150 or so tour groups which comes to Mapleside each year. On these occasions, Apple Bill will sometimes climb on the tour bus and belt out his signature lines:

> I'm Apple Bill,
> On top of the hill;
> I welcome you here today—
> *Boop-Boop!*

Apple Bill and Johnny Appleseed: they have formed a certain partnership. Just outside the Mapleside store door is a Cortland apple tree to which a very special twig was grafted long ago. The twig came from a tree believed planted by Johnny Appleseed on a farm in Jeromesville, near

Ashland. "Oh, it's a terrible apple," Apple Bill, says, curling his nose at what comes from that historic branch. It is small and pink, not good to eat—but like most such apples—good for cider. And that's what the Eyssens do with their historic Johnny Appleseed apples: mix them in with others for cider production.

The Eyssens think their "Johnny Appleseed Tree" in Brunswick is the only one in Ohio with their degree of confidence that it's the genuine article. Even so, you can catch other glimpses of Johnny throughout the state. In southwestern Ohio, visitors can see a statue of John Chapman in Section 134 of Cincinnati's Spring Grove Cemetery. And in the Cincinnati suburb of Glendale, the Church of the New Jerusalem houses a Swedenborgian congregation and a bench on which Johnny Appleseed is said to have sat. In another corner of Ohio, the southeastern town of Dexter City, is the Chapman family cemetery, near the present-day Johnny Appleseed Center for Creative Learning. While Johnny was buried in Fort Wayne, Indiana, where he died in 1845 at age 70, legend has it that his ghost returns each year to the Dexter City cemetery. It is said that he can be seen only by the "good and the innocent."

Such monuments and legends are interesting, but none has the power to persuade a skeptic that Johnny Appleseed was more than a legend. Doing that takes a trip to the Knox County shire town of Mount Vernon, located in the heart of Johnny Appleseed Country. What you see there may raise goose bumps. After parking on the picturesque town square, you need walk only a few steps up a side street to the recorder's office, on the second floor of a county office building. Ask to look at the deed records in the back of the office; they are kept in ponderous gray books on shelves with rollers. Pull down Book G and turn to page 504.

There you can touch the actual page and see the original writing set down there on Wednesday, November 5, 1828, by an unknown person with neat penmanship. That long-forgotten recorder's clerk had held a deed in his hand and copied it into this official record, word for word, as he had many others. Signed two days before and duly witnessed, the deed stated that, for $30 lawful money, Mount Vernon inlot number 145 was changing hands. The buyer was one Jesse B. Thomas. And the seller?

"Know all men by these presents that I John Chapman (by occupation a gatherer and planter of appleseeds) of...the State of Ohio...in testimony thereof...have hereunto set my hand and seal this third day of November in the year of Our Lord One Thousand Eight Hundred and Twenty Eight."

The parenthetical explanation after Chapman's name was as unusual then as it would be today; he must have wanted to make sure that no one missed who he was. Today, that little notation on page 504 is like a message from the past: *Believe in me.*

You can see it for yourself.

The Ohio Farmer, August 16, 1917

FACES OF THE LAND

Finding Johnny Ipil-Seed

We will agree, up front, that Dave Deppner certainly doesn't *look* like John Chapman, a.k.a. Johnny Appleseed. Johnny Appleseed was skinny as a rail, nervous and quick, fond of spreading the Gospel—the kind of guy you might find handing out tracts in an airport. Deppner is a solid rock of a man, craggy faced, with big hands and a deep, rumbling laugh; he keeps his religion to himself. And, he says with a grin, "So far I have not used a saucepan for a hat."

But just like Johnny Appleseed, Dave Deppner is a roamer who makes the hillsides bloom wherever he goes. Johnny did it for the Midwest. Deppner does it for the world.

In fact, Deppner just may plant more trees than any other human being alive. He doesn't do them all himself, of course: instead, he plants ideas, and the people who need them plant the trees. You might say he gets people to see the possibilities—the way Johnny did.

Seeing possibilities is what got Deppner going in the first place. Born in Dayton the son of a General Motors executive who also kept a farm, he earned a degree in animal science at Ohio State University in 1954. By the early 1970s, he was a Miamisburg poultry farmer, prosperous and bored. A friend just back from Africa told him how children there were withering mentally for lack of protein. A few weeks later Deppner found himself at a poultry meeting where the talk was all about dumping protein-rich eggs to keep the price up. Angrily telling his fellow farmers what he thought of wasting food, he walked out and—answering some voice deep in his soul—signed up for the Peace Corps.

Sent to the Philippines in 1972, Peace Corpsman Deppner was assigned to "a rather strange veterinarian—he spent all day planting trees." Until then, all that Deppner knew about trees was that, in his words, "they were green on top and brown on the bottom, and nice to sit under." But helping the native vet plant 60,000 trees, he learned how they could restore land devastated by clear-cutting. And he learned about the project's "miracle tree"—the *Leucaena leucocephala*, a native of the American tropics which Spanish explorers had carried to the Philippines. People there call it the Ipil-Ipil.

Most trees offer erosion control, wind breaks, natural fences, lumber and some fuel. But the modern *Leucaena*, beefed up by breeding at the

University of Hawaii, can overwhelm your expectations: a hectare (about 2.5 acres) can produce 46 cubic yards of dense, clean-burning firewood in one year; amazingly, the trunks grow right back, faster every time they're cut. The same amount of acreage can also yield 18 tons of dried leaves for animal forage: its leaves have about 26% protein and about three times as much vitamin A as alfalfa meal. *Leucaena* bark provides tannin and dye, and the tree's young leaves and pods can add vitamins to human diet. Even the roasted seeds can serve as a coffee substitute. In all, research has identified some 28 products of the Ipil-Ipil.

Best of all, this tree grows like crazy in the humid tropics. From a standing start as a seed the new, improved *Leucaena* can reach 24 feet in height in just one year—a growth rate remarkable by ordinary standards. As Deppner explains, "When you're working in developing countries they've got to see a benefit in an incredibly short time." He laughs as he remembers a government official telling poor people in Nicaragua they should plant hardwoods that take 25 to 30 years to mature: "I walked out with some campesino farmer, and he said, 'Look, I don't know what my kids are going to eat next week—I don't know for a fact they're going to be eating anything. How can this guy come in here and tell me I should plant trees for my grandchildren?'"

Dave Deppner

Deppner can't. Instead, he'll tell a Third World farmer that if he plants the seeds of the *Leucaena* in January, he'll see some benefit by July, and a lot more by December. "Normally we start planting them about five months before the rainy season begins, and one of the first benefits people see is erosion control on hillsides," explains Deppner. "They save a tremendous amount of soil. We have one project in Belize where we built 11 inches of soil around these trees in one rainy season."

An acre of Ipil-Ipil will produce about 16,000 pounds, dry weight, of leaves. The leaves contain almost 4% nitrogen, organic fertilizer. So, Deppner tells the farmer, "At six months, when they're 12 to 14 feet tall, you'll already be getting that benefit. So even in that first year you can greatly increase food production. And by the end of the year you've got trees that are two and a half inches in diameter, and you can start harvesting firewood."

Deppner has the blunt-talking, can-do spirit of the American pioneer, tempered by a farmer's horse sense. He's a big, hearty guy who's not shy about sharing his opinions. U.S. foreign aid projects to developing countries, for example, bring a snort of disgust. Most, according to Deppner, "involve spending a lot of the taxpayers' money to help corporations send sophisticated technology to people who don't know what to do with it or can't use it." Worst of all, he says, they are run by remote bureaucrats trying to *impose* solutions on people instead of asking them what they want solved.

By contrast, Deppner believes in getting up close and personal "one village at a time," asking people what their problems are, then showing them how they can get a quick payoff by planting trees. Globally, an area equal to the size of Ohio is deforested every year, some by greedy timber companies but most by poor farmers using self-defeating "slash-and-burn" methods to clear land for planting. But as over-cutting continues, hillsides wash away, water tables go down, crop production falls and so does income. And the price of firewood, the fuel of choice in most of the world, climbs out of sight.

When the locals begin to realize they need help, Deppner (or his agent) is ready with his miracle trees. Greeted with skepticism, he starts by persuading just a few families—15 or 20 in a village—to try out his trees. *Leucaena* is easy to plant and hard to kill: it grows readily in hot, dry conditions, quickly giving a cooling leaf canopy above and a root system below which reaches deep into the soil to bring up nutrients which benefit neighboring plants. When the Ipil-Ipil begins to perform its miracles, word spreads rapidly: "A year later we don't have to sell the idea. Everybody has seen it," Deppner says with a grin. "So the idea is planted, and the trees are now beginning to bear their own seeds, and the project can rapidly expand from that point on." Suddenly, the villagers are realizing new sources of fuel, fertilizer and animal forage; as the Ipil-Ipil trees renew their forests, other species of trees, including prized hardwoods, begin to return naturally, bringing the promise of cash income.

So Deppner believes in getting people to help the environment by appealing to their immediate self-interest. "I suppose this is what separates our organization from the majority of people in Washington," he says. "There's no argument on our part that there is an environmental disaster taking place. But there are those who say the only way this can be solved is to punish ourselves, we've got to tax ourselves into oblivion, we've got to cut our standard of living." By contrast, Deppner says, "every experience" he has had with properly planned reforestation is that it "creates jobs, it creates new industries, it generates a terrific amount of new income. It doesn't cost, it pays. It's time to start using our brains instead of our tax money. I think all you can offer somebody is an idea."

And in 20 years, Deppner has offered plenty of people plenty of ideas, many of them involving trees. After two terms in the Peace Corps in the 1970s, he returned to the United States, his first marriage in shambles. He later went back to the Philippines to teach for two years; there he met his second wife, a widow who had grown up in the barrios and "who knows what it's like when there's no food in the house and nobody to buy it. She knows things [about poverty] that I can only sense as an outsider. So we team up. I do all my technical wizardry and she goes out for hearts and minds, and once in a while we get something good done."

Doing "something good" means running Trees for the Future, a nonprofit organization based in Silver Spring, Maryland. After working for other aid programs for several years, Deppner began his own in 1989 with $8,400; since then Trees for the Future has been responsible for planting over 30,000,000 trees in 89 countries (37 of which Deppner has visited personally). At last report, Trees for the Future was planting over half a million trees a month, 86% of them the Ipil-Ipil. With a budget of scarcely $200,000, the organization employs only five people including

Dave and Grace Deppner, but relies heavily on an international network of volunteers.

Support for the organization comes from more than 5,000 contributors, who give amounts ranging from a dollar to $21,000. Among the supporters is Garry Trudeau, creator of the Doonesbury cartoon strip. Someday, says Deppner, he'd like to see Trees for the Future with a staff of perhaps 20, with an international network of 10,000 volunteers. He'll need them: the world is losing 40 billion trees a year, about an acre of forest per second.

Johnny Appleseed died a century and a half ago, and Dave Deppner doesn't claim to be his reincarnation, although he does call his newsletter the "Johnny Ipil-Seed News."

"We're both rather strange," says Deppner of himself and Johnny Appleseed. "I was fascinated by that story from the time I was very young. Not too bad a guy to pattern yourself after. But if I had to criticize, I'd have to say Johnny didn't have a long-range plan. He got his kicks out of watching something grow; the apple tree was an end in itself. To us, the Ipil-Ipil is the beginning of something."

So Dave Deppner neither sounds nor looks nor even thinks like Johnny Appleseed. And Johnny was buried a long time ago. You just can't claim that Johnny Appleseed roams the earth again.

And yet....

POSTSCRIPT: *For more information on Dave Deppner's work and how to support it, contact Trees for the Future, P.O. Box 1786, Silver Spring, Maryland 20915, or telephone 1-800-643-0001.*

RECIPES

Hot Cider Punch

Makes about 1-1/2 quarts

1 quart apple cider
2 cups cranberry juice cocktail
1 cup orange juice
1/2 cup firmly packed light brown
  sugar
4 whole allspice
4 whole cloves
2 cinnamon sticks

Apple cider, the harder the better, was a popular drink on the frontier and for many years in the rural areas. Many farmers had orchards and would set up cider presses in them, which yielded a saleable product more convenient than apples. The cider could be put in barrels and transported on river boats. Even before the War of 1812, cider was being squeezed in "prodigious amounts" in Washington County, which fronts on the Ohio River. A thirsty Cincinnati was downriver.

In large saucepan, combine ingredients; bring to a boil. Reduce heat; simmer uncovered 10 minutes. Remove spices. Serve hot in mugs with additional cinnamon sticks if desired.

George Voinovich's Favorite Pork Chops

Makes 6 to 8 servings

6 to 8 loin pork chops
Pepper
3/4 cup apple cider or juice
1/2 cup firmly packed light brown
  sugar
1/2 cup soy sauce
3 tablespoons catsup
2 tablespoons cornstarch
1/2 teaspoon ground ginger
2 all-purpose apples, cored and
  sliced in rings

This savory pork chop dish is a recipe from the *Family Favorites* cookbook written by Janet Voinovich and Fran DeWine in 1990. Mrs. Voinovich says the Governor likes these pork chops served with rice and broccoli.

Preheat oven to 350 degrees. Arrange chops in single layer in lightly greased 13x9-inch baking dish. Season with pepper; cover with foil and bake for 30 minutes. Drain; turn chops over. In small saucepan, combine remaining ingredients except apples. Cook and stir until thickened. Top chops with apple rings; pour sauce over. Cover with foil; bake an additional 30 minutes.

Ohio Apple Maple Chutney

Chutney is a condiment we associate with the British empire (the word comes from the Hindi), but this recipe is thoroughly Ohioan. It comes to us from Quail Hollow—Ohio's only four-diamond resort—in Concord (30 miles east of Cleveland). Executive Chef Tim Rios was kind enough to share this recipe, one of several they create with Ohio ingredients. The Quail Wagon dining room serves it with a pork loin baked in a crunchy pecan coating.

In large skillet, cook apples, peppers and onion in hot oil until softened. Add sugar, raisins, vinegar, syrup and spices; cook until tender. In small bowl, combine sherry and cornstarch; add to apple mixture. Cook until thickened. Cover; refrigerate 6 hours or overnight. Just before serving, add cilantro.

Makes about 2 cups

4 medium all-purpose apples, peeled, cored and chopped
1 green pepper, finely chopped
1 red pepper, finely chopped
1 small onion, finely chopped
2 tablespoons vegetable oil
1/2 cup firmly packed light brown sugar
1/2 cup raisins
1/4 cup cider vinegar
1/4 cup maple syrup
1/2 teaspoon each ground cinnamon, ginger and nutmeg
2 tablespoons dry sherry
2 teaspoons cornstarch
1 tablespoon chopped fresh cilantro

Autumn Harvest Soup

In recent years, Ohio has ranked either first or second among states in the production of Swiss cheese. It is also one of the nation's largest producers of chickens, onions and apples. This recipe brings these and other bounties of the Ohio harvest together in a new way. Although the recipe seems to fit autumn best, it can enjoyed any time of year, and will keep your guests guessing as to its exact ingredients.

In large saucepan, cook onion in butter until tender. Add squash, apples and chicken broth; bring to a boil. Reduce heat; cover and simmer 20 minutes or until tender. In blender or food processor, puree one third of the squash mixture, repeat until all mixture is pureed. In saucepan, combine half and half and cheese with squash puree; heat until cheese melts (do not boil). Add salt and pepper to taste. Sprinkle each serving with nutmeg.

Makes about 1-1/2 quarts

3/4 cup chopped onion
2 tablespoons butter or margarine
1 acorn squash, peeled, seeded and coarsely chopped*
2 medium all-purpose apples, peeled, cored and cut into eighths
4 cups chicken broth or stock
1 cup half-and-half or light coffee cream
1 cup (8 ounces) shredded Swiss cheese
Salt
Pepper
Ground nutmeg

* If squash is difficult to cut, pierce with a large fork and microwave on 100% power (high) for 2 to 3 minutes. This softens squash and makes it easier to halve and peel.

Apple-Stuffed Pork Loin with Raspberry Sauce

Makes 8 to 10 servings

1 cup chopped onion
1-1/2 cups chopped celery
1/2 cup butter or margarine
3 cups cored and chopped tart red
   apples
1/2 teaspoon ground allspice
1/4 teaspoon ground cardamom
5 cups dry bread cubes
1/2 cup raisins or chopped pecans
1 (3 to 4 pound) boneless single pork
   loin roast
Dash each garlic powder, pepper and
   salt

Raspberry Sauce
Makes 1-3/4 cups

2 cups fresh raspberries, or 2 cups
   frozen raspberries, thawed and
   undrained
1/2 cup apricot nectar
1/2 cup red currant jelly
2 tablespoons brandy (optional)
1 tablespoon honey or sugar
4 teaspoons cornstarch
1 tablespoon water

Nearly 180 years ago, stagecoach drivers pulled up at The Buxton Inn in Granville, Ohio. Today, former school teachers, Ralph and Audrey Orr, are busy restoring not just the Inn, but a whole block in this town amid Ohio's Welsh Mountains. It is a treat to stay at the Buxton, as each room is furnished in period antiques. The food served in the dining room is well known, prompting diners to drive many miles. This recipe is a favorite at the Inn. It combines pork and apples, two Ohio favorites.

In large skillet, cook onion and celery in butter until tender. Add apples, allspice and cardamom; cook, uncovered, for 5 minutes, stirring occasionally. In large bowl, combine apple mixture with bread and raisins; toss gently until bread is coated.

Preheat oven to 325 degrees. Trim excess fat from meat; split lengthwise almost through. Spoon about half of stuffing over meat; fold, tie with string to secure. Place remaining stuffing in 1-quart baking dish. Place meat on a rack in 17x12-inch roasting pan. Sprinkle with garlic powder, pepper and salt; insert meat thermometer. Roast meat, uncovered, 60 to 70 minutes or until thermometer registers 160 to 170 degrees. Cover and heat remaining stuffing during the last 40 minutes of roasting. To serve, slice pork; serve with additional stuffing and Raspberry Sauce.

Raspberry Sauce
In medium saucepan, combine raspberries, nectar, jelly, brandy and honey. Over low heat, stirring frequently, cook until mixture boils. Strain to remove seeds; return mixture to saucepan. In small bowl, combine cornstarch and water; add to raspberry mixture. Cook and stir until clear and thickened, stirring constantly.

Apple Cashew Pasta

Frannie Packard, who was trained at Paris's La Varenne Cooking School, is the chef at the Ohio Governor's Residence and coordinates the Heartland Cuisine Program at the Ohio State Fair. She teaches cooking classes at La Belle Pomme and Columbus's North Market. She even has her own "Frannie's Honey Mustard" salad dressing on the market and sells specialty bakery items throughout Ohio.

In large skillet, melt butter; add 2 tablespoons olive oil, onions and apples. Cook until tender. Add red pepper, zucchini and 1 cup cashews; cook 2 minutes, stirring constantly. In large bowl, combine hot pasta with remaining oil and 1/2 cup cheese. Pour apple mixture over pasta; toss. Season with salt and pepper. Sprinkle each serving with remaining cashews and cheese.

Makes 6 to 8 servings

6 tablespoons butter or margarine
3 tablespoons olive oil
2 large yellow onions, thinly sliced
3 large Red Delicious apples, cored and sliced
1 red pepper, cut into strips
1 medium zucchini, thinly sliced
1-1/2 cups roasted and salted whole cashews
12 ounces fettucine or linguine, cooked and drained
1 cup grated Parmesan cheese
Salt
Pepper

Mike DeWine's Favorite Apple Dumplings

Fran DeWine, the wife of Lt. Gov. Mike DeWine, graduated from Miami University in 1971, with a degree in home economics. In 1980, when her husband first ran for State Senate, Fran wrote a campaign cookbook entitled *Family Favorites*. She included her own recipes along with those of family and friends, and also had recipes for children to prepare. Since then, she has written a new cookbook for each election, seven in all. All the cookbooks are illustrated by her children. In 1990, Fran and Janet Voinovich wrote a cook book featuring favorites from both families.

Preheat oven to 350 degrees. In medium bowl, combine flour and salt. With pastry blender, cut shortening into flour mixture until it resembles coarse crumbs. Sprinkle water over mixture a tablespoon at a time, mixing lightly with a fork until pastry just holds together. With hands, shape pastry into 2 balls. On lightly floured surface, roll out each ball to 1/8-inch thickness; cut into quarters. Repeat with second pastry ball.

In small bowl, combine sugar, tapioca and cinnamon. Divide apples and sugar mixture evenly among the 8 pastry wedges; top each with dot of butter. Bring up corners of pastry; moisten with water, pinch edges to seal. Place in 13x9-inch baking dish. In small saucepan, combine syrup ingredients; boil until sugar dissolves. Pour over apple dumplings. Bake 40 to 45 minutes or until fruit is tender and pastry is golden brown.

Makes 8 servings

Pastry:
2-1/4 cups flour
1/2 teaspoon salt
3/4 cup solid vegetable shortening
5 to 6 tablespoons cold water

Filling:
1-1/2 cups sugar
1/2 cup minute tapioca
2 teaspoons ground cinnamon
10 all-purpose apples, peeled, cored and sliced
2 tablespoons butter or margarine

Syrup:
2 cups water
1 cup sugar
1/4 cup butter or margarine
1 teaspoon ground cinnamon

Cranberry-Apple Crisp

Makes 6 to 8 servings

*5 cups peeled, cored and sliced all-
  purpose apples*
3/4 cup fresh cranberries
*1 cup firmly packed light brown
  sugar*
1 teaspoon grated orange rind
3/4 cup flour
3/4 cup oats
1 teaspoon ground cinnamon
1/2 cup butter or margarine

Cranberries are associated with the eastern shore areas, such as Cape Cod and New Jersey. Most people don't know that Ohio has its own cranberry bog, too. Part of Buckeye Lake, it is a living remnant of the ice age and is believed to be the only floating cranberry bog in the world. It is gradually disappearing, and is now about 14 acres in size, surrounded by 4,000 acres of lake. The bog is teeming with plants, including some carnivorous ones. Because of its ecological frailty, visitors must obtain special permission from the Ohio Department of Natural Resources, or visit the last Saturday each June when an "open house" is held.

Preheat oven to 350 degrees. In large bowl, combine apples, cranberries, 1/4 cup sugar and rind; toss gently until fruit is lightly coated. Place in 8-inch square baking dish. In medium bowl, combine remaining sugar, flour, oats and cinnamon. Add butter; mix until crumbly. Sprinkle evenly over apple mixture. Bake 45 to 50 minutes or until fruit is soft and topping is crisp. Serve warm with vanilla ice cream or heavy cream.

Biddie's German Apple Cake

Makes one 13x9-inch cake

Cake:
2 cups flour
2 cups sugar
1 cup vegetable oil
3 eggs
2 teaspoons ground cinnamon
1 teaspoon vanilla extract
1 teaspoon baking soda
1/2 teaspoon salt
*4 cups pared, cored and chopped all-
  purpose apples*
1 cup chopped pecans

Frosting:
*1 (8-ounce) package cream cheese,
  softened*
1-1/2 cups confectioners' sugar
*3 tablespoons butter or margarine,
  softened*
1 teaspoon vanilla extract

This cake is a specialty at Biddie's Coach House in the historical village area of Dublin. The building was constructed in the mid-1800s and at one time was a stagecoach stop. "Biddie" is owner Mary Marsalka's mother and hostess at the quaint tea room.

Preheat oven to 350 degrees. In large bowl, combine flour, sugar, oil, eggs, cinnamon, vanilla, soda and salt; mix well. Stir in apples and pecans. Pour into greased and floured 13x9-inch baking dish. Bake 45 to 50 minutes or until wooden pick inserted near center comes out clean. Cool 20 to 30 minutes. In small mixer bowl, combine frosting ingredients; beat until light and creamy. Spread on cake.

Di's Dutch Apple Pie

Every year the cooks of Ohio fire up their ovens and begin baking pies for the county fair competitions held throughout the state. The biggest fair of all, of course, is the Ohio State Fair in Columbus. The following recipe is for the pie that earned a blue ribbon for Diane Cordial of Powell.

Diane is a registered nurse who works in a hospital. She has been entering and winning pie-baking contests at the Ohio State Fair for more than a quarter century.

Preheat oven to 400 degrees. In large bowl, combine all filling ingredients except apples and lemon juice; mix well. Add apples and lemon juice; toss gently until fruit is lightly coated. In medium bowl, combine topping ingredients; mix until crumbly. Turn apples into unbaked pastry shell; sprinkle topping mixture evenly over apples. Bake 20 minutes. Reduce oven temperature to 350 degrees; bake 45 minutes or until golden brown.

Makes one 9-inch pie

Filling:
3/4 cup sugar
1/4 cup firmly packed light brown sugar
3 tablespoons flour
1 teaspoon ground cinnamon
1/4 teaspoon salt
1/8 teaspoon ground nutmeg
6-1/2 cups peeled, cored and sliced Granny Smith or other tart juicy apples
2 teaspoons lemon juice

Topping:
1/2 cup butter or margarine, softened
1/2 cup flour
1/4 cup firmly packed light brown sugar
1/4 cup sugar
1/4 cup chopped pecans
1 tablespoon oats
1/2 teaspoon ground cinnamon
1 (9-inch) unbaked pastry shell

Rhubarb Pie

Makes one 9-inch pie

6 cups rhubarb, cut into 1/2-inch
  pieces
1-1/4 cups sugar
3 tablespoons minute tapioca
1 tablespoon red sugar (decorating
  sugar)
Pastry for 2-crust pie
1 tablespoon butter or margarine

Every farm used to have a rhubarb patch, usually by the back door of the farmhouse. Rhubarb was baked into so many pies that it became known as pieplant.

Pat Bruns is director of the Mercer County Council on Aging, in Celina. She remembers her father saying you should always pick rhubarb right after a rain, for the best flavor. As a child she peeled rhubarb, sprinkled it with salt, and ate it as a snack. She remembers her mother baking 8 rhubarb pies at a time. This recipe for rhubarb pie is her own. She prefers using small rhubarb stalks. What makes this pie unique is the addition of the red sugar (decorating sugar).

In large bowl, combine rhubarb, sugar, tapioca and red sugar; toss gently until fruit is lightly coated. Let stand 20 minutes.

Preheat oven to 425 degrees. Divide pastry in half; on lightly floured surface, roll each half out to 1/8-inch thickness. Line pie plate; trim edges even with plate. Turn rhubarb filling into pastry lined plate; dot with butter. Moisten edges of pastry in pie plate; lift second pastry circle onto filling. Trim 1/2-inch beyond edge of pie plate; fold top edge under bottom crust, flute edges. With sharp knife, slit top pastry in several spots for steam vents. Bake 40 to 45 minutes or until golden brown. (If crust is getting too brown during last few minutes of baking, cover edges loosely with aluminum foil.)

Variations: 1-1/2 cups fresh sliced strawberries, or 1 (16-ounce) can tart red pitted cherries, drained, may be substituted for 1 cup of the rhubarb. Proceed as above.

Fresh Peach Cobbler

The agricultural historian Robert Leslie Jones tells us that the first fruit the pioneers cultivated in Ohio was the peach. They were grown as early as the 1780s in Ohio, and more than 200 years later, are still being grown here.

Betty, Buckle, Crisp, Crumble, Pandowdy and Cobbler are all names for old-fashioned desserts. With some variations, they all refer to desserts made with fruit and a topping, crust or batter. Ohio community cookbooks almost always contain at least one of these made with apples, peaches, blueberries or other seasonal fruit.

Preheat oven to 350 degrees. In lightly greased 8-inch square baking dish, arrange peaches. In medium bowl, combine flour, sugar, baking powder, salt and butter; mix until crumbly. In small bowl, beat egg until thick and lemon colored; add milk and extracts. Add to flour mixture, stirring until just moistened. Spread batter evenly over peaches. Bake 35 to 40 minutes or until golden brown. Serve warm with vanilla ice cream or heavy cream.

Makes 4 to 6 servings

3 cups pared, sliced fresh peaches
1 cup flour
1/2 cup sugar
1 teaspoon baking powder
1/8 teaspoon salt
1/4 cup butter or margarine
1 egg
3 tablespoons milk
1/2 teaspoon vanilla
1/8 teaspoon almond extract

Peach Mountain Muffins

Marilyn and Larry Bagford own the Bayberry Inn in Peebles. Their Victorian home was built circa 1888 by Dr. James Murphy Wittenmyer, a distinguished physician and leading citizen in Adams County. The Bagfords opened it in 1985 as a bed and breakfast. The Bayberry is located on historic Zane Trace in Adams county and is not far from the historic Serpent Mound. This peach muffin recipe is one of Marilyn's favorites, and is named after the nearby mountain where the peaches grow.

Preheat oven to 400 degrees. In large bowl, combine flour, sugar, baking powder, baking soda, nutmeg and salt; cut in shortening until crumbly. In medium bowl, combine yogurt, egg and vanilla; add to dry ingredients, stirring just until moistened. Add peaches. Fill muffin cups 3/4 full. Sprinkle almonds evenly on each muffin. Bake 15 to 20 minutes or until golden brown. Cool 5 minutes; remove from pans.

Makes 12 muffins

2 cups flour
1/2 cup sugar
1 teaspoon baking powder
1/2 teaspoon baking soda
1/2 teaspoon ground nutmeg
1/4 teaspoon salt
1/3 cup solid vegetable shortening
1 (8-ounce) container low-fat peach
  yogurt
1 egg
1 teaspoon vanilla extract
1-1/2 cups peeled and chopped fresh
  or frozen peaches
1/4 cup slivered almonds

Rhubarb Crunch Cake

Makes one 13x9-inch cake

Cake:
2 cups rhubarb, cut into 1/2-inch
   pieces
2 tablespoons flour
1-1/2 cups sugar
1/2 cup solid vegetable shortening
1 egg
2 cups flour
1 teaspoon baking soda
1/2 teaspoon salt
1 cup buttermilk
1 teaspoon vanilla

Topping:
3/4 cup sugar
1 teaspoon ground cinnamon
1/4 cup butter or margarine, soft-
   ened

Lawrence Dunn was born in Sidney and lived in Piqua for 67 years before moving to Celina. Mr. Dunn, who is 90 years old, does all the baking in his family! He became interested in baking when he married for the third time, at age 73. He also bakes black walnut cookies and angel food cakes, but says this rhubarb cake is one of his favorites.

This moist cake is delicious as is or can be served with a topping of whipped cream or ice cream. If fresh rhubarb is not available, frozen works well too.

Preheat oven to 350 degrees. In medium bowl, combine rhubarb and 2 tablespoons flour; toss gently until rhubarb is lightly coated. In large mixer bowl, combine sugar and shortening; beat well. Add egg; beat well. Sift together 2 cups flour, baking soda and salt; add alternately with buttermilk, stir well. Add vanilla and rhubarb. Turn into greased 13x9-inch pan.

In small bowl, combine topping ingredients; mix until crumbly. Sprinkle evenly over cake. Bake 35 to 40 minutes or until cake springs back when touched lightly with finger.

Apple Butter

Makes four pints

3 quarts fresh apple cider
8 pounds juicy apples,* cored and
   quartered
2-1/2 cups firmly packed light brown
   sugar
2 teaspoons ground cinnamon
1/2 teaspoon each ground allspice,
   ground cloves and salt

* Jonathan, Winesap, McIntosh or Russet
   apples may be used. Janet prefers Winesap.

The Geauga County Historical Society, in Burton, began an annual Apple Butter Festival in 1948. About 400 gallons of apple butter are cooked over open fires in antique copper kettles and bottled for sale. At least 2,500 servings of apple fritters are prepared at the snack bar. Freshly pressed cider and hot mulled cider are also served. This recipe comes from the files of Janet Wood, of London, who calls apple butter "a bread spread from long ago that still tastes good today."

In large enamel kettle, boil cider 30 minutes or until reduced by half; add apples. Cook over low heat until apples are tender, stirring constantly with wooden spoon or paddle. Press through food mill or sieve. Return to kettle; add remaining ingredients. Cook over low heat, stirring constantly until sugar dissolves. Continue cooking and stirring about 30 minutes. (Constant stirring prevents mixture from sticking and burning.) Pour mixture into hot, sterilized jars; seal at once.

Apple-Pumpkin Streusel Muffins

This recipe is a favorite of Lorine Simmons, a Columbus native. She first sampled the muffins at a neighbor's home and subsequently asked for the recipe. Lorine likes to make them in the fall when the flavors of pumpkin and apples come to mind.

Preheat oven to 375 degrees. In large bowl, combine flour, sugar, cinnamon, baking soda, ginger, salt and nutmeg. In medium bowl combine eggs, pumpkin and oil; add to dry ingredients, stir until just moistened. Add apples and nuts. Fill paper-lined or greased muffin cups 3/4 full. Combine topping ingredients; sprinkle evenly over muffins. Bake 20 to 25 minutes or until golden brown. Cool 5 minutes; remove from pans.

Makes 18 to 24 muffins

Batter:
2-1/2 cups flour
2 cups sugar
1 teaspoon ground cinnamon
1 teaspoon baking soda
1/2 teaspoon ground ginger
1/2 teaspoon salt
1/4 teaspoon ground nutmeg
2 eggs, slightly beaten
1 cup (8 ounces) canned pumpkin*
1/2 cup vegetable oil
2 cups peeled, cored and grated all-purpose apples
1/2 cup finely chopped nuts

* Since pumpkin usually comes packed in 16-ounce cans, use half the can and freeze the remainder for another batch of muffins at a later date. You'll need it, and not much later, either.

Topping:
1/4 cup sugar
2 tablespoons flour
1 tablespoon butter or margarine
1/2 teaspoon cinnamon

Grandma Failor's Cranberry Relish

Our family serves jellied cranberry sauce with our turkey, but we ALWAYS have Grandma Failor's Cranberry Relish. Grandma's relish even survived Grandma. She passed away at 80, between Thanksgiving and Christmas. After she had passed away, we still had some leftover cranberry relish in our refrigerator that she had made for Thanksgiving. We still enjoy the recipe.

In food processor, finely chop cranberries in batches until all are chopped; place in large bowl. Finely chop oranges (yes, rind and all), then pecans; add to cranberries. Stir in sugar, sweetening to taste. Cover; refrigerate at least two days. Serve as an accompaniment to holiday meals.

Makes about 4 cups

2 (1-pound) bags fresh cranberries, washed, sorted and drained
3 to 4 medium oranges, UNPEELED, cut into quarters (center membrane removed)
1 cup pecans or walnuts
1 cup sugar (or to taste)

Since the early 1800s farmers have been undergoing an industrial revolution of their own, replacing horsepower and manpower with machines and chemicals. This picture, taken on an Ohio farm in the late 1930s, captures in one scene the transition from old to new. A team of draft horses waits with its load while a five-man crew uses a threshing machine getting its power from a gasoline tractor (right). Today, one farmer and a diesel combine have replaced them all.

Big Ag and Little Ag

Early in 1993 Ohio moviegoers were flocking to see *Lorenzo's Oil*, a better-than-average tearjerker that earned three and a half stars from many critics and four hankies from most audiences. It was the story of a boy stricken with a mysterious disease for which, The Experts solemnly told his parents, there is no cure. The parents went ahead and discovered one anyway, proving once again The Experts don't have all the answers.

It's an old story: The Experts, the Tribal Elders, or Mom and Dad—in other words, The Establishment—declaring What's So; some lonely individuals stubbornly disagreeing. Often The Experts are right—after all, how did they get to be experts in the first place? Once in a while, though, the little guy gets it right instead, and, thanks to Hollywood, the dramatic story will be coming soon to a theater near you. And sometimes, both sides learn from each other, not without some Sturm und Drang, of course, and the world changes.

One of these scenarios is unfolding right now in Ohio. It arrays The Establishment of modern conventional agriculture versus certain folks who are pushing alternatives. Modern conventional agriculture is what's usually taught in the schools, practiced by most farmers, big and small, and supported by heavyweight authorities like the U.S. Department of Agriculture. Collectively, they form Big Agriculture—Big Ag, for short. By *alternatives* to Big Ag, we mean a whole passel of things—organic farming, sustainable agriculture and holistic resource management, to name a few. These are practiced by fewer people, folks who usually work on a smaller scale and see themselves outside the mainstream—not because of their size but because of their ideas. Collectively, they are Little Ag.

Big Ag and Little Ag. Together, they are players in a very human and thoroughly fascinating drama. Little Ag thinks Big can be overbearing or uncaring, while Big Ag thinks Little can be hopelessly romantic or tiresomely zealous. But deep down is a shared perception: each side thinks the other is naive. Each expresses the thought a little differently. Big Ag's message to Little Ag is, *Get real*. Little Ag's message to Big is, *Get a life*.

We oversimplify, of course, and no doubt will be hearing soon from both sides. Little Ag has its own retinue of experts, for example, and Big Ag is not heartless. Moreover, each side gives the other credit (sometimes, anyway) for good, if misguided, intentions. ("They are not evil people," a spokesperson for one side said of the other, although no one had suggested they were.) Still, you get the drift: a voice from Little Ag deriding the Ohio State University College of Ag as a "lumbering bovine;" a faculty member there calling such critics the "counter-culture"—deftly marginalizing them as Not Our Kind of People.

But what's exciting to even a citified onlooker is that something important is going on here—something linked to the nation's heart and soul as well as its body. For years we have endured angst-generating media reports on the Farm Crisis, the poisoning of the countryside and the disappearance of rural society. Now we are beginning to get better news. So far, the net improvement in this area is not too much bigger than a man's hand. But something IS happening in the 1990s, something that puts us on the leading edge of change. The fussing and fuming from Big and Little Ag are proof of it.

First, some history.

For hundreds of thousands of years our ancestors roamed in packs, hunter-gatherers with no fixed addresses. Then—oh, say, 10,000 years ago—a few people learned how to plant seeds and raise crops. In this, the First Agricultural Revolution, some of the hunter-gatherers settled down, built houses and created villages. A few of the villages even grew into cities, but most folks continued to live close to the land.

Then, scarcely 200 years ago, the wealth and knowledge that had been fermenting in those cities hit critical mass and began exploding into mass production, mass communication, and mass-just-about-everything. We call this the Industrial Revolution, and it goes on yet. It changed whole nations from being mostly rural societies, in which most people were farmers, into urban societies, in which few people are farmers. But production has skyrocketed as agriculture uses machinery and chemicals and big bucks to industrialize itself. Farming once was plows and cows, but now it's a lot more complicated, and called agribusiness. The Second Agricultural Revolution.

This revolution has given America such a bounty of food and farm products that the U.S. government has had to provide subsidies and other help for farmers unable to profit from their own plenitude. But American consumers would seem to be winners. Carla Moore, a certified home economist who works for the Ohio Department of Agriculture, notes, "One American farmer or rancher provides food and fiber for 128 people—94 in the United States and 34 abroad. In the U.S., we spend ten percent of our income on food. In France, it's 16 percent; in Japan, 18 percent; China, 48 percent; India, 53 percent." A government official summed it up this way: "Modern agriculture has done a tremendous job of providing high-quality and reasonably priced food for consumers." How right you are, says Big Ag.

Hey, wait a minute, says Little Ag: everyone has been paying a price for all this. Listen to the voices:

• Rachel Carson, whose 1962 classic, *Silent Spring*, warned how farm pesticides were threatening the balance nature. Her larger message: some of the "miracles" of modern science and agriculture have a dark side.

• The Rodales, who began preaching the connection between soil health and human health in the 1940s. The Rodale organization has been researching organic, chemical-free growing methods ever since and arguing in books and magazines that "you really are what you eat."

• Ohio's own Louis Bromfield (1896-1956), a globetrotter, novelist, and Hollywood scriptwriter, who returned to his native Richland County to reclaim the home place, which he called Malabar Farm. Using new tillage methods, he revived several worn-out farms, writing eloquently as he did so about the need for preserving land instead of exploiting it.

• Gene Logsdon of Upper Sandusky, who farms 32 acres while raising a bumper crop of books and articles about Little Ag. Sometimes adopting the fractious persona of The Contrary Farmer, the scrappy Logsdon declares: "A nation with a strong fabric of small family farms is better for society, better for the food supply and better for the environment than what we have now"—namely, fewer and bigger farms.

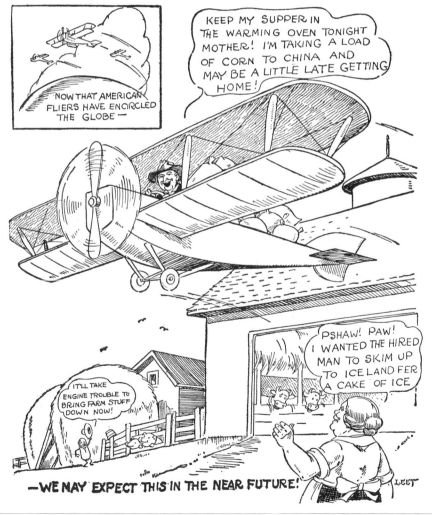

The Ohio Farmer, August 2, 1924

Voices like these have been having an effect. Across the country, interest has been growing in organic agriculture, for example. Organic farmers try to conserve natural resources and the environment, protect country life and the rural economy, and, most of all, avoid the synthetic chemicals that are a hallmark of modern conventional agriculture. Instead of depositing chemicals on their land, they try to build life into their soil. "Stewardship" is a popular word in their vocabulary.

In 1979, some of these farmers formed the Ohio Ecological Food and Farm Association, a name neatly bypassing the hippy-dippy farmer image sometimes stuck on organic agriculture. OEFFA (pronounced "OH-fa" by friends and critics alike) has been expanding ever since. It offers farm tours, a state-wide conference each winter, and a program for farmers who want to earn the "certified organic" label defined by state law. It also gives a sense of community to growers who might otherwise feel isolated; organic is very much Little Ag.

OEFFA's annual winter conference is a cheerful affair drawing a thousand organic farmers and wannabes who chat up hot topics like non-chemical disease control for fruit, successful composting with earth-worms, and farming with draft horses (the latter being of great interest but limited use to organic farmers, most of whom use tractors or hand labor like anyone else). Rather than being turned-off and tuned-out hippies, organic farmers are hard workers driven by the idea of better living *without* chemistry; they tend to be well educated, politically alert, and vocal.

Todd and Holly Harman Fackler are examples. They are college gradu-ates who run an organic grain and livestock farm near Plymouth. Re-cently they set up a small factory to make something called "EweMulch," a biodegradable mat of wool for use as a planting aid. The OEFFA business office is in the Fackler living room and Holly, a former newspaper re-porter, edits the organization's thoughtful newsletter. Periodically, she writes "A Call to Farms," in which she worries about American agriculture's shift to fewer and bigger farms: "Come the next century, Who will grow our food? Who will care for the soil? What land will they steward? Where will the future farmers come from?"

A hail of such questions come, machine-gun fashion, from another OEFFA leader, Dr. Kamyar Enshayan. At first glance, Enshayan seems an unlikely activist for America's Heartland: he grew up in rural Iran, son of a lawyer and a schoolteacher. Enshayan fled the country just before the Islamic Revolution, then earned a Ph.D. in agricultural engineering at OSU and spent a year on a Maine farm. Perhaps he has just exchanged one revolution for another: a Third Agricultural Revolution to reform Big Ag, get it off its so-called "chemical fix," and revitalize small farming.

"How long can we keep producing the way we have when the resource base—our soil and water—is declining in quality?" demands Enshayan. "We have massive soil erosion rates in this country. It cannot go on for very long. And the food system is not cheap. We are paying $35 billion in subsidies. We are paying $10 billion to reclaim costs of soil erosion. We are paying $8 to $11 billion a year is going just to clean things up after agriculture. The cash economy does not necessarily reflect these ecological and social costs."

Like many others in OEFFA, Enshayan's concerns go beyond the use of chemicals. "There's the loss of community," he says of industrialized agriculture, asking, "Why is the economy of agriculture in such a shape that we are getting more and more land in the hands of fewer people?" And, arguing for more local production of fresh produce, he wonders, "What policies have led to Ohio growing all corn and soybeans? What would Ohio be like if we were more self-reliant and ate from this landscape? Why is everything we're eating coming from California and Florida?"

Enshayan is not only a member of OEFFA, but also fulltime education coordinator for another force on Little Ag's side: the Sustainable Agriculture Program at OSU. (The term "sustainable" covers a range of resource-saving alternative approaches, of which organic is only one; it favors reduced use of chemicals, not necessarily their abolition.) A beachhead in the bosom of what some see as a citadel of Big Ag, the program was set up in 1986 to support research and provide educational outreach. It is directed by Dr. Clive Edwards, former chair of OSU's entomology department, who's kept it going mostly on soft money from foundations and government agencies. (Starting with the 1985 Farm Bill, the U.S. government has provided a small amount of money for such programs.)

Make a Tractor of Your Car

The Ohio Farmer, July 5, 1919

The rapid fire of questions from people like Enshayan is supported by the heavy artillery of the prestigious National Research Council. The NRC is a Washington-based group of big thinkers who advise government and such. In 1989 it fired off a 448-page blockbuster called *Alternative Agriculture,* warning that conventional agriculture is causing water pollution, soil erosion, and hard-to-assess but still worrisome residues of chemicals in food. On a more hopeful note, it predicted, "Today's alternative farming practices could become tomorrow's conventional practices."

The Spray Farm, near Mount Vernon in Knox County, is one of the success stories described in the NRC book. Organic farms are apt to be small operations, but Rex Spray, his brother and nephew have been organically farming 700 acres of grain, plus livestock, for 20 years. The Sprays tried organic when they noticed the more herbicide they used, the less weed control they got. Now the Sprays, pampering their humus, use a four-year crop rotation system, employ mechanical weed control, apply only natural (non-synthetic) nutrients for their crops and animals, get yields better than neighbors at lower cost, and sell at a premium price. Farm neighbors used to ridicule the Sprays, but, says Rex, "They don't laugh so much anymore."

While Kamyar Enshayan is sounding trumpet blasts for alternative agriculture on one side of the OSU campus, Dr. Luther Tweeten is playing a different tune on another. Tweeten, who holds an endowed professorship in agricultural marketing, policy and trade, has some terse advice for the agitators of Little Ag: "Cool it."

"These are doomsday people, apocalyptic in their view of the world, and that's just not justified," says Tweeten of the NRC report and its believers. Tweeten, who has built a reputation researching many of the issues which worry Little Ag, admits there are problems in the farm sector, but "they are manageable."

Says Tweeten: "In general, farmers are using a very different set of practices than they did a few years ago, and consequently we have massively reduced our erosion rates." Furthermore, "the EPA did a rather extensive survey, and the finding was that [less than] two percent of wells are contaminated [by pesticides]. That's not good, but it's not catastrophic. Two percent is manageable—we can deal with that."

Even the decline in the number of farms isn't as bad as billed, says Tweeten. "It's slowing substantially...[and] will be less than 1% a year in the 1990s." In any case, says Tweeten, concern over the declining number of small farms "is almost totally a political issue. Economists and sociologist really can't identify on objective grounds any basis to say we'd better off to have smaller or bigger farms or medium-sized farms." Tweeten, who grew up on an Iowa farm himself, is as plain-spoken as any countryman. "The sky is not falling," he says of the critics' claims; their ideas about more regionalism in food production, for example, are "just nonsense."

Tweeten points to Big Ag's reply to *Alternative Agriculture*—a 1990 broadside from the Council for Agricultural Science and Technology. A coalition of farm science groups, CAST lined up 44 scientists to fire back at the NRC's report. Their views varied, one damning it as "propaganda and blatant advocacy," another cautiously praising it as "a means toward a profitable and more environmentally sound agriculture." Nonetheless, Tweeten says, their basic message is that alternative agriculture's ideas could mean "a substantial cut in output and with higher food prices, and perhaps as much environmental damage."

Bill Swank, executive vice president of the Ohio Farm Bureau Federation, agrees. "Big commercial farming is going to be done in the foreseeable future with chemicals," he says. "The alternative would be higher price for everybody. We'd produce less per acre without chemicals, and we'd have to have much more labor input."

Like Tweeten, he praises the Sprays, but regards them as exceptionally skillful, dedicated workers who most other farmers probably couldn't imitate. Organic farming is "hard work," explains Swank. It requires so much labor and close management that the conventional farmer wonders, "Why should I put up with it? I did it that way 50 years ago, and I'm not going to today."

That's why many in Big Ag predict that organic growers will never serve more than niche markets. Organic farmers snap back that they certainly could if they just had the kind of marketing support and university research that Big does. Big Ag grumbles in return that its critics are "small farmers with an attitude." Little Ag replies that Big needs an attitude adjustment of its own.

The arguing goes on, but talk to conventional farmers, and you get this message: when you have a thousand acres to farm, plus taxes and bank loans to pay, you use the best technology available for spurring plant growth and defeating predators—and right now, that's chemistry. But many farmers also echo Mitch Lynd, who raises apples, a crop especially vulnerable to predators. "I would LOVE to use fewer chemicals," he says. "They're expensive. But right now, that's what I have to work with." Still, things are changing. For example, Mike Pullins, spokesman for the state's fruit and vegetable growers, says they are "doing all they can to reduce chemicals and still put out a product consumers like."

In fact, Tweeten, Swank and other voices for Big Ag say the commotion from Little Ag, combined with public opinion and scientific concern, is having an effect. "They may have learned something from the organic farmers," Swank says of conventional growers who are reducing chemicals and improving tillage systems. Mike Pullins says organic and conventional farmers are "finding a lot of common ground." The mainline farm magazines all see fewer chemicals and better tillage in their readers' future.

The signs are everywhere. The Ohio State University Extension used to declare its mission was "to improve the productivity and efficiency of agriculture"—pure Big Ag talk. Now Extension pays attention to Little Ag hot buttons like "alternative agricultural opportunities," "conservation and management of natural resources," and "revitalizing rural America." And a spokesperson for the OSU College of Ag says that 70 or 80 percent of its research these days in production agriculture seeks ways to cut chemical inputs. Just one example: OSU horticulture scientists are working to bring back a gene, which had been bred out the potato plant, as a natural defense which could substitute for pesticides.

The Ohio Farmer, November 20, 1926

But chemistry, ecology and economics are only part of what's going on here. The story of Little Ag is also a human story, the story of people trying to fulfill their dreams: dreams of living close to the land, a place where you can be master of your destiny and feel at home. Perhaps, in part, it's a yearning for what German sociologist Ferdinand Tönnies called the warm sense of community felt in rural settlements (*Gemeinschaft*) versus the impersonal, even hostile quality of urban life (*Gesellschaft*). Something in our soul needs the family farm to be out there somewhere.

Voices of Big Ag are apt to counsel realism in this matter. "Yes, there's value in the family farm," says Bill Swank. "I grew up on one, I own one, but the bulk of farming is not going to be done that way in the foreseeable future. We're losing something important, but it's reality." However, Swank also says, "We'll have small farms for a long time, but they'll be part-time farms. These people think of themselves as farmers who happen to work in town. I don't think they will ever be pushed off the land."

Not only will they not be pushed off the land, other sources suggest their numbers just may be growing. The surprising news is that, even as farms get bigger and fewer at one end of the scale, a grassroots movement is reportedly swelling the ranks of farmers at the other. *The New York Times* has seen the trend, reporting in a front-page story in 1992 that "a new type of farm—and a new type of farmer—is sprouting up across America: modest plots tended by savvy, part-time farmers who plow, weed and water as much to cultivate a way of living as to grow profitable crops."

And Andrew Stevens has seen it, too. An agricultural journalist in Ohio for much of his life, he persuaded an out-of-state publisher to start a new magazine, called *American Small Farm*, and name Stevens editor of it. From his editorial office in Columbus, Stevens declares, "American small-scale agriculture is about to find its place in the sun." Rodale Institute editor Craig Cramer is blunter: he predicts a "bleak future" for big farms and says that instead we'll see "more farms—not fewer—dotting the landscape." Even that bastion of Big Ag, the U.S. Department of Agriculture, knows something is up: a few years ago it established the Office for Small Scale Agriculture, which keeps track of small farmers and publishes a newsletter.

That doesn't necessarily mean the future belongs to Little Ag. It's hardly that simple. As Tweeten predicts, big farms may keep getting bigger, perhaps delivering even more of our food and fiber. In any case, Big Ag will keep on feeding and clothing many of us for some time to come, doing it even as critics are holding its feet to the fire. But Big Ag also will keep learning alternative techniques that conserve resources and reduce chemicals. Scientists at OSU and other places will keep researching those techniques. Recent trends are clear: Many of today's alternate ideas for farming really will be tomorrow's conventional ones. You can bet on it.

Meanwhile, Little Ag, led by stalwarts like OEFFA, will keep serving as a goad, a pioneer of alternative techniques, and perhaps a source of so many new, small farms that some sense of rural community may return. Ohio is especially fertile ground for small farms, because it has so many urban areas offering markets and second jobs to country dwellers.

Big Ag and Little Ag: an odd couple that need each other, though they'd be loathe to admit it. And we need them both, even if we can't be sure just what scenario they will write for us. One thing IS for sure, however. Even if one of our worst nightmares was to come to pass—every inch of open land in Ohio merged into one corporate mega-farm—there would still be some lonely individual tending a window box of vegetables and protesting, protesting, protesting. And that voice—probably a member of "OH-fa"— would be heard to quote from Abraham Lincoln:

"The greatest fine art of the future will be the making of a comfortable living from a small piece of land."

POSTSCRIPT: *To join a Farm Bureau, contact the one for your county; it should be listed in the phone book. (If necessary, call 614/249-2400 for information on how to find it). Anyone interested in agriculture may join. OEFFA membership is open to "farmers, gardeners and consumers working together to promote sustainable agriculture and wholesome foods." Contact the Ohio Ecological Food and Farm Association, 65 Plymouth Street, Plymouth, Ohio 44865 (419/687-7665).*

FACES OF THE LAND

Life Among the Vegetables

If you can imagine Tennessee Williams with a playful streak (admittedly, a stretch), you can imagine a play by him about the life of Molly Bartlett. Born in a privileged suburb, she began a modeling career as a child, eventually appearing for photographers in New York. She spent three years in Russian studies at Yale and many more wearing the natty uniforms of corporate life: first in retailing, then with a company that makes expensive custom clothing.

Now look at her: in overalls and muddy boots, she crawls on her knees, helping a sheep give birth on an old Ohio farm. It's a long way from her native Shaker Heights (although it's scarcely an hour's drive). The dramatic question: whatever brought Molly Bartlett to this?

The slightly less-than-dramatic answer: athlete's foot in an apple orchard, for one thing. An overdose of suburbia for another. And a desire to live as a steward of the land, not an exploiter.

Molly Bartlett, 47, is doing just what she wants to do at this point in her life: running a highly diversified farm. And, like the farmers who settled northeastern of Ohio nearly two centuries ago, she and her husband are pioneers in a changing landscape.

Molly and her husband, Ted, 54, own Silver Creek Farm near Hiram, about 40 miles east of Cleveland. She is a full-time farmer; he is a full-time professor of philosophy at Cleveland State University, who also works on the farm. Their 123-acre spread is both old and new. It is old because it recreates a way of life that has almost faded away in America. It is new because the way the Bartletts do this differs from most other farmers, past and present.

Four different families have owned their land since it was first settled about 165 years ago and, says Molly, "probably every family has farmed it differently." The Bartletts are farming it organically, meaning they use no synthetic fertilizers, pesticides or antibiotics—which is dramatically different from most other farmers in Ohio. The past 50 years have seen a veritable chemical explosion in agriculture, with most farmers using pesticides to defeat unwanted insects and weeds, synthetic fertilizers to spur growth, antibiotics and other drugs to raise animals. Simultaneously, farms have been getting bigger and more specialized—*industrialized*, you might say. The homey, diversified, self-sufficient family farm

Molly Bartlett

where Grandpa and Grandma grew up has mostly receded into memory.

Except for people like the Bartletts. Organic farming isn't just farming without chemicals: it means farming smart, working hard, and thinking big. For Ted and Molly Bartlett in particular, that means running a mini-conglomerate of small business enterprises, raising much of their own food, and volunteering their spare time (ha!) to defending the rural landscape (they are active in the land preservation efforts of the area's Headwaters Landtrust). This self-sufficient mixed farming does not mean going back to the 40 acres and a mule of their pioneer ancestors, however. The Bartletts are attacking their personal frontier not just with their hands but with tractors, a computer and a fax machine.

At the heart of the enterprise is a fresh produce business, yielding more than 15 different fruits and vegetables, all certified organic. Among the haul from the Bartletts' summer gardens are blueberries, kale, chard, summer squash, peas, peppers, eggplant, beets, broccoli. In fall, carrots, winter squash and root crops come into season. The farm also produces herbs (about 12 varieties) and shiitake mushrooms (a tasty Japanese variety grown on hardwood logs). This bounty is recorded on a computer, then sold in the farm's own market, to fine restaurants, and to the Food Co-op, a non-profit, full-service grocery store in the University Circle area of Cleveland.

Silver Creek's produce even goes to outlets as far away as Washington, D.C. In 1992 the Bartletts grew four acres of carrots—perhaps the largest retail planting of carrots in Ohio—and shipped as many as a thousand pounds of carrots a week. "Sometimes we were up washing carrots by moonlight," recalls Molly. The carrots went out on a truck, operated by a West Virginian, who made twice-weekly 1200-mile round trips through several states. He would pick up wholesale lots of organic produce at some stops and drop them off at others—a sort of magical bus ride for vegetables.

This saved individual growers some time, letting them specialize a bit. But specialization will never be the name of the game in organic production; diversity and a high degree of self-sufficiency always will be. For example, avoiding synthetic chemicals that would defeat pests and spur growth means finding alternate methods—usually right on the farm. Among these are mulching to prevent weeds, and fertilizing with animal as well as green manure. Thus, many organic farms raise livestock for manure as well as food and fiber; Silver Creek farm uses sheep.

The Bartletts have upwards of a hundred ewes, housed in a barn near the farmhouse, where they can be heard blatting at each other. (By the way, sheep say M-A-A-A instead of B-A-A-A. And not softly, either.) During lambing season, Molly checks the barn every four hours, ready to help any ewe having trouble giving birth. In winter, newly born lambs may be brought into the house and placed in a box by the stove until their first hearty M-A-A-A. Then it's back to the barn and their real Ma.

The sheep provide fertilizer for the garden and the lambs provide meat for the Bartletts to sell ("Very few Americans know what really good lamb is," Molly says; the Bartletts make sure what they sell is young and ten-

der.) While most of the flock—black-faced Suffolks and Polypay/Cor-
riedales—is raised for meat, part—also Polypay/Corriedales as well as
Lincolns—provide wool. Their wool is mixed with mohair from the farm's
own angora goats (who sound like E-E-E-K), and spun and dyed, off the
farm, into luxuriantly soft two-ply yarns, which the Bartletts sell retail.
(Molly will even custom knit you a sweater, if you like.) As well as sheep
and goats, the Bartletts raise about a thousand broilers a year: like Old
MacDonald's operation, Silver Creek has a cluck-cluck here and a M-A-A-
—M-A-A-A there.

There is no Moo-Moo, at least not yet, but milk is one of the few foods
the Bartletts buy off the farm. Molly estimates that scarcely 20 percent of
their food—coffee, spices, sugar and such—comes from the conventional
supermarket. They raise more than half on their own farm, and the rest
comes from other area growers (the Bartletts are great believers in
supporting regional food production). They store food in four freezers and
a 10-by-12-foot "cold room."

"We're very self-sufficient. I was talking with our eldest child, in Ann
Arbor, and she said, 'You don't realize how easy it is for you. When you
want to prepare a meal, you either look in the freezer or on the shelves.
The rest of us have to write a list and go to the grocery.'"

IT WON'T BE LONG, NOW!

The Ohio Farmer, November 5, 1927

The Bartlett see themselves becoming even more self-sufficient. "It gets easier," Molly says. "You just sort of limit your needs and diet wants more and more to what you have available. If you have 110 pounds of winter squash in your storage room, and you'd rather have green beans but you don't have them, you just learn to work with the winter squash. It's real simple."

Even most of the Bartletts' heating comes from the farm. The house has an oil furnace for backup, but most of the heat comes from a stove fed with wood from the farm's own trees. (Small fans circulate the heat throughout the house.) About an hour a day is spent getting firewood. Silver Creek Farm has about 65 acres of woods (including some sugar maples the Bartletts may someday tap); 25 acres are used for crops and another 20 for sheep pasture. The farm also has three wells and two ponds.

Located in an area of the state settled by many New Englanders, the farm looks as if it came from there, too. The old white farmhouse is furnished country style, making a pleasant setting for dinners a Cleveland chef occasionally stages there. Several old barns and sheds, including the former outhouse, are on the property, and a creek really does run through it. The farm welcomes visitors, but they should be careful not to poke those funny little white boxes: they are beehives.

"This is a very diverse farm," Molly explains. "We try to think of it as a 12-month farm. We have something going on basically every month, and right now [February] we're into lambing." Spring, summer and fall, of course, are devoted to crops; winter is when Molly catches up with her pottery business, making bowls, cups and pots on her wheel for retail and two wholesale accounts. A highlight of spring is Silver Creek's annual sale, on Mother's Day weekend, of five to six thousand heirloom tomato plants raised in the farm's greenhouse. Every October the farm sponsors a harvest festival, attracting several hundred people for sheep shearing and craft demonstrations. Activities like these have helped bring the new farm, with all its start-up costs, to about the break-even point; the Bartletts think they are "about a year away" from turning a profit.

"We've been at this particular farm for six years," says Molly. "We have no children at home—all five are either in college or through college and living as far away as Sri Lanka with the Peace Corps. So here we are without any farm help, unlike our Amish friends down the street who may have eight children at home to help." The Bartletts get the job done with long hours, tractors and workers hired at peak times.

Organic farming is hard work. Avoiding herbicides means the Bartletts must mechanically cultivate their fields or use mulch, while avoiding insecticides means they may have to hand-remove insects. Avoiding synthetic fertilizers requires building compost piles and collecting manure instead of simply opening bags or bottles. And, as always, farming means always keeping an eye on the weather and the calendar; every season offers its own tasks and opportunities.

But the Bartletts prefer all this to conventional chemical agriculture. "I am passionate about organic," says Molly, who is a member of the board of the Ohio Ecological Food and Farm Association. She also is an OEFFA examiner who inspects farms for certification as organic, a label which state law defines.

Still, the Bartletts "sort of backed into organic" when they first moved to Silver Creek Farm and tried to save old apple trees with pesticides. "After the first year of spraying them in 90-degree weather, wearing yellow rubber suits from head to toe, my husband realized he had developed an incredible case of athlete's foot from spraying in hot weather," Molly recalls. "He said, if we can't even figure out what all these chemicals mean, and I'm standing out there spraying with all this garb on, I don't think I want these apples or these apple trees." So the apple trees were sacrificed (the county agent now uses them for pruning classes), but the farm was saved for organic growing.

Life on a farm had become increasingly attractive to the Bartletts, both of whom had their share of apartment living in various parts of the country before returning to Ohio. Molly grew up in the wealthy Cleveland suburb of Shaker Heights ("Yes, I had a very fine life"), but she couldn't face returning to it. "When I think of Shaker Heights...I think of houses on either side of me, and houses to the rear. I get a claustrophobic feeling," she says.

"One thing we had decided was that we wanted to be in a business together. Ted's a philosopher and I'm a potter, so we kept saying, 'That's not going to work!' So this [farming] is what we enjoy doing together. Just the idea of being outside, without so much of this 9-to-5 routine. It's very, appealing not to have the same routine every day."

Dull routine it's not. It's "a whole way of life," as Molly puts it, one in which you can get up close and personal with nature, the animals—and your vegetables.

At a speaking engagement, Molly recalls showing a slide of her barn with the entire harvest of hard winter squash and pumpkin arrayed in front of it. "It looked just incredible, the quantities," she says. " I don't know how many thousand pounds there were. I looked at that slide and took immense pride in what was there. I looked at each one of those squash and pumpkins, and said, 'I remember you!'"

POSTSCRIPT: *Silver Creek Farm (216/562-4381) is located at 7097 Allyn Road in Hiram (ZIP 44234), east of Ohio 700. From Mother's Day through New Year's Day, the farm's market is open Saturdays 10 a.m. to 4 p.m.; visitors are welcome other days, but should call first.*

RECIPES

Wendy's Pesto

Makes about 1 cup

2 cups fresh basil leaves
1/4 cup pine nuts, walnuts or
* pistachios*
1/2 cup grated Parmesan cheese
2 to 3 cloves garlic, finely chopped
1/2 cup (approximately) olive oil

Fisher's Fresh Herbs is located in Gibsonburg, about 25 miles southeast of Toledo. Wendy and Willie Fisher began growing and selling fresh herbs to restaurants in 1988, and have added edible flowers, baby vegetables and speciality vegetables. Among the flowers raised by the Fishers (using no chemicals) are baby rose, dianthus, fuschia, lilac, nasturtium, tulips and pansies. Their customers include some of the nation's finest restaurants.

The blossoms really can be eaten, although Wendy realizes that about 75% of the blossoms are not. Those diners are missing something, because edible flowers have interesting flavors. The tuberous begonia has a tart citrus taste, while carnations taste a little like cloves, and nasturtiums have a peppery watercress flavor.

In blender or food processor, blend all ingredients except olive oil until smooth. With machine running, add olive oil in a steady stream; blend until a paste-like mixture forms. Use immediately with pasta, rice, fish, vegetables, salads or soups; or add a thin layer of olive oil on top of mixture and refrigerate or freeze.

Stuffed Nasturtiums

Makes about 32

1 (8-ounce) package cream cheese,
* softened*
1 teaspoon each chopped fresh
* chives, parsley, rosemary and*
* thyme leaves*
Nasturtium blossoms (about 32)

In small mixer bowl, beat cream cheese until smooth; add herbs. Carefully stuff each nasturtium blossom; serve.

Ohio Field Greens with Sprouts and Orange Segments

We met Gary and Kathy Zay, from Sunnyside Farms, Johnstown, at the North Market in Columbus. They were selling a beautiful assortment of fruits and vegetables from their small, diversified family farm. The Zays raise sheep and broilers, and are certified organic producers of fruit and vegetables. One of their best sellers at North Market were bags of mesculun greens, tossed with edible flowers. The colorful bags were eye-catching. This recipe is their favorite way of eating these assorted greens.

Replacing chemicals on the Zay farm are parasitic wasps, ladybugs, praying mantises and barn swallows, which control damaging insects. Weeds are pulled with old-fashioned elbow grease and a tractor-drawn cultivator. Fertilizer comes from prepared from sheep and chicken manure, ground-up leaves and biodegradable foodstuffs. Kathy is also a food service instructor at Licking County Joint Vocational School, Newark, and Gary an architect and contractor who works out of his home. He designed and built the passive solar home in which they live.

In blender or small mixer bowl, combine all dressing ingredients except oil and celery seed; blend until well mixed. On medium speed, continue blending, slowly adding oil. Stir in celery seed. Chill to blend flavors. Just before serving, in large salad bowl, combine salad ingredients. Toss with dressing.

Makes 6 to 8 servings

Dressing:
3/4 cup sugar
1/2 cup cider vinegar
2 tablespoons grated onion
1-1/2 teaspoons dry mustard
1 teaspoon salt
1-1/2 cups vegetable oil
1 tablespoon celery seed

Salad:
8 cups field grown mesculun greens, torn into bite-size pieces*
1 cup chopped red cabbage
2 cups alfalfa sprouts
4 oranges, peeled, sectioned and drained
1/2 cup sunflower seeds, toasted
Assorted edible flowers, nasturtiums, pansies, red clover and rose petals

* Field grown mesculun greens are usually a combination of endive, bibb lettuce, romaine and leaf lettuce.

Boursin Cheese

Boursin cheese and herb butter (below) are favorite herb recipes of Marilyn Hartley. Marilyn and a friend put together an herb cookbook with some of their favorite recipes to use for teaching an herb class at Columbus' Ameriflora celebration in 1992.

Balls of boursin cheese may be made ahead of time and frozen. Marilyn often rolls them in chopped fresh parsley for a pretty variation. The leftover cheese is delicious when melted over cooked vegetables.

In small mixer bowl, beat cream cheese and butter until smooth. Add remaining ingredients; mix well. Chill slightly; form into balls or logs. Wrap tightly in plastic wrap; store in refrigerator. Before serving, bring to room temperature. Serve with crackers or assorted fresh vegetables.

Makes 3 cups

2 (8-ounce) packages cream cheese, softened
1 cup butter or margarine, softened
2 cloves garlic, finely chopped
1 tablespoon each chopped fresh basil, chives, marjoram, and parsley leaves
1 teaspoon chopped fresh thyme leaves
1/4 teaspoon pepper

Herb Butter

Makes about 1/2 cup

*1/2 cup butter or margarine,
  softened
2 tablespoons chopped fresh parsley
2 tablespoons chopped fresh chives
2 teaspoons chopped fresh tarragon
  leaves
1 teaspoon dry mustard*

Herb butter, made from this recipe by Marilyn Hartley, is delicious on warm bread or as a topping for grilled meats or vegetables.

In small mixer bowl, combine all ingredients; beat well. Turn or pack into serving dish; chill. Serve with cooked vegetables or grilled meats.

Beside The Point's Split Pea Soup

Makes about 2 quarts

*8 cups water
1 (1-pound) bag split peas, rinsed
  and drained
1 ham bone with meat or 1 large
  ham hock
2 large onions, chopped
2 to 4 leeks, white part only,
  chopped
2 ribs celery, chopped (include some
  leaves)
1 large carrot, peeled and chopped
1 cup dry white wine
1 clove garlic, finely chopped
1/2 teaspoon marjoram leaves
1/4 teaspoon thyme leaves
Salt
Pepper*

Akron's fabulous West Point Market (1711 West Market Street, 216/864-2151), under the direction of proprietor Russ Vernon has become known as one of the most elegant and innovative food and wine stores between New York and California.

Carol Moore is director of "A Moveable Feast," the store's catering division. Thanks to her, no Akronite need resort to fast food after a late day at the office. The selection of prepared foods is enormous and a different meal could be brought home each night for weeks with no one ever suspecting you didn't make it yourself. Of course, you can also eat in West Point's restaurant or have a feast catered to your home.

This is Carol's choice of a "typically Ohio" recipe. Strictly Midwestern in origin, split pea soup is enhanced by West Point's special touches.

In large kettle, combine all ingredients except salt and pepper; bring to a boil. Reduce heat, cover and simmer 2- to 2-1/2 hours or until peas are soft. Remove ham bone; cool slightly. Remove meat from bone; return to kettle. Add salt and pepper to taste.

Sausage and Kale Soup

Linda Stewart and Dean Johnstown own Harpersfield Organic Garden in Geneva, in the northeastern corner of the state. Their five acres were once part of a large dairy farm. Linda was born in Ohio and raised on her grandparent's farm where they grew grapes, peaches and grandma's flowers. Ancestors on both side were homesteaders, so her love of animals, plants and concerns with the land came naturally. They are founding members of the Covered Bridge Organic Farms Co-op.

Linda and Dave strongly feel that the soil is a living thing which must be tended and nurtured for future generations. They use the French Intensive method of producing organic vegetables. In 1992, Linda and Dave grew about 25 varieties of vegetables including bok choy, Chinese cabbage, kale, leeks, onions, lettuces, radishes and others. They keep growing new vegetables, some of which they had never tasted before. Kohlrabi and kale are examples. They first tried kale in this delicious soup and loved it.

In large kettle, brown kielbasa; remove from skillet, drain on paper towels. Discard drippings in kettle; cook carrots, celery, onions and garlic in oil and butter until tender. Return kielbasa to kettle; add broths, potatoes, tomatoes, kale and basil. Bring to a boil. Reduce heat; cover and simmer 30 to 40 minutes or until vegetables are tender. Add salt and pepper to taste.

Makes about 3 quarts

1 pound kielbasa or smoked sausage, cut in bite-size pieces
1 cup sliced carrots
1 cup chopped celery
1 cup chopped onions
3 cloves garlic, finely chopped
1/4 cup butter or margarine
3 tablespoons olive oil
6 cups (1-1/2 quarts) chicken broth or stock
3 cups beef stock or broth
5 medium potatoes, peeled and chopped
2 (14-1/2-ounce) cans whole tomatoes, undrained and broken up
1 pound kale leaves, washed, drained, leafy sections removed from stems
2 tablespoons chopped fresh basil leaves or 2 teaspoons dried
Salt
Pepper

Homestead Grilled Mushrooms

Mike Omler and his staff at Homestead Mushrooms in Hillsboro grow shiitake, oyster and angel trumpet mushrooms indoors under environmentally controlled conditions. The growing rooms have an eerie quality, the misty air simulating a humid morning in Ohio. Originally from Napoleon, Mike began growing button mushrooms in his basement fifteen years ago and the business has been expanding ever since. Homestead, the only operation of its kind in the state, ships fresh mushrooms to restaurants throughout the country.

In shallow glass dish, place mushrooms. In small bowl or jar with tight-fitting lid, combine remaining ingredients; shake well. Pour over mushrooms. Cover and let stand at room temperature for 1 to 2 hours, stirring occasionally. Drain; grill or broil until lightly browned. If desired, serve with hot mustard, sweet and sour sauce or pesto.

Makes 4 to 6 servings

1 pound fresh shiitake mushrooms
1/2 cup olive oil
1/3 cup lemon juice
3 tablespoons dijon-style mustard
1 tablespoon crushed fresh rosemary leaves (or fresh herb of your choice)
Dash hot pepper sauce

Chilled Melon Soup

Makes about 1 quart

3 cups coarsely chopped muskmelon
2 cups orange juice
1/3 cup lemon juice
3 tablespoons honey
1/2 to 3/4 teaspoon fresh rosemary
   leaves, optional
2 cups sparkling white grape juice
   or ginger ale

"The Sweetest and Best Melons are in Milan" is the motto of the Milan Melon Festival held Labor Day weekend in the town square. Melon growers in the Milan area go all-out for this festival, planting a special crop of muskmelons to ripen in time for the festival. Muskmelon ice cream and Watermelon sherbet are specially made for the festival by Toft's Dairy in Sandusky. Melon candy, melon milk shakes, slices of watermelon, and halves of Milan muskmelons filled with vanilla ice cream, are served at the festival.

Mrs. Louis Weiss, who has been involved with the Melon Festival for many years, says that most people erroneously think that muskmelon is an old-fashioned word for cantaloupe. There are differences: muskmelon meat is thicker than that of a cantaloupe, and a deeper orange color. And a muskmelon smells sweet, while a cantaloupe has no aroma at all.

In blender or food processor, combine 2 cups melon, orange juice, lemon juice, honey and rosemary; puree. Add grape juice and remaining melon; chill well. If desired, garnish with mint leaves and strawberries.

Spaghetti Squash with Garlic and Parmesan

Makes 6 to 8 servings

1 (2- to 3- pound) spaghetti squash
1/4 cup grated Parmesan cheese
2 tablespoons butter or margarine
2 to 3 cloves garlic, finely chopped
Salt
Pepper
Chopped fresh parsley

Molly and Ted Bartlett own Silver Creek Farm in Hiram, an organic farm raising fresh produce certified by the Ohio Ecological Food and Farm Association. Molly gets many requests for recipes using what they grow. Customers are always looking for new ways to prepare the many varieties of squash. This is one of her favorites. Microwave cooking makes spaghetti squash quick and easy to prepare.

Pierce squash in several places with large fork or knife. Place on paper towel in microwave oven. Cook on 100% power for 10 minutes or until squash yields to pressure and feels soft. Cool slightly; halve crosswise. Scoop out seeds and fibers; twist out long strands of pulp with fork, place in 2-quart microproof baking dish. Add remaining ingredients, except parsley; mix well. Cover; cook at 100% power (high) for 4 to 6 minutes or until heated through. Top with parsley.

Rosemary Scalloped Potatoes

Karen and Mark Langan run Mulberry Creek Farm in Sandusky. He has a degree in ornamental horticulture, she in agricultural research and greenhouse production. They make a young, enthusiastic team with plenty in common. Karen and Mark grow ornamentals, mainly wildflowers for seed, as well as organically produced grains like vinton soybeans, adjuki beans, black turtle beans, corn, wheat and clover. Presently they have seed growing contracts in California, New Mexico and Germany, and hope to turn most of the 65-acre farm into all flowers some day. They also sell herbs, dried herb packets, fresh and dried cut flowers and a few farm items.

Preheat oven to 350 degrees. In lightly greased 12x7-inch baking dish, arrange one layer of potatoes; sprinkle with rosemary. Repeat; making 2 or 3 more layers. Dot with butter; sprinkle with pepper. Pour cream over top of potatoes. Cover; bake for 1 hour. Uncover; bake 20 to 30 minutes longer or until golden brown.

Makes 4 to 6 servings

4 large (or 6 medium) potatoes, peeled and sliced
2 tablespoons crushed fresh rosemary leaves or 1 tablespoon dried
3 tablespoons butter or margarine
1/4 teaspoon pepper
1 cup (1/2-pint) light cream or half-and-half

Sauteed Zucchini with Walnuts

After Adele Straub's son entered school, she had always thought she would go back to teaching. But, instead, she woke up at 2 a.m. one morning and thought, "I'm going to be a farmer!" So this forty-something wife, mother, Phi Beta Kappa, former world traveller and teacher became "The Farmer is Adele" in Grafton. She had no formal farming or business training, but she read, took commercial horticultural classes, studied, talked, listened and learned. And she came up with the idea of "surrogate farming."

"Surrogate farming" means that she sells memberships for a nominal fee to her FEAST (FarmEr Adele's Surrogate Team) Club. Now all her produce is sold before it is even planted. Her membership is mostly busy professionals who appreciate freshness and quality but do not have time or space to grow their own produce. So, Adele grows the produce organically for them and sets up delivery spots throughout growing season.

Adele says, "Squash is truly American in origin. They are naturally sweet, nutty, and exceptionally high in vitamin A." This recipe is from Mary Beth and Ted Lundgren, members of Adele's FEAST club. It is simple to prepare, and tasty to serve when zucchini is so prolific in the garden.

In large skillet, cook zucchini in hot oil 2 to 3 minutes, stirring occasionally. Add walnuts; cook until zucchini is tender.

Makes 4 servings

8 small zucchini, sliced
2 tablespoons walnut oil, butter or margarine
1/2 cup chopped walnuts

Bison Stew

Makes 4 to 6 servings

2 pounds cubed Bison meat
2 tablespoons vegetable oil
2 medium onions, chopped
2 (8-ounce) cans tomato sauce
1 (14-1/2-ounce) can whole tomatoes, undrained and broken up
1/2 cup water
1 teaspoon salt
1/2 teaspoon pepper
3 medium potatoes, peeled and
   cubed
2 medium carrots, peeled and sliced

In 1797, Freddie Perkins's ancestors, Rubin and Elizabeth Perkins, ventured into the wilderness of Ohio. Today, Freddie and Bunny Perkins own Whitefeather Farm in Wadsworth (the white feather is a sign of peace). The Perkins family raise bison and sell the meat. Bison meat is tender, moist and satisfying. It is not gamey or wild-tasting, but has a sweet, rich flavor. And it is lower in fat and calories than beef or chicken.

In large kettle, brown bison cubes in oil; add onions, cook until tender. Add tomato sauce, tomatoes, water, salt and pepper. Bring to a boil; cover and simmer 1 hour or until meat is tender. Add vegetables; cook 20 minutes or until tender. Serve in individual bowls.

Variation: Transfer stew to a 2-quart baking dish; top with favorite biscuits. Bake at 425 degrees 15 to 20 minutes or until biscuits are golden brown.

Sunnyside Farms Roast Leg of Lamb Dijon

Makes 8 to 10 servings

Fresh garlic cloves, peeled, thinly
   sliced
1 (about 8-pound) leg of lamb,
   bone-in
Salt
Pepper
3 slices whole wheat bread, toasted
Olive oil
Fresh rosemary
1/2 (8-ounce) jar dijon-style mustard

Gary and Kathy Zay own Sunnyside Organic Farm in Johnstown, a highly diversified 25-acre family operation. They raise both crops and livestock.

Local chefs have taken an interest in the Zays' organically raised lamb and several chefs, including Frannie Packard at the Governor's Residence, cook with it.

Preheat oven to 350 degrees. On top of leg of lamb, make small slits with sharp knife; insert garlic clove slices into each slit. Salt and pepper entire leg. In food processor, blend remaining ingredients until a paste-like consistency forms. Spread paste over fat side of leg; place in large roasting pan. Cover; bake 3 to 4 hours or until of desired doneness. (It is best to cut into lamb to check for degree of doneness.)

Rider's Inn Lake Erie Walleye

Rider's Inn is Painesville's oldest hostelry, dating back to 1812 when it was a stagecoach stop between Erie, Pennsylvania, and Cleveland. Owned and operated by Elaine Crane, who, with her mother, Elizabeth Roemisch, refurbished it, this bed-and-breakfast inn has nine guest rooms furnished with Western Reserve antiques. Overnight guests can have their breakfast served in bed, with head chef Art Bennett custom-designing pastries to fit their personalities. (Are you a bran muffin type of person, or a cream-filled napoleon type?)

Mistress Suzanne's Dining Room serves dinner entrees based on recipes from the early 1800s, with an emphasis on regional cuisine. Mr. Joseph's English Pub is a cozy place to gather after a busy day.

Art Bennett was happy to share this recipe with us. It is a delicious way to prepare walleye from the nearby waters of Lake Erie.

Place fillets in shallow dish; pour cream over fillets. Cover; refrigerate 3 to 4 hours. In another shallow dish, combine coating ingredients. Remove fillets from cream, dip both sides in coating mixture, pressing firmly so coating adheres evenly. In large skillet, cook fillets in butter, skin side up, 3 to 4 minutes, turn and cook other side until golden brown; sprinkle with salt and pepper. Remove fillets from skillet: drain off excess butter. Add lemon juice and white wine; stir well to remove any brown bits from skillet. Pour sauce over fillets; sprinkle with parsley.

Makes 4 servings

Fish:
4 (3- to 4-ounce) Lake Erie Walleye fillets
2 cups (1-pint) whipping cream or half-and-half

Coating:
1 cup flour
1/2 cup yellow cornmeal
1 teaspoon salt
2 teaspoons baking soda
1 teaspoon paprika
1/2 teaspoon garlic powder
1/4 teaspoon cayenne pepper
1/3 cup butter or margarine

Sauce:
1/2 teaspoon salt
1/4 teaspoon pepper
2 tablespoons lemon juice
2 tablespoons dry white wine
Fresh chopped parsley

Apple Pie Bars

Makes one 13x9-inch pan

Crust:
2 cups flour
1/2 cup sugar
1/2 teaspoon baking powder
1/2 teaspoon salt
1 cup butter or margarine

Filling:
4 cups peeled, cored and thinly
  sliced all purpose apples
1/2 cup sugar
1/4 cup flour
1 teaspoon ground cinnamon
1/4 teaspoon ground nutmeg

The Jackson Apple Festival is held the third week of each September. The entire area turns out to honor the apple, which is a big part of the local economy. There are over 1,000,000 apple trees within a 35-mile radius of Jackson.

The Jackson Junior Federated Women's Club produces a benefit cookbook entitled *50 Golden Delicious Years of Recipes*. This recipe was contributed to the book by Margaret Conway, the group's 1991-1992 president. It's an easy alternative to traditional apple pie.

Preheat oven to 350 degrees. In large bowl, combine flour, sugar, baking powder and salt; cut in butter until crumbly. Reserving half of the crumb mixture for topping, press remainder firmly on bottom of 13x9-inch baking pan.

In large bowl, combine filling ingredients, toss gently until fruit is lightly coated. Arrange filling evenly over crust; sprinkle reserved crumb mixture evenly over top. Bake 45 to 50 minutes or until golden brown. Cool. If desired, drizzle with thin confectioner's sugar icing.

Chocolate Angel Pie

Makes one 9-inch pie

Crust:
2 egg whites
1/8 teaspoon cream of tartar
1/8 teaspoon salt
1/2 cup sugar
1/2 cup chopped nuts
1/2 teaspoon vanilla extract

Filling:
1 (4-ounce) package German Sweet
  Baking Chocolate, melted
3 tablespoons hot water
1 teaspoon vanilla extract
1 cup (1/2-pint) whipping cream,
  whipped and slightly sweetened

Karen Palmer has been food editor of the News Journal, Mansfield, since 1978. Each week she writes a Recipe File column about a regional food subject or personality, so she is well acquainted with good food in her area. Raised on a dairy farm in Mansfield, she now lives in Bellville, but her parents, Jason and Ruth Kisling, still live on the third-generation family farm. Karen remembers her mother baking this Chocolate Angel Pie for special occasions.

Preheat oven to 300 degrees. In small mixer bowl, beat egg whites until foamy; add cream of tartar and salt. Beat until soft peaks form; gradually add sugar, beat until stiff peaks form. Fold in nuts and vanilla. Turn into lightly buttered 9-inch pie plate, mounding slightly at edge. Bake 50 to 55 minutes or until crust is slightly dry. Cool thoroughly.

In medium bowl, combine chocolate and water; add vanilla, mix well. Cool slightly. Fold chocolate mixture into sweetened whipped cream. Turn mixture into pie shell. Refrigerate 2 hours.

Glazed Raspberry Pie

The Beam Road Berry Farm is located in Crestline, and is owned by Ken and Lyn Chapis who purchased the property in 1984. The very next spring they began the process of establishing a certified organic market garden, a subsistence homestead and a demonstration garden and retail sales area. Seasonal produce is available from the store March 15 to October 15.

In large saucepan, combine sugar, cornstarch and salt; gradually stir in water. Cook over medium heat until mixture comes to a boil, stirring frequently. Remove from heat; cool 20 minutes. Arrange berries in pastry shell. Pour glaze evenly over berries.

Refrigerate at least two hours. Before serving, top with dollops of whipped cream.

Makes one 9-inch pie

3/4 cup sugar
2 tablespoons plus 2 teaspoons
  cornstarch
1/4 teaspoon salt
1 cup water
1 (9-inch) baked pastry shell or
  graham cracker or vanilla wafer
  crumb crust
4 cups (1 quart) red raspberries,
  washed and drained
Whipped cream

Great Grandma Porter's Applesauce Cake

This cake is the product of of two families. Jim Miles, a Bowling Green certified public accountant remembers his great grandmother, Sadie Porter, making it. She used a burnt sugar frosting. But in recent years Jim's wife, Gerry, has used a recipe for Penuche Icing from her grandmother, Avis Sutton Haskins.

Preheat oven to 350 degrees. In medium bowl, combine applesauce and baking soda; mix well. In large mixer bowl, combine butter and sugar; beat until fluffy. Add applesauce mixture; beat well. Add 3 cups flour, cinnamon and vanilla; beat well. In small bowl, combine nuts, raisins and 1 tablespoon flour; mix well, add to batter. Turn into two greased and floured 9-inch cake pans. Bake 30 to 40 minutes or until wooden pick inserted near center comes out clean. Remove from pans; cool thoroughly. Fill and frost cake with Penuche Icing.

Makes one 9-inch layer cake

1-1/2 cups unsweetened applesauce
1 tablespoon baking soda
1 cup butter or margarine, softened
2 cups sugar
3 cups flour
1 tablespoon ground cinnamon
1 tablespoon vanilla extract
1 cup chopped nuts
1 cup raisins
1 tablespoon flour

Penuche Icing

In medium saucepan, melt butter; stir in brown sugar. Bring to a boil, boil 2 minutes, stirring constantly. Add milk; bring to a boil; boil 1 minute, stirring constantly. Remove from heat; cool to lukewarm. Stir in confectioners' sugar. Place saucepan in bowl of ice water; stir until creamy and spreadable.

Frosts one cake

1/2 cup butter or margarine
1 cup firmly packed light brown
  sugar
1/4 cup milk
1-1/2 to 2 cups confectioners' sugar

Freshwater Farms Rainbow Trout with Orange-Basil Sauce

Makes 6 servings

6 Freshwater Farms of Ohio Rainbow Trout, deboned
1/4 cup frozen orange juice concentrate, thawed
3 tablespoons olive oil or vegetable
  oil
2 tablespoons chopped fresh basil
  leaves
2 tablespoons water
1 tablespoon chopped fresh tarragon
  leaves
1 tablespoon Worcestershire sauce
2 cloves garlic, finely chopped

Thanks to Dave and Carol Smith of Freshwater Farms of Ohio, diners in Ohio restaurants can order rainbow trout that was swimming earlier that day. Rainbow trout and other farm fish are raised in Freshwater's modern facility in Urbana, designed by Dave, who has a master's degree in marine biology and a Ph.D. in nutritional sciences. This is a family operation: Dave's wife, Carol, does the bookkeeping. His mother is in charge of the fish "nursery" and his dad also works in the operation as an engineer.

In shallow glass dish, place fish. In small bowl or jar with tight-fitting lid, combine remaining ingredients; shake well. Pour over fish. Cover and refrigerate 4 to 6 hours, occasionally spooning marinade over fish. Grill or broil for 6 to 8 minutes or until fish is opaque and flakes easily with a fork.

Carol suggests using a lightly oiled grill basket or porcelain coated grill topper for cooking the fish. This makes turning it on the grill much easier and eliminates sticking. She also advises not to overcook the fish, remembering the "1-inch" rule of cooking fish: allow 10 minutes of cooking time for every inch of thickness of fish.

Corn Pone

Makes one 9x5-inch loaf

1-1/2 cups yellow cornmeal
1-1/2 cups flour
1 tablespoon baking powder
1 teaspoon salt
1/2 teaspoon baking soda
1 cup sugar or 2/3 cup honey
1/2 cup solid vegetable shortening
2 eggs
1 cup plus 5 tablespoons milk

The North Ridgeville Corn Festival, first held in 1975, takes place the second weekend in August. In 1988, Dayle Noll, executive director of the North Ridgeville Chamber of Commerce and Visitor's Bureau, won first prize in the Corn Crafts and Cuisine contest with this corn pone recipe. Corn pone is different from cornbread as it has the texture of pound cake and is slightly sweeter and less crumbly than cornbread. It should be served as an accompaniment to main dishes or as a dessert.

Preheat oven to 300 degrees. In medium bowl, combine cornmeal, flour, baking powder, salt and baking soda. In large bowl, combine sugar and shortening; beat well. Add eggs; beat well. Add dry ingredients, alternately with milk, stirring just until moistened. Turn into greased and floured 9x5-inch loaf pan. Bake 55 to 60 minutes or until wooden pick inserted near center comes out clean. Cool 5 minutes; remove from pan. Slice slightly warm or at room temperature.

Baking Powder Biscuits

Edna Stahl Schaefer was born in Meigs County in 1900 and lived to age 88. Her daughter, Ferndora Schaefer Story, remembers her as a talented, active lady who square danced and walked two miles a day. For much of her life she raised her family's food and preserved much of it for the long winter. Every morning Edna prepared a big farm breakfast of eggs, bacon or sausage, and these baking powder biscuits, with sausage gravy.

We came upon Edna's biscuit recipe in *Treasured Recipes Of The Past*, a cookbook published by the town of Pomeroy for its sesquicentennial in 1990. Pomeroy, "The Heart of the Valley," is located on the Great Bend of the Ohio River, midway between Cincinnati and Pittsburgh. The business district is located on so narrow a strip of land beside the river that there are no cross streets, a fact noted in *Ripley's Believe It or Not*. Most buildings in the business district are over 100 years old and listed on the National Register of Historic Places. "A few miles away and a hundred years ago," Pomeroy is off the beaten path, deep in the foothills of Southeastern Ohio, and a pleasant place to visit.

Preheat oven to 400 degrees. In medium bowl, combine flour, salt and baking powder; cut in shortening until crumbly. Add milk; stir until just moistened. On lightly floured surface, knead lightly. Roll out to 3/4-inch thickness; cut with 2-inch biscuit cutter. Place biscuits 1-inch apart on ungreased cookie sheet. Bake 12 to 15 minutes or until golden brown.

Makes 4 to 6 servings

2 cups flour
4 teaspoons baking powder
3/4 teaspoon salt
1/4 cup solid vegetable shortening or lard
2/3 cup milk

The impish gentleman with the goatee wants you to observe his fellow worker sampling the boss's product. Probably Mr. Wehrle could afford it. By 1871, Andrew Wehrle and partners had built the nation's largest winery on Middle Bass, one of Lake Erie's "Wine Islands." The limestone wine vault seen in this view from the period 1888-1905 remains today. The structure above it, however, has been replaced by the Lonz Winery.

Return of the Vines

Ohio and wine seem a perfect dichotomy, a pair of absolutely exclusive terms. Ohio is corn and steel and football; wine is grapes and green glass and five-course meals as recreation. Ohio sticks to the ribs; wine caresses the palate. Ohio gets up at dawn to tend to the animals and goes to bed at dusk; wine stays up late and then sleeps in.

What is most odd about this is how untrue it is. Wine and Ohio share a long and lustrous history; in another decade, perhaps, the history will be even more lustrous, as the wines Ohioans are making now increase their following. And they are going to do that; for at least the third time in the state's history, Ohio wine is beginning to capture national attention.

A quirky but enterprising nineteenth-century Cincinnatian named Nicholas Longworth made the Ohio River Valley the nation's first big wine producer. Longworth—who also pioneered strawberry production in the state and was its first art patron—laid out his first vineyards in the 1820s. After failing to grow varieties of Europe's delicate *Vitis vinifera*, he had great success with the hardier domestic *Vitis labrusca* grapevines. Ohio became so well known for its Catawba that Longfellow rhapsodized from his poet's seat in New England that "the richest and best is the wine of the West"—meaning Ohio. The state became the nation's largest wine producer in the nation by 1850, a year when California was still a place of bearded men in their undershirts, sleeping in tents and shooting each other over gold claims.

The Civil War and a blight brought an abrupt end to Ohio's first wine era, however. And, by the 1870s, California was using its climate to advantage to grow the European *vinifera*. In Ohio, the focus shifted north to the Lake Erie shore, where climate, tourism, and shipping connections permitted the industry to rebuild. Though less prestigious than wines made from the *vinifera*, Lake Erie *labrusca* wines, especially those from the islands, were shipped around the world. The Catawba was largely replaced by the more versatile Concord, another domestic vine which was popular for jams, jellies and juice (even today, two-thirds of Ohio's grape production goes to uses other than wine). But Prohibition, in force from 1919 to 1933, wiped out Ohio's wine industry once again, and so its second era ended.

When Repeal came in 1933, California and New York aggressively re-entered the market with the tonier *vinifera* and hybrid vines while Ohio languished with its native *labrusca*, producing what wine writer Roger Gentile has called "cheap jug wines and brown-bag fare." Much of Ohio's wine had only a regional appeal.

And, until about 1960, that was the story of Ohio wine. Since 1960, however, Ohio viticulture has been notable for innovation, improvement and invention. State government has developed a commitment to wine production, with viticultural research stations at Ripley and Wooster. Meier's, Ohio's oldest and best-known name in wine, supported research on the French-American hybrids, and they have risen to prominence in Ohio wine culture. Hybrids—Baco Noir, Chambourcin, Seyval and Vidal are among the best-known names—capture some of the quality of Europe's *vinifera* while retaining some of the hardiness of American *labrusca* vines. Wineries such as Lonz, on Middle Bass Island, still offer their share of old-fashioned sweet wines from native American grapes, but the contemporary focus in Ohio wine making is on French-American hybrid varieties, with interest also growing in the lofty *vinifera*—the same grapes grown for European wine making for centuries.

Best of all, a number of new vineyards and wineries have opened throughout the state; quality is rising, too, and Ohio wines are beginning to hold their own with the Californians and New Yorkers who eclipsed them years ago. As Gentile puts it in his guidebook, *Discovering Ohio Wines* (Canal Winchester; Enthea Press, 1991): "We are witnessing ...something which rarely happens, an agricultural and technological transformation from alcoholic Kool-Aid to vinous gold."

It takes certain ingredients—certain *tools*—to make good wine, of course, although some are much more important than others. Soils, for example, are important to a point, but only to a point: Lou Jindra, an Ohio wine maker, likes to point out that the mystical qualities of the supposedly unbeatable European vineyards are "deep subsoils with gravel and limestone, which makes for excellent drainage. The soils of the Lake Erie region, though, are also deep limestone and glacial stone subsoils, with excellent drainage. Go figure."

The real keys to wine are climate and the wine maker, and of course, the grapes and grapevines, although the order of importance here is open to interpretation. Wine makers who buy their grapes rather than grow them themselves believe it is the vintner who makes the wine; vintners who grow their own ascribe much more power to the actual plants. And the weather, while certainly a factor, is beyond anyone's control, although that doesn't stop wine makers from talking obsessively about it. (Wine makers rarely establish eye contact when speaking: if they're outside, they're looking at the sky or the clouds or the thermometer or the barometer; if they're inside, they're looking out the window.)

The ideal microclimate for wine in Ohio is the Lake Erie region, because Lake Erie is a textbook example of a weather-making natural resource. Lake Erie is large and shallow; in the spring, it is a natural air conditioner, sending cool air south across the flat, glacial-scraped northern counties. This cold air slows vine growth in the spring and, except in catastrophic years, insures that the vines won't blossom until all danger of frost has passed. The vines thus begin the summer growing season in good and hardy shape.

In the fall, after the lake has spent the summer absorbing the sun's heat, the breezes are warm, lengthening the growing season. That permits the vintner to harvest the grapes when the vintner wants to, rather than when the weather demands it. Wes Gerlosky, whose Harpersfield Vineyard in Geneva is in the epicenter of the lake-effect vineyards, has a complicated and subtle theory about the lake effect that has to do with malic acid and the malic bacterium. It's a theory that places his twelve acres of vines in, well, exactly the right spot to make great wine. But it is also true that Wes Gerlosky runs a wine-making operation that permits him to be on all but a first-name basis with each of his vines.

This is at least as important as the lake effect, this small-scale and perhaps most Frenchified aspect of Ohio wine making: of the forty or so wineries in Ohio, four of them make ninety per cent of the wine, and the rest of the vineyards produce the rest. This state of affairs is analagous to France, where three-quarters of the vineyards and winemakers work on a scale so small that export to the United States is unheard of; likewise in California, three-quarters of the wine made there is consumed there.

What this means in practice is what wine makers have instinctively known for six thousand years: wines are not widgets and each batch will be unique. Big wine makers get around this through a blending process that levels the wine out to a common denominator. But most Ohio vineyards make only distinctive wine; the scale is so small that this is inevitable. Wine in Ohio is mostly a boutique industry, where the owner is almost always on the premises.

In Ohio, the owners are apt to be people who not only are passionate about wine, but who helped pick the grapes and run the presses. Their workers are apt to be family members, neighbors, and assorted vinophiles: one vineyard had the volunteer services of a priest who was a wine fancier. The priest also blessed the vineyard, a European custom of ancient origin. The charming practice of blessing the vineyard—in this case, at Shamrock Vineyards in Waldo, just north of Columbus—is another example of how beguiling the culture of wine can be.

Shamrock is but one example of how wine in Ohio is usually the product of individuals who cherish what they do. Tom Quilter, M.D., and his wife, Mary, operate Shamrock among the corn and bean fields. They planted their first vines in 1971 and now have a small vineyard tended so lovingly it looks manicured. Their wine-pressing shed is fitted with imported Italian equipment. Far from the lakeshore, the Quilters face up to winter's vagaries with *labrusca* and hybrids, but with Irish stubbornness Tom insists he will make a *vinifera* succeed there yet. The Quilters' car bears the vanity plate SEYVAL, and, indeed, estate-bottled Shamrock Seyval can be highly recommended. So is the Quilters' hospitality: visitors are treated to tours, lectures on wine making, and tastings of the product.

The Ohio Farmer, March 11, 1922

Visitors are even invited to bring picnics.

Down the road in Columbus is a different kind of operation: Bill and Jane Butler's Wyandotte Wine Cellar and Wm. Graystone Winery. The Butlers prefer to buy their grapes and press them at these sister wineries. The atmospheric Wm. Graystone winery was established in 1990 in the cavernous cellars of a former German Village brewery. Wyandotte, which the Butlers established earlier, makes highly praised (and handsomely labeled) wines of many kinds, from *labrusca* to *vinifera*. One of the couple's offerings is memorably named Rhedd Butler.

Up on the lakeshore, in Harpersfield Township, is a prototypical wine-making family of still another stripe: Wes Gerlosky and his wife, Margaret, are vintners who would be absolutely at home in the Chablis region of France. Grown on a farm that was operated by Wes's father, their grapes are true French *vinifera*—twelve acres of Chardonnay—and the wine-making process positively archaic. The result, produced in very small quantities and under stringent conditions, is a Chardonnay that is better than 75 or 80 per cent of the Chardonnays made in any given year. It would confound all but the most dedicated wine snobs.

The Quilters, Butlers and Gerloskys are among a number of Ohioans who have made lifestyle changes to make fine wine: Tom Quilter retired from medicine, Bill Butler changed from being an agronomist, Wes Gerlosky switched emphasis from conventional farming. Other examples include a pediatric dentist (Dave Rechsteiner, Willow Hill Vineyards, near Johnstown); an investment realtor (Dalton Bixler, Breitenbach Wine Cellars, Dover), and an engineer, Arnie Esterer (Markko Vineyards, Conneaut). And there are many others, large and small, scattered throughout the state.

The result of this for those who love wine is astonishing: Ohio wines can be very, very good. But the result of this for those who try and entice people to try Ohio wines is frustrating: there has been, to date, little snob appeal for wines from the Buckeye State. Just try to find Ohio wine on the list at your favorite restaurant; odds are you won't, even in many places in Ohio.

The craze for white Zinfandel from California is a galling example of this. The American hybrid varietals like Seyval and Vidal Blanc are generally superior to any "blush" wine advertised in national magazines; to put it bluntly, the Vidal Blanc and Seyval Blanc produced in many Ohio vineyards is exactly the wine that the drinkers of white Zinfandel should be looking for and drinking. Ohio hybrid whites are better tasting and more distinctive while at the same time appealing to the tastes that have made white Zinfandel so popular: a little lighter, a little less dry. A good Seyval Blanc tastes like a very light, very young Chardonnay; a good Vidal is a little fruitier, a little less dry, but far more drinkable than most of what people drink. It is worth mentioning that in the 1990 Ohio Wine Challenge a "blush" Baco Noir from Ohio's largest winery, Meier's, beat in a blind tasting the most popular and largest selling white Zinfandel in the United States.

The Ohio Wine Challenge is an attempt to prove to those who select wine according to taste, rather than pedigree, that Ohio makes some fantastic wines. A sort of continuing dog-and-pony show, The Challenge pits Ohio wines against wines from California and Europe in the same price range. When wines compete against one another on a fairly level playing field, Ohio's hold up surprisingly well. In other regional, national and even international competition as well, Ohio's wines are beginning to show up, particularly those from the Firelands Winery and Chalet Debonné. These are two of the state's big operations: Firelands processes grapes from four area wineries and is operated by Paramount Disitillers, a Cleveland corporation; Chalet Debonné has involved four generations of the Debevcs and is said to be the state's largest family winery.

To cap (or cork) it all off, Ohio wines offer a price advantage. After all, fifty acres in Geuaga County, Ohio, contributes less to the overhead than fifty acres in, say, Sonoma County, California: the upper price range for good Ohio wines hovers around twenty dollars, with the vast majority around, or under, ten.

But as much as the search to replicate France in Ohio may occupy some vintners, it is impossible to ignore the wines that put Ohio on the wine-making map in the first place. These would be the Catawbas and Niagaras, on the one hand, and the dessert wines on the other. Many Ohio vineyards still bottle and sell Catawba wine, a vestige of a time when wine tasted, forthrightly, of grapes. Pink Catawba wine tastes emphatically of grapes. The most steadfast example of this is certainly the Mantey Vineyards in Sandusky, which makes Pink Catawba, Cream Catawba, White Catawba and, most endearingly, "Blue Face," or Concord, grape wine, with a picture of Grandpa Mantey on the label. Concord grape wine is an acquired taste that would tax the vocabulary of the most metaphorical wine writer. Suffice to say, it is not dry, and it is not light. It is an institution.

The dessert wines are an interesting story in themselves, particularly the Madeiras and ports and sherries. Since these wines are supposed to be sweet, their makers get sensitive about something else: the suggestion that Madeira or port from anywhere but Spain is only good for cooking will earn one a bath in a wine vat. Indeed, it is hard to compete with the real thing, but the "3 Islands" Madeira produced by Lonz comes very close. Although they have expanded their line, Meier's is perhaps best known for its ports and sherries, and rightfully so. As much as they might hate to hear it, their wines have a permanent place in the cook's kitchen, the Ruby Port especially; no duck should be cooked without it.

Which brings the story of Ohio wine full circle, in a way; from the kitchen (where it was relegated, untasted, by wine snobs) and back to it. But it really belongs on the table.

POSTSCRIPT: *More information about Ohio wines, including a directory of wineries, can be obtained from the Ohio Wine Producers Association, 822 North Tote Road, Austinburg 44010. Telephone 800/227-6972.*

FACES OF THE LAND

Farmer with a Vision

In his farmer's clothes, Arnie Esterer doesn't look like a spit-and-polish Navy officer, which he once was (four years active duty, 21 years in the reserves) nor even a Fortune 500 industrial engineer, which he also was (17 years with Union Carbide). Instead, Arnie Esterer has become someone more formidable: a pioneer and a visionary.

Or, he will admit when pressed, "a farmer with a vision." That vision is of the Lake Erie region as one of the great wine-making areas of the world, rivaling California and, yes, even France.

Arnie Esterer is a wine maker. A wine maker with big ideas. Big, *world-class* ideas.

Those who can't keep from laughing had better not underestimate the quiet man from Conneaut. With his beard, wire-rimmed glasses and little blue cap, Esterer may have a detached, professorial air; with his calm manner of speaking, he may sound as if he's politely leading a seminar instead of thinking about a viticultural revolution.

But make no mistake about it: Arnie Esterer is tough-minded and serious about wine. Serious enough to be the first to grow the delicate *vinifera* grapevines of Europe in the northeastern Ohio snowbelt. Serious enough to grow grapes the hard way, using natural soil additives instead of commercial chemicals. Serious enough to have built a reputation with connoisseurs for his Reisling, Cabernet Sauvignon and Chardonnay. Wine and food writers have described them as "a delight to drink," "extraordinary," and "some of the best wines in the country."

And serious enough, more than 20 years ago, to have transformed himself from "a desk-bound paper-pusher into a living, breathing, dirty-fingernails farmer." Now Esterer and a partner, Tim Hubbard, own Markko Vineyards in northeastern Ohio. The vineyard is located on a high ridge overlooking Lake Erie, barely a shout from the Pennsylvania line.

That makes it part of the Lake Erie viticultural region, which includes Ohio, Pennsylvania and New York. It also makes it part of the snow belt of which Buffalo is the notorious capital. The story of how Esterer decided to face up to this blustery land and bring bouquet and, yes, nose out of it deserves to become one of the legends of the Ohio pioneers...latter-day pioneers, of course, but pioneers nonetheless.

Esterer, who has a master's degree in business from the University of

Michigan, had been working for Union Carbide in northeast Ohio, doing what he calls "engineering the cost of processing things"—worker productivity, plant layout, time studies. And he was a Navy Reserve cryptologic (codebreaker) officer.

But at age 26, Esterer was in the Union Carbide cafeteria one day when an old Finnish janitor told him he was too old to drink milk: he should be drinking wine instead. "That got me interested," Esterer recalls; he had seen vineyards in the region and knew northeast Ohio was "a great area for growing grapes, but the wine was terrible." In his opinion, the problem was the kind of grape used—Concord, a native American *labrusca* variety which some people like but which Esterer regards as best for juice.

Esterer got more and more interested and eventually, in 1967, was able to arrange a kind of internship with Dr. Konstantin Frank, an expert on growing grapevines in upstate New York. In effect, Esterer traded his labor for a crash course in growing grapes for wine.

Frank scorned the sturdier hybrid vines many American vineyards used instead of the *vinifera*, the delicate, aristocratic grapevines of Europe. "He said the hybrids caused mutations and deformities in children," recalls Esterer. "He always said, 'Americans deserve to drink the best!'"—meaning wine made from *vinifera*.

Esterer was a rapt pupil; even today he wears a cap like Frank's. And he has a philosophy with which Frank could agree: "The important thing in a wine is what kind of grape it's made out of. That's number one. The second most important thing is the climate, the third is the soil, and the fourth is the wine maker."

Lake Erie offered the cooler springs and warmer autumns that grapes like, and the soil was acceptable, too. So Esterer set out to learn from Frank how to grow the best vines—the *vinifera*—in the face of snowbelt conditions that Lake Erie also offers.

Arnie Esterer

Frank taught Esterer such cultural practices as the spacing of vines and how to protect them against winter winds and snow. Frank also picked varieties of *vinifera* most apt to survive Lake Erie's bluster and explained how the process of natural selection and adaptation will, over time, sort out the right vines for the climate. "The French did it over a thousand years," Esterer says; "They got it down to just one vine for each region. They know precisely which work there and which don't. We do not. That's the work that needs to be done, and that's what I'm doing."

He opened Markko Vineyards in 1968, while still working at Union Carbide; in 1972—two days after his 40th birthday—he left the Fortune 500 corporation and became a full-time wine maker. The early years were difficult, as ice and cold wiped much out of his stock. Like a frontiersman trying to turn a wild land into a productive farm, Esterer had to take defeat, pick himself up, and try again. Between 1975 and 1985 the area suffered the "ten coldest years on record," according to Esterer. But gradually, through persistence, he has been able to build a vineyard 10,000 vines, producing an average of 5,000 gallons of wine a year.

A 5,000-gallon annual production is not tiny, but it's probably not big enough to ever make Esterer rich. But rich is not why he's growing grapes and making wine: "It's a more spiritual kind of thing," he explains. "I still feel this is what God asked me to do. You have to be of service to society in a lot of different ways. We're a demonstration vineyard—we were the first to pioneer these grapes in this region and to focus very specifically on this, not necessarily as a money maker."

And, indeed, inspired by Esterer's example, several other Ohio vineyards have begun growing *vinifera*, and still others are considering it. Now, where there once were only those American stalwarts, Concord or Catawba, you may find Chardonnay, Cabernet, Reisling—the aristocrats of Europe. And like most pioneers, Esterer has been generous with helping his fellow frontiersmen; after all, they are all in this together. But there's a larger reason, too, for Esterer to welcome competitors: his eye is set on a larger goal than simply making Markko a commercial success.

"The Lake Erie region can produce some of the nicest, finest white wines in the country—or the world," says Esterer. But more than that, it just might be that some day the region could, in its own way, become the world's best. How is that?

"Dr. Frank used to say that there were five great wine grapes in the world: Pinot Noir, Cabernet, Chardonnay, Reisling, and Pinot Gris," explains Esterer. And, of the world's great wine-growing regions, several can claim to have "its own grape"—one variety for which it is the sweet spot, as athletes call that rare place where ball and bat connect perfectly. When that unsurpassable combination occurs, it may said the region *defines* the wine, making it the number-one place in the world for it.

In Esterer's opinion, four of the five great wine grapes are already locked up, already defined by a region: Pinot Noir, by Burgundy; Cabernet, by Bordeaux; Chardonnay, white from Burgundy; Reisling, by Germany. Sure, you can produce a good Chardonnay elsewhere, for example, but only one with its own character, and not a copy; the French growers simply define that wine. Oh, California can try to beat the French, but, says Esterer, "They're only copying. They'll never win. It's impossible. Their place in the world is to grow Zinfandel."

But Pinot Gris? *That* is the greatest wine grape in the world, according to Konstantin Frank. And nowhere, insists Esterer, *nowhere* "is it number one." Perfection is still to be achieved; Pinot Gris remains to be defined. By someone.

And guess who that someone could be: "There's going to be a race to produce and define Pinot Gris," says Esterer. "Somebody is going to define it. I see a big race between Oregon and the Lake Erie viticultural region."

Not soon: "We're looking at 40, 50 years down the road, but we're going to see some big plantings of Pinot Gris." Esterer himself is just getting into planting Pinot Gris, some 200 vines out of 10,000: most of his 14 acres is planted to Chardonnay and Reisling, with some Cabernet Sauvignon and Pinot Noir. But, he says, "I think you'll see an explosion of Pinot Gris in this area." Esterer is already planning to convert some of his Reisling root stock to Pinot Gris. "It has a lovely character," Esterer says of Pinot Gris. "It's something like a Chardonnay, but more versatile. It has power and strength. It's just interesting."

And if Esterer is correct and Lake Erie comes to define Pinot Gris, comes to be one of the world's great wine regions, the impact could be enormous. Esterer sketched out his vision at a speech at Kent State University: "I said, 'Take the Lake Erie region. It's 250 miles long, five miles wide, from Buffalo to Toledo. Put a thousand wineries in there, each worth a million dollars, each having, say, 40 acres of grapes. We could produce a tenth or a fifteenth of the national consumption rate. This a multi-billion dollar industry...It's wine sales, but it's also an industry using barrels, tanks, farm machinery, trellises, wire, advertising—you name it.'"

Most of all, says Esterer, northern Ohio and its neighbors have the possibility of transforming itself from rust belt to something else: the mind's eye sees verdant images of gently rolling hillsides covered with vineyards, hundreds of little wineries squeezing out the vintage, of diners in five-star restaurants around the world raising their glasses of Lake Erie Pinot Gris.

But right now, says Esterer, "This region has no perception of itself as a wine-making region. It has to have a perception of what it is, a vision, a sense of how good it is and how good it can be."

And Arnie Esterer has that vision.

POSTSCRIPT: *Markko Vineyard, open year-round, is on South Ridge Road, Conneaut 44030 (Exit 235 on Interstate 90, then S.R. 193 to Main Street. Turn right on to Main Street and then take South Ridge). Tel. 216/593-3197.*

RECIPES

Chalet Debonné Famous Shrimp Dip

Makes about 2 cups

1 (8-ounce) package cream cheese,
   softened
1 cup salad dressing (not mayonnaise)
2 (6-1/2-ounce) cans tiny de-veined
   shrimp, rinsed and drained
1/4 cup chopped celery
1/4 cup sliced green onions
2 tablespoons Debonné Vineyards
   Seyval, Reisling or Reflections wine

Beth Debevc, of Chalet Debonné calls this her "famous" shrimp dip because it is the recipe for which she gets the most requests. Chalet Debonné Vineyards in Madison (7734 Doty Road, 216/466-3485) is the largest family winery in the state and one of the most progressive wine operations in the country. The winery began producing wine in the mid-1970s from native American *Labrusca* varieties. But with an eye to the future, the Debevcs hired professional oenologist, Tony Carlucci, and began planting Chardonnay, Reisling, and Cabernet grapes. As a result, Chalet Debonné has won many awards for its wines and attracts the sophisticated wine drinker.

In small mixer bowl, beat cream cheese until fluffy. Add salad dressing: beat well. Stir in remaining ingredients. Chill before serving. Serve with crackers or bagel chips.

Shamrock White Sangria

Makes 6 servings

1 (750 ml) bottle Shamrock Seyval
   wine
1/2 cup Curacao (triple sec)
2 tablespoons sugar
1 each lemon, lime and orange,
   thinly sliced
6 fresh strawberries, halved
1 (10-ounce) bottle club soda,
   chilled
Ice cubes

You'll get a friendly, personal welcome to the wine industry in Ohio when you visit Shamrock Vineyard, which calls itself "the micro-winery in the heart of Ohio" (Rengert Road in Waldo (614/726-2883). Every bottle is the product of Tom and Mary Quilter, who prune, pick, press, bottle and label by hand.

This recipe uses their Shamrock Seyval wine. The wine itself has a pleasing taste of peaches, apples and citrus that makes it perfect to use in this light white sangria. We like to make a pitcher on those lazy summer afternoons when we are having friends over for a barbecue.

In large glass pitcher, combine wine, Curacao and sugar; stir until dissolved. Add fruits. Cover; refrigerate at least one hour to blend flavors. Just before serving, add soda and ice cubes; stir gently to mix. Serve in wine glasses or champagne flutes.

Meier's Sparkling Catawba Punch

Meier's, Ohio's "oldest and largest winery," has been making wines for well over 100 years. Meier's spans the state: its vineyards are in the north, on Lake Erie's Isle St. George (designated a specific viticultural area by the federal government) and its wine-making facilities are in Silverton, in southern Ohio near Cincinnati.

The winery (6955 Plainfield Pike, Cincinnati, 513/891-2900) offers tours that show wine-making first hand, a massive tank farm with its 1.8 million gallon capacity, and the wine cellars with century-old casks.

Meier's produces a great variety of wines, including Labrusca and fruit wines, premium sherries, classic French-American varietals and award-winning sparkling wines. Meier's is especially known its #44 Cream Sherry, and Walleye White, and non-alcoholic juices, both still and sparkling.

In punch bowl, combine water, juice concentrates and grenadine. Refrigerate. Just before serving, add sparkling juice and ginger ale. Float ice ring in bowl or add ice cubes.

Makes 24 1/2-cup servings

2 cups cold water
1 (6-ounce) can frozen lemonade concentrate, thawed
1 (6-ounce) can frozen pineapple juice concentrate, thawed
1/2 cup grenadine
1 (750-ml) bottle Meier's Sparkling Pink or White Catawba Grape Juice, chilled
3 (12-ounce) cans ginger ale, chilled
Ice ring or ice cubes

Turkey Cutlets in Catawba Cream Sauce

Lou Jindra is is executive director of the Ohio Grape Industries Program, which works with the Ohio Department of Agriculture to provide research and promotion. Jindra enjoys using Ohio wines in almost everything he cooks...not a bad way to promote Ohio wines. The Catawba used here reflects one of the most famous names in American wine; wines from Catawba Island (actually a peninsula) were popular throughout ninetheenth-century America.

We should mention that the turkey is a very b-i-g bird in Ohio. According to the Ohio Department of Agriculture, in 1991 the state raised over 4.8 million turkeys, produced nearly 127,000,000 pounds of turkey meat, and exported between 20 and 25 million young turkeys.

In large skillet, cook bacon until crisp; remove from pan. In shallow dish, combine flour, salt and pepper. Coat both sides of turkey with mixture. Brown turkey on both sides in bacon drippings; remove from skillet, keep warm. Add mushrooms and garlic; cook until tender. Add wine; scraping to loosen brown bits from skillet. Bring to a boil; reduce heat, simmer until liquid is reduced by half. Add cream; bring to a boil. Reduce heat; simmer 5 minutes. Pour sauce over cutlets and garnish with parsley.

Makes 4 to 6 servings

4 slices bacon, chopped
1/4 cup flour
1/4 teaspoon salt
1/8 teaspoon pepper
1 package (about 1-1/4 pounds) boneless fresh turkey breast slices
1 cup sliced fresh mushrooms
2 cloves garlic, finely chopped
1/4 cup Pink Catawba wine
1 cup (1/2 pint) whipping cream or half-and-half
Chopped fresh parsley

3 Islands Madeira Cheesy Chowder

Makes about 2 quarts

1 medium carrot, peeled and
   chopped
1 rib celery, chopped
1 leek, white part only, chopped
1 medium onion, chopped
1/2 teaspoon thyme leaves
3 tablespoons butter or margarine
2 large potatoes, peeled and diced
6 cups chicken broth or stock
1 pound smoked sausage or Polish
   kielbasa, diced
4 tart apples (Granny Smith,
   Spygold or Melrose) peeled and
   diced
2 cups (8 ounces) shredded premium
   Ohio cheese (Jersey Jack or
   Smoked Baby Swiss)
1 cup 3 Islands American Madeira
   wine
1 cup (1/2-pint) whipping cream or
   half-and-half
1/2 teaspoon crushed rosemary
   leaves
Sea salt, cayenne pepper and
   ground allspice

Many Ohioans consider 3 Islands American Madeira a staple item in their kitchens. Madeira wine has a history in America, too. Familiar with English Madeira, the colonists adopted it as their national wine. Since the 1700s it has been a vital flavoring for sauces, soups, glazes, entrees and desserts. Today many cooks kept an open bottle on hand for these dishes; it is also perfect for deglazing a pan and capturing every last bit of flavor.

This recipe combines the goodness of Ohio ingredients with 3 Islands American Madeira for a savory chowder. It comes to us from Tom Johnson of Paramount Distillers, who produce the American Madeira under the Lonz label. Lonz Winery is located on Middle Bass Island and is a popular spot for fishermen, boaters and vacationers who want a sandwich and a glass of wine.

Formerly of Shaw's in Lancaster, and Lindey's and L'Armagnac, both in Columbus, Tom has broadcast on WOSU in Columbus and was "State Chef" for the Ohio Department of Agriculture. He is also a regular cooking instructor at La Belle Pomme and Cookery/Zona Spray, as well as "Gilded Vine" cooking classes at Firelands Winery.

In large saucepan, cook carrot, celery, leek, onion and thyme in butter until tender. Add potatoes and stock; bring to a boil. Reduce heat; simmer 30 minutes. In large skillet, cook sausage until brown; drain on paper towels. Add sausage to chowder along with apples, cheese, wine, cream and rosemary. Heat until cheese melts (do not boil). If desired, sprinkle each serving with sea salt, cayenne and allspice.

Valley Vineyards Pork Ragout

Valley Vineyards is located in Morrow in the southwestern part of the state (2276 East U.S. 22 & 3. 513/899-2485). Ken Schuchter produces good wines, ranging from dry red Blue Eye to sweet Honey Mead. He also produces food and entertainment. Steak cookouts are conducted weekly, and on the last Thursday, Friday and Saturday of September Valley Vineyards holds its annual Wine Festival. Events include wine-stomping and amateur wine-making contests.

Valley Vineyards' DeChaunac wine is so good that we developed this recipe using it. The wine is a hearty red that complements this pork stew. It is a great dish to get simmering on your stove and then have company walk in; the aroma of rosemary and basil is heavenly.

In large kettle, brown pork cubes in oil; remove as browned. Add potatoes, carrots, onion, celery, green pepper and garlic; cook 5 minutes stirring frequently. Add flour; mix well. Return pork cubes to skillet; add remaining ingredients. Bring to a boil; cover and simmer 1 hour or until meat is tender. Serve in individual bowls.

Makes 4 to 6 servings

2 pounds boneless pork shoulder or sirloin, cut into 1-inch cubes
2 tablespoons vegetable oil
3 medium potatoes, cut in 1/2-inch cubes
2 medium carrots, peeled and sliced in 1/4-inch rounds
1 medium onion, chopped
1 cup sliced celery
1 cup chopped green pepper
2 cloves garlic, finely chopped
3 tablespoons flour
4 cups beef broth or stock
1-1/2 cups Valley Vineyards DeChaunac wine
2 tablespoons Dijon-style mustard
2 tablespoons brown sugar
1-1/2 teaspoons crushed rosemary leaves
1 teaspoon basil leaves

Grilled Lamb Markko

Makes 6 to 8 servings

1 (5 to 6 pound) leg of lamb, boned
  and butterflied
2 cups olive oil
1 cup Markko Cabernet Sauvignon
1 medium red onion, thinly sliced
1/3 cup chopped fresh oregano
  leaves or 1 tablespoon dried
1 tablespoon crumbled fresh rosemary leaves or 1 teaspoon dried
3 bay leaves
3 cloves garlic, finely chopped
1 teaspoon whole peppercorns

"Gladden thy heart" (from Psalm 104) is the motto of Markko Vineyards in Conneaut. Markko wines, which do indeed gladden the heart, are the creation of Arnie Esterer who, with partner Tim Hubbard, pioneered the raising of *vinifera* in Ohio. Markko Cabernet Sauvignon is a hearty mouth-filling red wine, blended with Chamborcin, Cabernet Frank and Merlot. It adds a wonderful, robust flavor to the marinade.

Place lamb in 13x9-inch glass baking dish; pour oil and wine over top. Add remaining ingredients; turn once to coat. Cover; refrigerate 6 hours or overnight, turning occasionally.

Bring lamb to room temperature before grilling. Remove lamb; drain. Placing close to hot coals, cook 5 minutes per side or until browned. Adjust grill so lamb cooks more slowly; cook about 8 to 10 minutes per side or until meat thermometer reaches 140-145 degrees. Remove to cutting board; let stand 10 minutes. Carve in thin diagonal slices.

Walleye White Walleye

Makes 4 servings

1/4 cup olive oil
1/4 cup Meier's Walleye White Wine
1 clove garlic, finely chopped
1 teaspoon salt
1/2 teaspoon pepper
1/4 teaspoon crushed bay leaf
4 (3- to 4-ounce) Lake Erie Walleye
  fillets
2 green peppers, seeded and thinly
  sliced
2 medium onions, thinly sliced
4 cherry tomatoes, quartered

More than 4 million walleye pike are caught annually in Lake Erie, most of them in the western basin, which has been dubbed the "Walleye Capital of the World." In the midst of this walleye paradise is Isle St. George, where Meier's Wine Cellars grows the Reisling and Vidal Blanc grapes that go into Meier's Walleye White Wine.

Walleye White is one of Meier's most popular wines. A proprietary blend of *labrusca* and hybrids, it is medium-dry, fruity and refreshing. It is a natural, not only with walleye, but with any fish or chicken entree.

In small bowl, or jar with tight-fitting lid, combine oil, wine, garlic, salt, pepper and bay leaf. In shallow baking dish or resealable plastic bag, pour marinade over fish. Cover; refrigerate 1 hour.

Preheat oven to 350 degrees. On 4 large pieces of heavy-duty aluminum foil, place walleye fillet; top each with equal amounts of green pepper and onion slices. Pour a small amount of marinade over vegetables; top with tomatoes. Wrap foil securely around fish, leaving room for expansion. Bake for 30 minutes or until fish flakes easily with fork. (Fish packets may also be prepared on the barbecue grill. Cook over hot coals for 20 to 30 minutes.)

Portage Hills Chinese Chicken and Peanuts

Portage Hills Vineyard in Suffield (1420 Martin Road, 216/628-2668) believes in the family approach to making wine. The three principals are Cordell Glaus and his two sons, Kent and Gary. All three men left careers in other fields to become wine makers: Cordell is a former architect, Kent is an ex-genetic biologist, and Gary was trained as a teacher.

The winery hosts annual Junefest and Oktoberfest, food and wine events, and Cooking with Wine demonstrations. Tours of the winery are offered year round. The winery has a comfortable hospitality room for tasting. This recipe is a favorite from the Portage Hills Cooking with Wine demonstrations. Its unusual list of ingredients reflects the creativity of the Glaus family.

In non-aluminum bowl, combine soy sauce, Chablis and ginger root; add chicken. Cover: refrigerate at least 1 hour. Drain chicken. In medium bowl, combine egg white and cornstarch; add chicken, stirring to coat. Cover; refrigerate. Heat oil in wok; cook peanuts until lightly browned, stirring constantly. Remove peanuts from wok. Drain chicken; cook in hot oil until tender, stirring constantly. In small bowl, combine bean sauce, chili paste, Hoisin sauce, Chambourcin, sugar and garlic; add to chicken. Heat through; top with peanuts.

Makes 4 servings

1/2 cup soy sauce
1/4 cup Portage Hills Garden Chablis Wine
1/2 teaspoon grated fresh ginger root
4 boneless skinless chicken breast halves, sliced
1 egg white, slightly beaten
2 tablespoons cornstarch
1/2 cup peanut or sunflower oil
1/2 cup raw peanuts
1/4 cup brown bean sauce
2 tablespoons chili paste with garlic (Szechwan paste)
2 tablespoons Hoisin sauce (Peking sauce)
2 tablespoons Portage Hills Chambourcin wine
1 tablespoon sugar
8 garlic gloves, pressed

Strawberry Rosé Crepes

Makes 10 servings

4 cups sliced fresh strawberries
1/2 cup Mon Ami Lake Erie Rose
  Wine
2/3 cup sugar
2 tablespoons cornstarch
10 prepared crepes
Sour cream

Mon Ami Winery (3845 East Wine Cellar Road, Port Clinton, 419/797-4445) serves up atmosphere, food and wine, all under one roof. The building was constructed of native materials in 1872 and has limestone walls four to six feet thick. In the vaulted cellars below are huge casks where once a bandstand and dance floor stood during Prohibition.

In 1980 Mon Ami was added to the Paramount Distillers wine group and has undergone a great deal of renovation. Wines are not made on premises, but are produced, bottled and labeled at Paramount's Firelands facilities. Mon Ami produces 26 varieties of wine, but is especially noted for its sparkling varieties. The Mon Ami restaurant is open year round.

Strawberry Rosé Crepes, made with Mon Ami Lake Erie Rosé, shows the versatility of cooking with Ohio wines. It's a great dessert to make when Ohio strawberries are in season.

In medium saucepan, crush 1 cup strawberries; add wine. Cook over medium heat until soft. In blender or food processor, puree mixture. Return to saucepan; add sugar and cornstarch. Cook over medium heat until thickened, stirring constantly. Cool slightly; stir in remaining strawberries. Fill crepes; fold over. Chill. Serve topped with sour cream.

Ohio Cream Sherry Pound Cake

Makes one 10-inch cake

1 (18-1/4-ounce) package yellow
  cake mix
1 (4-serving size) package instant
  vanilla flavor pudding mix
3/4 cup Meier's No. 44 Premium
  American Cream Sherry
3/4 cup vegetable oil
4 eggs
1/2 teaspoon ground nutmeg
Confectioners' sugar

This unusual recipe is made with award-winning No. 44 Cream Sherry from Meier's Wine Cellars in Silverton. The wine is full-bodied, smooth and sweet wine with the "nutty" flavor characteristic of fine sherries.

Preheat oven to 350 degrees. In large mixer bowl, combine cake mix, pudding mix, cream sherry and oil. Beat on low speed until moistened; add eggs one at a time, beat well after each addition. Add nutmeg; beat on medium-high speed 6 minutes. Pour into greased and floured 10-inch bundt pan; bake 40 to 45 minutes or until wooden pick inserted near center comes out clean. Cool 5 minutes; remove from pan. Cool. Sprinkle with confectioners' sugar.

Wm. Graystone Wine Omelet

Established in 1990, Wm. Graystone is owned by Bill and Jane Butler, who also own Wyandotte Winery. Graystone is located in the historic Brewery District of Columbus, in the old Schlee Bavarian Brewery building, built in 1875 and now on the National Historic Register (544 South Front Street, 614/228-2332).

In the morning, the Graystone winery is set up to offer light breakfasts, while at lunch they serve salads, soups and light deli foods as well as tastings of their wines. After lunch the emphasis is on wine tours, catered events and retail wine sales.

Each bottle of Columbus Classics (Wm. Graystone label) features an original watercolor painting of a Columbus landmark by artist Bonnie Weir. Some people collect the bottles and keep them, unopened!

Arrange bread in lightly greased 13x9-inch baking dish; pour melted butter over bread. Sprinkle with Monterey Jack and Swiss cheeses, meat and onions. In medium bowl, beat together eggs, milk, wine, mustard and peppers; pour over bread, moistening completely. Cover with foil; refrigerate overnight.

Remove dish from refrigerator 30 minutes before baking. Preheat oven to 325 degrees. Bake 1 hour. Remove foil; top with sour cream and Parmesan cheese. Bake 10 minutes longer or until golden brown. (For a crisper top, omelet may be browned under broiler for 5 minutes.) Allow to stand 5 minutes before cutting into squares.

Makes 6 to 8 servings

8 cups (about 8 ounces) French bread cubes
3 tablespoons butter or margarine, melted
1 cup (4 ounces) shredded Monterey Jack cheese
1 cup (4 ounces) shredded Swiss cheese
4 ounces hard salami or ham, thinly sliced
1/4 cup sliced green onions
8 eggs
1-1/4 cups milk
1/2 cup Columbus Classics (Wm. Graystone) Grandstand or Wyandotte Winery Delaware wine
2 teaspoons Dijon-style mustard

Firelands Braised Beef Noir

Makes 4 to 6 servings

6 slices bacon, diced
1 (1-1/2- to 2-pound) bottom round
    steak, cut into 1-inch cubes
2 medium carrots, peeled and sliced
    in 1/4-inch rounds
2 ribs celery, chopped
1 medium onion, chopped
1 tablespoon chopped fresh parsley
1-1/2 teaspoons thyme leaves
2 cloves garlic, finely chopped
1/2 teaspoon salt
1/4 teaspoon pepper
3 tablespoons flour
1-1/2 cups beef broth or stock
1-1/2 cups Firelands Pinot Noir wine
2 bay leaves
2 cups sliced fresh mushrooms
1 cup frozen pearl onions
Cooked noodles or rice

Firelands Winery in Sandusky is part of Paramount Distillers, a Cleveland firm that owns four separate wine operations in the state of Ohio. (Meier's, Lonz and Mon Ami are the others.) The Paramount success story is in no small part due to the leadership of its chairman, Bob Gottesman.

The Firelands facility (917 Bardshar Road, 419/625-5474) is spacious and provides an enjoyable tour. (The Firelands name originated in 1792 when the state of Connecticut set aside part of the land it held in Ohio for people whose homes had been burned during the Revolutionary War.) Many bus charters stop here. Firelands wines are highly regarded by wine critics; a recent issue of the *Wine Spectator*, a national wine publication, singled three Firelands wines for high marks, a notable accomplishment for a regional winery.

This recipe is especially suited for a cold winter night with a roaring fire in the fireplace. Serve it with a green salad and crusty French bread.

In large kettle, cook bacon until crisp; remove from kettle. Brown beef cubes in bacon drippings; remove as browned. Add carrots, celery, onion, parsley, thyme, garlic, salt and pepper; cook 5 minutes. Add flour; mix well. Return bacon and beef cubes to kettle; add broth, wine and bay leaves. Bring to a boil; cover and simmer 1 hour or until meat is tender. Add mushrooms and pearl onions; continue cooking 30 minutes. Serve over noodles or rice.

Harpersfield Chicken

Meg and Wes Gerlosky own Harpersfield Winery in Geneva (6387 State Route 307, 216/466-4739). Their motto is "Always make the best wine you can." After purchasing the farm, which grew only apples, they planted *vinifera*. To this day they make only white wine, feeling the Lake Erie region is best suited for the growing of Chardonnay, Gerwurtztraminer and Reisling grapes.

The Gerloskys cook with their own wines all the time, and were kind enough to share this favorite recipe with us. It uses only part of the bottle, but wine connoisseurs will know what to do with the rest.

In small bowl or jar with tight-fitting lid, combine all ingredients except chicken. In large shallow baking dish or resealable plastic bag, pour marinade over chicken. Cover; refrigerate 6 hours or overnight. Drain chicken, reserving marinade. Grill or broil as desired, basting frequently with marinade. (The Gerloskys suggest grilling the chicken over apple or cherry wood chips if using a conventional barbecue grill.)

Makes 8 to 10 servings

2 cups Harpersfield white wine
  (Chardonnay, Gerwurtztraminer
  or Reisling)
2 tablespoons each Dijon-style
  mustard, honey mustard and
  Pommery mustard
1 teaspoon soy sauce
1/2 teaspoon sesame oil
1/2 teaspoon worcestershire sauce
Fresh herbs (lemon thyme, english
  thyme, oregano and tarragon, or
  combination of herbs of your
  choice), amounts as desired
Freshly ground black pepper
8 to 10 boneless chicken breast
  halves, skinned

Aunt Ruth's Concord Grape Pie

Concord grapes have long been popular in Ohio for wine, juice and jelly production. In autumn the air is heavy with their sweet, ripe aroma along the shores of Lake Erie. Ruth Wale, aunt of Bill Failor, the co-author's husband, was born and raised in Ohio and is known as a great cook.

Slit and pop grape pulp from skins into medium saucepan; reserve skins. Simmer pulp for 5 minutes; press through sieve to remove seeds. Discard seeds; in saucepan, combine pulp and skins; bring to a boil. Remove from heat; add remaining ingredients, except pastry; mix well.

Preheat oven to 425 degrees. Divide pastry dough in half; on lightly floured surface, roll each half out to 1/8-inch thickness. Line pie plate; trim edges even with plate. Turn grape filling into pastry lined plate. Moisten edges of pastry in pie plate; lift second pastry circle onto filling. Trim 1/2-inch beyond edge of pie plate; fold top edge under bottom crust, flute edges. With sharp knife, slit top pastry in several spots for steam vents. Bake 10 minutes. Reduce oven temperature to 400 degrees; bake an additional 25 to 30 minutes or until golden brown.

Makes one 9-inch pie

4 cups Concord grapes
1 cup sugar
1/4 cup flour
1 teaspoon ground cinnamon
1/2 teaspoon ground nutmeg
1/8 teaspoon salt
Pastry for 2-crust pie

Reminders of why Cincinnati was nicknamed Porkopolis in the 1800s remain today. For example, there's Kahn's, Ohio's biggest meat packer and still the last stop for many Ohio hogs. The business was started with a meat market that German immigrant Elias Kahn opened in Cincinnati in 1882. In this 1938 picture, the "Kahn's girls" are making weiners.

The Mother of All Food Plants

As one Ohioan knows all too well, being a public beauty isn't easy, even if she WAS born with drop-dead good looks. For one thing, there's the same carefully managed diet, day after day, with absolutely nothing sinful. Then there's the hair care: brushing and trimming and washing, until a girl could just bellow. And the travel! Up at dawn to get stared at by thousands of people, then to bed in another city, over and over again. With a life like that, sometimes it just happens that she—how do we put this delicately?—defecates in public.

But, hey, if you're Elsie the Borden Cow, people understand and even *expect* it of you, so it's n-o-o-o problem. It all goes with the job of being official spokescow for one of the nation's biggest food companies. Trouper that she is, Elsie cheerfully endures weeks on the road, appearing at fairs and festivals, children's hospitals and camps. Still, she's always glad to get back to her home on an Ohio farm, chew a cud with the old gang, and just ruminate.

Most people don't know Elsie is an Ohioan. Many don't even know that Ohio is the nerve center for America's largest dairy processor, Borden, Inc. The company, which also leads the nation in pasta, canned seafood, packaged lemon juice and bouillon, is America's fourth largest food packager. But it's dairy products that got the firm started (in the 1850s, when Gail Borden, a New Yorker, invented condensed milk), and it's dairy products that many people still think of first when the name Borden is mentioned.

Today, Borden plants are scattered across the country. However, the company's administrative center is on East Broad Street in Columbus, and one of Borden's ice cream plants is also located in the city. (By the way, Borden is the biggest ice cream maker in the *world*.)

Borden, which has other plants in Ohio as well, helps make Ohio one of the top ten dairy states in the nation. Yet cows are one of the last things to come to mind when "Ohio" is mentioned. It is yet an another sad reflection of the state's one-dimensional smokestack image. Most Ohioans know their state is big in car, truck and bus production, but few realize how many of the biggest names in food are just down the street. In fact, food processing is a $15.6-billion-a-year industry in Ohio, with companies ranging from Ma-and-Pa operations in the basement to world-class giants. (Restaurants and institutional food services account for another $10.4 billion per year; grocery stores and food wholesalers, $8.4 billion; production agriculture, $8.1 billion.) Food is so big a business in Ohio that most Americans don't get through a single day without some contact with an Ohio food industry. Consider, for example, a day in your own life:

• Your breakfast very likely includes a ready-to-eat cereal, and there's a good chance, too, that it's Cheerios. Cheerios roll off the production line by the billion at a General Mills plant in Toledo. Introduced in 1941 as Cheeri Oats, those little round O's are now the nation's first choice in breakfast cereal, when ranked by dollar sales.

• Like some fruit on that cereal—a banana, perhaps? Believe it or not, an Ohio firm is the biggest supplier of bananas in the world. No banana boats have been seen traveling the Ohio River lately, but Chiquita Brands International, Inc., has its headquarters in Cincinnati. Chiquita Brands is descended from the old United Fruit Company, once based in New York. Cincinnati financier Carl H. Lindner took control in 1984, moved the firm to his hometown, and changed its name.

• Don't forget jam for your toast. The J. M. Smucker Company of Orrville boasts it is America's number-one producer of jams, jellies, preserves, ice cream toppings and fruit syrups. It started when Jerome M. Smucker opened a cider mill in Orrville in 1897 and signed the paper lid on each crock of apple butter. Today Smucker's has plants in England and Australia, but headquarters are still in Orrville (on Strawberry Lane) in rural Wayne County. A spokesperson says of her company, "They try to keep a low profile," but with a name like Smucker's...

• Being "aw, shucks" types, the Bob Evans Farms folks make no claim to being the biggest or only, but their bright-red family restaurants are probably where most Ohioans head first when they go out for breakfast. There really is a Bob Evans, who got things started back in 1946 when he made sausage, on the home farm, for his tiny diner in Gallipolis. That 12-stool hole-in-the-wall has turned into a chain of more than 290 family restaurants from Michigan to Florida; company headquarters are in Columbus. Ohio leads the pack with 100 Bob Evans restaurants, and they still serve sausage for breakfast...and lunch...and dinner.

• How could we forget the coffee? A lot of Americans wake up to theirs from an automatic drip maker made by Mr. Coffee, one of nation's biggest names in counter-top appliances. The Bedford Heights firm introduced the device in 1975, answering the prayers of bleary-eyed Americans everywhere and giving brides something more to look forward to than a shower of toasters.

Time moves along, and we should start thinking about lunch. We won't have to look far.

• With his fingers crossed, the personable Dave Thomas opened his first Wendy's Old-Fashioned Hamburgers in 1969 at 257 East Broad St., Columbus. The restaurant is still there, and Thomas has added nearly 4,000 more. Headquartered in Dublin, the company named after Dave's little girl has become the third largest of the world's hamburger giants. If there isn't a Wendy's near you, wait a minute. There will be.

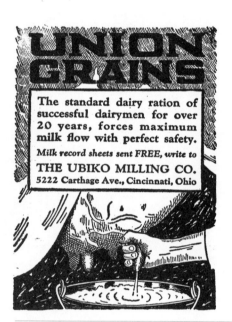

The Ohio Farmer, May 22, 1926

• Talking about personalities, we can't ignore Columbus-based White Castle Systems. With 269 outlets mainly in the Midwest, it's not the world's biggest fast-food hamburger chain, but, says a company spokesperson, it was the very first. It may also be the most unusual. White Castle opened in 1921 with a 5-cent burger, which has increased a bit in price, but lost none of its unique personality. Small, square, grilled with onions and usually purchased by the bagful, the White Castle burger has a following that's almost cult-like. ("If we knew why, we'd REALLY be rich," said the spokesperson.) Aficionados have a whole vocabulary for those little burgers, "Sliders," "Belly Bombers" and "Gutbombs" among them.

• All this talk of hamburgers brings ketchup to mind. Not all the ketchup in the world is made by Heinz—just more of it than anyone else. The biggest ketchup factory in the world is the H.J. Heinz plant in Fremont, near the heart of Ohio's tomato country. Established in 1937, the plant ships out more than 65 truckloads and two rail cars of finished Heinz products every day. That helps explain why, almost nine times out of ten, the ketchup bottle on your restaurant table is from Heinz; at least half the time the one you have at home is, too.

It's time to start thinking about dinner. Perhaps you'll have it at home tonight.

• If you need to stop at the grocery store, it may well be at a Kroger's. The Cincinnati-based firm is the nation's largest food retailer (based on revenue). At last count, the company had 1,274 food stores and 940 convenience outlets. Everything about Kroger is big: its sales in 1992 totaled $22.1 billion (bigger than the gross national products of many small countries) and it employed 185,000 people. Today, Kroger's modern 25-story headquarters building is only a few blocks from where Barney Kroger opened his first store in 1883.

• In Columbus, Teresa Marzetti, born in Italy and widowed at 28, turned an OSU campus restaurant into a student favorite early in this century. A downtown Marzetti's became so well known for its salad dressings that it began selling them in grocery stores. Today, Marzetti's is the nation's third largest manufacturer of salad dressing; for two decades it has also been the number-one seller of slaw dressing.

• Another Ohio family food enterprise that just growed like Topsy was that of Abraham and Mahala Stouffer. Starting with a stand-up dairy counter in downtown Cleveland, the Stouffers built a restaurant, hotel and frozen food empire. The Stouffer name may be best known for its Lean Cuisine line of calorie-controlled foods, the name many dieters think of when they're making New Year's resolutions. Now owned by Nestlé, Stouffer Foods headquarters are in the Cleveland suburb of Solon.

• In 1911 Procter & Gamble introduced a revolutionary vegetable oil shortening, called Crisco. Still made in P&G's Ivorydale plant in Cincinnati, Crisco adds richness and tenderness to cakes. It is made primarily from soybeans, of which Ohio farmers grew 3,800,000 acres in 1991.

• Perhaps the kids would like some candy after dinner. Around Christmas they might ask for candy canes, which just happen to be made in

Bryan by Spangler Candy Co. Founded by a Spangler in 1906, the company is still run by Spanglers. Their northwest Ohio candy factory produces one and half million candy canes a day, as well as six million of those famous Dum-Dum lollipops. Yes, Dum-Dums come from Bryan, Ohio. Be careful where you say that.

These Ohio firms are giants in the food industry, but for sheer size, all in one place, nothing beats the Behemoth of Northwest Ohio. Sprawled along on the south bank of the Maumee River is the giant of giants: Campbell Soup's Napoleon factory. As Saddam Hussein might put it in his inimitable way, this is the mother of all food plants.

Conventional wisdom has it that this is the biggest food processing plant in the world. Company spokesperson Tim Thompson, a little more cautious, prefers to call it only the world's biggest *thermal processor* (meaning the food is cooked right in the can). A fellow worker, hearing this, tells him he is splitting hairs and the Colossus of the Maumee is unsurpassed. Whatever; this is one humongous soup kitchen by any standard.

The Napoleon plant doesn't produce just soup, although Campbell's does make upwards of 350 different flavors, sizes and labels of the stuff. This plant also makes Prego spaghetti sauce, Open Pit Barbecue sauce, V-8 vegetable cocktail and enough other foods so that it takes 700 trucks every day to bring in the fresh ingredients and haul away the finished product. Campbell's employs between 2,600 and 3,300 people, depending on the season, and runs three shifts, meaning that "soup's on" in Napoleon 24 hours a day.

Campbell's came to Napoleon in 1948 when it bought a local beverage plant that was making V-8 vegetable cocktail. Northwest Ohio is tomato country, of course, and the region is lush with other vegetables as well, so what better place could there be to make soup and juice? Campbell's couldn't think of any, so in 1952, it began building its biggest soup plant, right next to the beverage factory. The new building is so big it took five years to build, but the Campbell's people had their thinking caps on: first they built the world's largest on-site can factory—"a factory within factory," Tim Thompson calls it—so they would have some place to put all that soup.

Even an introductory tour of the soup plant, conducted by Thompson at a relentless pace, takes nearly three hours; it covers 55 acres and, combined with the beverage plant, stretches for nearly a mile along the river. A visitor has the feeling he has entered a world created from Charlie Chaplin's *Modern Times* and Stanley Kubrick's *2001: A Space Odyssey*. The highly automated facility is a cacophony of sounds, soupy aromas and flashing images, with only an occasional human being, dressed in white, in sight. Parallel streams of vegetables—here, carrots; there, potatoes; mushrooms and celery further over—flow through washing, trimming and inspection, inexorably moving toward their doom in huge kettles that warm and mix 300 to 700 gallons of ingredients at once. Nearby, a noodle machine spins out endless sheet of pasta headed for a rendezvous with chicken. After blending, the ingredients pour into cans, which are sealed and then cooked before being popped into cartons and stacked on pallets by robots. Overhead, shining cans, not yet labeled, go glimmering by on a maze of tiny conveyor belts that resemble toy train tracks suspended in air. On the floor below, lift trucks race back and forth, sounding their horns as they lug ingredients to one end of the system and haul away finished product from the other. You get the feeling workers here know there are a lot of hungry people just beyond the plant walls, banging their spoons, and demanding their soup.

And apparently there are. Since inventing condensed soup nearly a century ago, Campbell's has become the ninth largest food packager in the nation, so big it introduced 70 new products in just one three-month period recently. Surveys show the Campbell's name is second only to Coca-Cola in brand recognition. Its command of the soup market is overwhelming, selling nearly two-thirds of all kinds of soup in the United States. Of condensed soup alone, Campbell's has an 81 or 82 percent market share. King of the American soup bowl, Campbell's now wants to become a world power. It is hungrily eying countries like China (which reportedly consumes more soup in one month than the United States does in a year) and saying to itself, "M'm! M'm good!"

But you don't have to be big to be successful in food in Ohio. One example is the Rothschild Berry Farm, where ingenuity has turned a raspberry patch into a gold mine. Robert Rothschild was a construction engineer in California who decided to make a lifestyle change and wound up on a 170-acre farm in Urbana. After several years of experimentation, the Rothschild family began to concentrate on growing raspberries and, in 1984, making of condiments from them: fruit sauces, vinegars, mustards, fruits in liqueur, conserves, and chutney. Fancy packaging became such a hallmark of Rothschild products that in 1991 they won the National Association of Specialty Food Trade's "Outstanding Product Line" award. Today Rothschild products are found in 4,000 gourmet and specialty food shops across the country, or they can be ordered direct: Rothschild Berry Farm, Inc., 3143 East Route 36, P. O. Box 311, Urbana 43078; 800/356-8933.

Marietta, lying at the intersection of the Muskingum and Ohio rivers, is the oldest pioneer settlement in Ohio. It dates to 1788, when Revolutionary War veterans came to explore what was then America's western frontier. Nearly 200 years later, another pioneer came along: John Rossi. *He* wanted to explore the frontiers of pasta. Rossi was an art student who got into the pasta business as an graduate student at OU; since then he has developed a line of pasta in over 30 flavors, ranging from tomato-basil-garlic to saffron. He also offers five varieties of sauces, and is adding more. Rossi's "designer pasta" is so successful that he and his crew now make 4,000 pounds a day in the busy season. Like Rothschild's, Rossi products are sold across the country. (For sale in specialty food stores or from Rossi Pasta, 114 Greene St., Marietta 45750. Tel 800/227-6774. The Rossi pasta catalog also offers recorded music; Handel's *Water Music* is the current best seller. We are not making this up.)

Rossi's and Rothschild's are among Ohio's best-known cottage industries, but there are many others, each building their own reputations. Success in such a venture requires a harmonious blend of many different talents. Which is why, perhaps, Yuval Zaliouk has been able to turn his grandmother's recipe for twice-baked cookies into a million-dollar business with more than 5,000 wholesale accounts. Zaliouk had been conductor of the Toledo Symphony Orchestra when he and management came to a parting of the ways. Zaliouk set up YZ Enterprises and began making Original Almondina Biscuits, wafer-thin almond and raisin cookies with no fat (except for the almonds), no cholesterol, no salt and no preservatives. The cookies come in five flavors and Zaliouk is working on new products as well, but if the bottom falls out of the cookie market, he won't be out of work: Zaliouk can go back to being an attorney, which he also once was. (For sale in specialty food stores or phone 419/893-8777, fax 893-8825.)

Rothschild's, Rossi's and YZ Enterprises are brand-new starts, but there are also cottage industries that build on the past by reviving some ancient business or tradition. Such is Fowler's Mill in Chardon, once the country mill of Milo and Hiram Fowler but today the dream come true of Rick and Billie Erickson. He was an engineer in Columbus, she worked for the Lazarus department store chain, when they bought the historic mill in 1985. The original Fowlers had started a sawmill on this site in 1828 and later opened a gristmill in 1834, which stands today, housing the Erickson operation. They have revived the stone grinding; their whole-grain meals and flours contain the three major grain components: bran, endosperm and germ. The result is a more flavorful, nutritious product than conventional flour. Today the Ericksons sell five flours and eleven mixes to wholesale and retail customers. They also do custom flour blending. (The mill store is open seven days, and Fowler's products are also for sale in specialty stores in Ohio and 30 states. The Fowler's Milling Company, 12500 Fowlers Mill Road, Chardon 44024. Tel. 800/321-2024.)

Where do new foods come from? From the test kitchens of food giants as well as the kitchen ranges of budding entrepreneurs. Sometimes, though, a little outside help is needed. Ready to serve as a midwife to food ideas are what may be the state's most unusual laboratories: the pilot plants operated by the Food Industries Center, part of the College of Agriculture at Ohio State University.

Housed in the basement of OSU's Howlett Hall, the main pilot plant is several miniature food factories rolled into one. It can peel, cut, blanch, heat, freeze, extrude, fry, homogenize, ferment, and package just about anything you can imagine. (A slightly smaller pilot plant in Vivian Hall concentrates on dairy and bakery products.) The Howlett pilot plant has production lines that can process green beans or tomato juice, for example, or make new kinds of popcorn, extrude any kind of cheesy-corny-potato chip, curl or twist, or pump out slush desserts. Dr. Winston Bash oversees it as part of his job as director of the Food Industries Center. The lab is not only used for teaching and research by the university, but as a place large or small food processors can test new food products and procedures. (They pay a fee to do so: the center is self-supporting.)

Columbus-based Glory Foods, which aims to be the first nation-wide producer of African-American foods, developed much of its product line here. Another firm learned how to use trimmings from matzos to produce a new snack food. And the Food Industries Center is researching ways to concentrate tomato juice at low temperatures, which would save both flavor and cost.

Bash has another job as well: answering the state's Food Safety Hotline (800/752-2751). Underwritten by the Ohio food industry, the Hotline's Bash and a helper answer upwards of 2,000 calls a year from Ohioan worried about chemicals in food, puzzled about canning peaches, or wondering whether that turkey that's been sitting in the freezer for five years is safe to eat. (Answer: whether it was safe or not, its quality would be too poor to eat.) "Every year we have several cases—up to 10—where we played a role in saving somebody's life," says Bash, explaining that botulism, from improper food handling, as in home canning, is one of the deadliest toxins known.

And so Winston Bash spends his days with food, giving a potential new product a helping hand down in his magical basement, then coming upstairs to lay a soothing hand—by telephone—on the worried brow of an Ohio eater.

"Anything that's food, I can work with, yes," says Bash. "We have lot of fun here. We do something a little different every day."

FACES OF THE LAND

Going for the Glory

In the early 1960s, Bill Williams was a skinny black kid using his smarts to survive in big-city high school football. Williams isn't quite so skinny today but he's still using his smarts to go head-to-head with the big guys. Only this time they're REALLY big: Like Stauffer's. Quaker Oats. Green Giant.

Bill Williams is an entrepreneur. But he's more than that: he's leading a black invasion of a very white world—and trying to do some good in the process. To hearts yearning for nourishment, to folks crying out for freedom, to people hungering for satisfaction, Williams is bringing...

Food. Soul food. *Healthful* soul food. Or, as his marketing manager, Toni Shorter, prefers to call it, "African-American cuisine."

That means canned greens, home-style corn bread mix, and a dozen other dishes—with more on the way—that blacks (and many southern whites) grew up with, as part of their heritage.

It's hard to believe, but in a nation with nearly 24,000,000 Americans of African descent, no one sells a full line of prepared food products just for them. There are companies specializing in Chinese, Jewish, Hispanic and other tastes, but no African-American equivalent. A little black firm here may sell a barbecue sauce and a big white corporation there may offer corn bread mix, but nobody does it all, in depth, just for African-Americans.

Bill Williams aims to change that, and change it in a big way. In 1989, Williams and two co-workers in the food business launched Glory Foods—a name intended to evoke the joy of a beautiful sunrise or an exultant church service. The name is also a deliberate reminder of the film, *Glory*, the hit about a regiment of black soldiers who triumphed against the odds in the American Civil War.

In their own way, Bill Williams and the Glory gang—now grown to 10—may be just as audacious. The Columbus entrepreneurs are creating the nation's first broad line of prepared products for African-American (or, if you prefer, Southern) tastes. They, a minority-owned firm, are doing it in the face of a food processing and distribution establishment that is almost exclusively white. And, from their Columbus base, they hope to take Glory coast to coast.

They just may do it. The first Glory products hit Columbus area store shelves in July, 1992, appearing in 40 Kroger supermarkets. By December

Glory foods had spread to 400 stores...100% of the market in central Ohio. And the products were also being test marketed in Atlanta, Georgia, to see how they'd be received by southern whites as well as blacks. Glory was hoping performance in Atlanta would signal their potential for sale nationwide; as Williams put it laughingly, "Atlanta today, tomorrow the world."

But despite Glory's seemingly fast start, Williams was still refusing to claim success at year's end, saying only, "We're probably ahead of plan." That was in character: Williams is a cautious businessman. Glory's first line of products was the result of two years of testing at the Food Industries Center at Ohio State University (where Glory paid full price for research services, like any other customer. "This is all our own money in this," stresses Williams; no public funds are involved.) Working with Dr. Winston Bash, the Glory people manipulated such variables as cooking times and ingredients to arrive at items, from blackeye peas to hot sauce, that are, according to the Glory slogan, "just about the best."

"*Just about* the best?" That's right: Glory knows they may come close but they can't beat the taste of Mother's own—so they shouldn't claim to do so. That air of humility may be deceptive, however, for in some ways Glory is trying to outdo Mother (probably to Mother's relief). One way is to reduce soul food's image problem and raise its nutritional value by cutting salt, fat, and other problem ingredients. (That is also why Glory people prefer the more elegant term, "African-American cuisine.") And the other—and really big—way Glory will outdo Mother is to make their foods more convenient than homemade.

"I hear a lot of feedback from women," says Toni Shorter about the reception Glory products received early on. "They come up to me in church and on the street and say, 'Thank you so much for saving me time, thank you for saving my evening.' We've taken the labor out of it for them." Fresh greens, for example, take an extraordinary amount of time to prepare, with the result that African-Americans pressed for time may pass up their own foods. "That's our biggest selling point—that we're making people's lives a little easier," she says. And also preserving the flavor—literally—of African-American culture.

Bill Williams

Concern for African-American culture is worthwhile in itself, but it's also smart business. Williams knows if Glory does well, giant corporations will jump in to compete. So, he says, "We're trying to anchor ourselves in our community," pointing, for example, to the company's choice of headquarters in an old storefront at 18th and Oak in Columbus, the same black neighborhood where Williams grew up. "That's not an accident," Williams says. "We hope we can build brand loyalty so that a Stouffer's, for example, will not have the nerve to attack us for that market."

Williams believes that unless his company has "a very strong presence" in the black community—is a *force*, in other words—it might just as well be any other company. So Glory makes a point of using African-American subcontractors and professional advisors whenever it can; it urges its brokers and vendors to use African-Americans. The company has also commissioned black artists to do the company Christmas card, has helped sponsor an evening with noted black photographer Gordon Parks, is supporting fund raising for settlement houses, and hopes to establish a fellowship for a graduate student in food technology at Ohio State University.

This is more than altruism and more than public relations: it's also part of a philosophy. "Integration has worked in some ways, but it's failed in others," says Williams. "We believe our problem today is that we're not investing our dollars back in our [black] community. And those who continue to make profits off us are not investing their dollars back. I've been committed to the black community for over 30 years. All my investments are in the black community."

Williams has been cooking for even longer than he's been investing. As a precocious teenager he became known for his sauces and soups; at 18 he was *chef saucier* at a downtown hotel. Then he went to the famed Culinary Institute of America, following which he completed the restaurant-hotel administration program at the University of Massachusetts. Eventually he returned to Columbus to run restaurants for the Lazarus department stores; then he opened his own, the Marble Gang, which became known among middle-class blacks as "the place to be." The idea for Glory Foods emerged about five years before the first products reached store shelves. Williams was running another food distribution business specializing in selling to state agencies when he and fellow workers Iris McCord and Dan Charna began wondering why no one offered a full line of processed foods for African-American tastes. The scattering of products already out there weren't as good as they could be, either. "We realized there was a void in the marketplace," recalls Williams.

Within five years, Williams and his colleagues had conceived, tested and packaged the company's first product line of seventeen items: five kinds of canned greens, two kinds of peas and two of beans, okra, sweet potatoes in two sizes, hot sauce in two sizes, peppered vinegar, and two kinds of cornbread mix. The canned goods are made for Glory in South Carolina, the hot sauce in Louisiana, and the cornbread mix in Ohio. Competitively priced, Glory products are brightly dressed in labels bearing the company's rising sun logo and the promise, "Good taste for the table... good taste for the soul."

It's too early to tell if Bill Williams and his little company will achieve their dream of becoming the first black national distributor of a line of African-American foods. But one thing's for sure: blacks, hitherto largely invisible in the food products industry, are going to be a lot more visible— as consumers, as distributors, as producers.

"The grocery industry, and the food industry as a whole, does not think of the African-American community as important to them," Williams observes. "I don't think they're aware we want to participate in this economy. They think we're satisfied with our food stamps and our second-rate housing."

But the leader of the Glory gang makes this promise: "I think before we're finished we'll shake up the world."

RECIPES

Montezuma Deluxe Nachos

Chuck and Karen Evans of Powell started Sauces and Salsas, Ltd. in 1987. The business began in Karen's kitchen where Chuck would whip up sauces in the blender. Now they produce about 40 products carrying the Montezuma label, and ship them direct to customers all over the country. Their line includes salsas, marinades, hot sauces, seasonings and tortilla chips.

Spread tortilla chips on 15x10-inch jelly roll pan. In medium skillet, cook ground beef using taco seasoning mix, following directions on label. Spread over chips (if using refried beans, spread over chips before meat); sprinkle with cheese. Heat in oven or microwave oven until cheese melts. Top with peppers, onions and tomatoes; add dollop of sour cream. Serve with salsa.

Makes 4 to 6 servings

*Montezuma Tortilla Chips or Blue
  Corn Tortilla Chips
1 pound lean ground beef
Montezuma Taco Meat Seasoning
  Mix
Shredded Cheddar or Monterrey
  Jack cheese
Sliced Jalapeño peppers
Sliced green onions
Chopped tomatoes
Sour cream
Montezuma Fiesta Salsa or Green
  Chile Salsa*

Optional:
*Refried beans, Guacamole or black
  olives.*

Cheerios Toasted Party Mix

Makes 6-1/2 cups snack mix

1/4 cup butter or margarine
1/2 teaspoon salt
1/2 teaspoon Worcestershire sauce
1/4 teaspoon celery salt
1/4 teaspoon garlic salt
3 cups Cheerios cereal
2 cups pretzel sticks
1-1/2 cups mixed nuts or peanuts

While most people eat Cheerios with milk, out of a cereal bowl at breakfast time, there are other ways and times to eat them. Here's one example of how to party hardy with those little round O's.

Preheat oven to 275 degrees. In 13x9-inch baking pan, melt butter in oven. Stir in salt, Worcestershire, celery salt and garlic salt. Add cereal, pretzels and nuts; stir until well coated. Bake 45 minutes, stirring occasionally. Store tightly covered.

Waldorf Slaw Salad

Makes 4 to 6 servings

6 cups coarsely shredded green
  cabbage
1 large all-purpose apple, cored and
  chopped
1/2 cup raisins
1 cup Marzetti Slaw Dressing
1/4 cup chopped walnuts

The T. Marzetti Co. of Columbus advertises its slaw dressing as, "The best you ever slaw." Imaginative cooks use it in a variety of ways in the kitchen—as a dip for shrimp or vegetables, for example, or to add to potato, chicken or tuna salad. The following recipe is an interesting variation on the classic Waldorf Salad.

In large bowl, combine cabbage, apple and raisins; mix well. Add dressing; toss lightly until ingredients are lightly coated. Refrigerate at least 1 hour to blend flavors. Just before serving, add walnuts; mix well. If desired, garnish each serving with additional apples slices dipped in lemon juice to prevent browning.

Heinz Super Burger Sauce

Makes about 1 cup

1/2 cup sour cream
1/4 cup Heinz Tomato Ketchup
1/4 cup finely chopped Heinz Dill
  Pickles or well-drained Heinz
  Sweet or India Relish
1 tablespoon prepared horseradish
1/4 teaspoon salt

Heinz, which introduced its ketchup in 1876, today sells the equivalent of more than one billion 14-ounce bottles a year. Its biggest ketchup plant is in Fremont. There is no condiment more midwestern than ketchup. Pickles are another important Ohio product, so this sauce is a good way to dedicate your burger to dear old Ohio.

In medium bowl, combine all ingredients. Cover; refrigerate at least two hours to blend flavors. Serve as a topping for hamburgers, cheeseburgers or cold beef sandwiches.

Johnny Marzetti

The story behind the T. Marzetti Company began in 1896, when 13-year old Teresa Marzetti left her home near Florence, Italy, and came to Columbus. From 1901 until 1972—the year of Teresa's death—there were Marzetti restaurants in Columbus. Today, Marzetti's is known for its salad dressings instead.

The following recipe is similar to the casserole served at Marzetti's early restaurant. Almost every Ohio community cookbook has a different recipe for this dish. It has been a favorite over the years among budget-pinched students, mothers of large families, and anyone needing an economical dish to pass at a social gathering. It also makes a good dinner for a busy family, as it can be prepared ahead of time and reheated before serving. Team it up with a salad and crusty bread, and it makes a complete, satisfying meal.

In large skillet, brown ground beef; drain. Add mushrooms, celery, green pepper, onion, and garlic; cook 5 minutes. Add tomatoes, tomato sauce, salt and pepper; bring to a boil. Reduce heat; add macaroni and cheese. Serve immediately, or place mixture in 2-quart baking dish; refrigerate. Bake at 350 degrees for 45 to 50 minutes or until hot.

Makes 4 to 6 servings

*1 to 1-1/2 pounds lean ground beef
1 cup sliced fresh mushrooms
1/2 cup each chopped celery, green pepper and onion
2 cloves garlic, finely chopped
1 (16-ounce) can tomatoes, undrained and broken up
1 (8-ounce) can tomato sauce
1/2 teaspoon salt
1/8 teaspoon pepper
1 (8-ounce) package elbow macaroni, cooked and drained
2 cups (8 ounces) shredded Cheddar cheese*

Bob Evans Farms Hearty Meat Loaf

Bob Evans Farms, Inc., headquartered in Columbus, operates 292 restaurants in 19 states and produces and distributes a variety of food products in 26 states. From Memorial Day through Labor Day the Bob Evans Farm in Rio Grande is a popular spot to visit. It offers riding trails, canoeing, a modern riding arena, hiking, picnic facilities, and, oh yes, a sausage shop. Sausage, of course, is a key ingredient in this homey recipe.

Preheat oven to 350 degrees. In small bowl, combine ketchup, sugar and mustard. In large bowl, combine remaining ingredients and 1/3 cup sauce; mix well. In 13x9-inch baking dish, shape into loaf. Bake 1 hour; remove from oven. Spoon remaining sauce over loaf; bake an additional 10 minutes.

MICROWAVE: Mix meat loaf as directed above. In 9-inch pie plate or casserole, shape into ring; cook at 100% power (high) 13 to 15 minutes or until loaf is firm, turning twice during cooking. Spoon remaining sauce over loaf; cook at 100% power 3 minutes. Let stand 5 minutes before serving.

Makes 6 to 8 servings

*1/2 cup ketchup
2 teaspoons brown sugar
1 teaspoon dry mustard
1 (1-pound) roll Bob Evans Farms Original Recipe Sausage
1 pound lean ground beef
1 cup quick cooking oats
1/2 cup chopped onion
1 egg, slightly beaten
1 teaspoon salt
1/4 teaspoon pepper*

Chef Tom's Honey Apple Chops

Makes 4 servings

4 boneless center loin pork chops
1-1/2 cups apple cider or juice
1/4 cup lemon juice
1/4 cup soy sauce
2 tablespoons honey
2 cloves garlic, finely chopped
1/4 teaspoon pepper

Tom Douglas is the certified executive chef for the Kroger Co. A resource person for those who shop in Kroger stores across the state, he gets many phone calls from customers who cannot find a certain ingredient or are unsure of what a recipe is calling for. He also develops recipes.

These savory marinated pork chops are ideal for the barbecue grill. Tom suggests serving them with a hot stuffed baked potato, steamed fresh asparagus and fresh fruit salad.

In shallow glass dish, or resealable plastic bag, place chops. In small bowl or jar with tight-fitting lid, combine remaining ingredients; shake well. Pour over chops. Cover; refrigerate 6 hours or overnight, turning occasionally. Grill or broil as desired, brushing occasionally with marinade.

Smucker's Apricot Chicken

Makes 4 to 6 servings

1/2 cup Smucker's Apricot Preserves
1/4 cup chopped onion
2 tablespoons soy sauce
1 tablespoon lemon juice
1 tablespoon chopped fresh parsley
1/8 teaspoon oregano leaves
1 (2-1/2- to 3-pound) broiler fryer
  chicken, cut up

Vickie Limbach, communications manager for the J. M. Smucker Co., the jam and jelly producer in Orrville, suggests serving this chicken with hot cooked rice. There is plenty of sauce from the chicken to spooon over it.

In shallow glass-dish, or resealable plastic bag, place chicken pieces. In small bowl or jar with tight-fitting lid, combine remaining ingredients; shake well. Pour over chicken. Cover; refrigerate 6 hours or overnight. Preheat oven to 350 degrees. Drain chicken, reserving marinade. Place chicken on 15x10-inch jelly roll pan; bake 45 to 50 minutes or until chicken is tender and lightly browned, basting occasionally with marinade.

Rossi Pasta with Peas, Onions and Eggs

Like John Rossi, the art-student-turned-pasta-entrepreneur of southeast Ohio, this recipe shows great versatility. Not just spaghetti any more, pasta here is deliciously combined with three Midwestern ingredients.

In large skillet, melt butter; add oil. Add onion and garlic; cook one minute. Add peas, pasta, eggs, milk and half the cheese; stir vigorously over medium-high heat. Add vinegar and tamari; stir well. Reduce heat to low; cover, cook 2 minutes. Uncover; squeeze lemon half over top of pasta, add pepper to taste. Serve with lemon wedges.

Makes 2 servings

2 tablespoons butter or margarine
2 tablespoons olive oil
1 medium onion, chopped
2 cloves garlic, finely chopped
1 cup frozen green peas, rinsed with
  hot water and drained
8 ounces Rossi Pasta (any flavor),
  cooked and drained according to
  package directions
3 eggs, slightly beaten
1/2 cup milk
1/2 cup grated Parmesan or Romano
  cheese
1 tablespoon balsamic vinegar
1 tablespoon tamari or soy sauce
Juice from 1/2 lemon
Pepper
Lemon wedges

Magic Cookie Bars

In the early 1900s cooks began using Eagle Brand Sweetened Condensed Milk to make desserts, although this was not the reason Gail Borden developed the milk. In the mid-1800s, he developed sweetened condensed milk, a vacuum-cooked milk product that would not spoil when left unrefrigerated. During the era of the Civil War, the product was used by the military and also for used in infant formulas; it was credited with saving lives in both situations.

Many recipes using Eagle Brand Sweetened Condensed Milk have become classics, one being Magic Cookie Bars. Similar recipes appear in many Ohio community cookbooks, under such names as "Hello Dolly Bars" or "7-Layer Bars."

Preheat oven to 350 degrees (325 degrees for glass dish). In 13x9-inch baking pan, melt butter in oven. Sprinkle crumbs over butter; pour sweetened condensed milk evenly over crumbs. Sprinkle with chips then coconut and nuts; press down firmly. Bake 25 to 30 minutes or until lightly browned. Cool; cut into bars. Store loosely covered at room temperature.

Makes 36 bars

1/2 cup butter or margarine
1-1/2 cups graham cracker crumbs
1 (14-ounce) can Eagle Brand
  Sweetened Milk (not evaporated
  milk)
1 cup semi-sweet chocolate chips
1 (3-1/2-ounce) can flaked coconut
  (1-1/3 cups)
1 cup chopped nuts

Krema Prima Peanut Butter Pie

Makes one 9-inch pie

1 cup milk
1 pound high quality semi-sweet
*   chocolate, finely chopped*
1 (9-inch) baked pastry shell
2 cups (1 pint) whipping cream
2 tablespoons sugar
2 tablespoons Krema Creamy
*   Peanut Butter*
Chocolate curls

Founded in 1898, Krema Products Co. is a Columbus institution and a regional producer of gourmet nuts, peanut butter and other nut products. Krema began producing peanut butter without preservatives or additives in 1909, making it the oldest producer of peanut butter in the nation. In the 1950s mass-produced peanut butters with preservatives began to dominate the market, but recent interest in health and natural ingredients has revitalized Krema sales. In 1988, R. Craig Sonksen, an investment banker for Chemical Banking Corp. in Tokyo, and three partners bought the Krema Co.

Claire Lehoux, former pastry chef at the Hyatt Regency, Columbus, developed this pie for the Ultra-Chocolata Dessert Bar in The Peppercorn Duck Club Restaurant.

In small saucepan, heat milk; pour over chocolate. Stir until melted; pour into pastry shell. Refrigerate one hour. In large mixer bowl, beat cream until soft peaks form; gradually adding sugar, continue beating until stiff peaks form. Fold in peanut butter. Turn mixture into pastry shell, spreading to edge of pie crust. Top with chocolate curls. Refrigerate at least one hour.

Lazarus-Style Cheesecake

Makes one 9-inch cake

Crust:
1-3/4 cup graham cracker crumbs
1/3 cup butter or margarine, melted
1/4 cup sugar

Filling:
3 (8-ounce) packages cream cheese,
*   softened*
1-1/2 cups sugar
4 eggs
1 tablespoon vanilla extract

Topping:
1-1/2 cups (12 ounces) sour cream
1/4 cup sugar
1 teaspoon vanilla extract

Today the Lazarus department store chain has 33 dining facilities in 19 stores. One of the favorite desserts served has been Lazarus's own cheesecake. Versions have appeared in many local community cookbooks. This recipe, inspired by one from Mary Rob Clodfelter, editor of the Delaware (Ohio) *This Week* community newspaper, is an amalgam of the best recipes for Lazarus-style cheesecake.

In medium bowl, combine crust ingredients; mix well. Press mixture on bottom and side of 9-inch springform pan. In large mixer bowl, beat cheese and sugar for 5 minutes; add eggs and vanilla. Beat 30 minutes on medium speed. Preheat oven to 300 degrees. Pour filling into crust. Bake for 1 hour; remove from oven, cool 20 minutes. In small mixer bowl, combine topping ingredients; pour over cooled cake. Return to oven for 10 minutes. Cool; refrigerate.

Di's Ohio Sour Cherry Pie

This is the recipe that won Diane Cordial of Powell the Grand Prize at Crisco's American Pie Celebration National Championship in 1991. A distinguished panel of food experts from across the country saluted Di and declared her Ohio pie the best pie in America, beating entries from the 49 other states. Crisco, of course, is a product of Ohio-based Procter & Gamble. Way to go, Bucks!

In medium saucepan, combine sugar and cornstarch; add cherries. Cook and stir on medium heat until mixture comes to a boil. Remove from heat; stir in butter, extracts and food color. Let stand for one hour at room temperature.

Preheat oven to 375 degrees. In medium bowl, combine flour, sugar and salt; cut in shortening until crumbly. Add egg and vinegar; stir until dough forms a ball. Divide into thirds. On floured surface, roll each third out to 1/8-inch thickness. Line pie plate; trim edges even with plate. Turn cherry filling into pastry lined plate. On second pastry circle, cut out the word "Ohio" and a shape of the state. Moisten edges of pastry in plate; lift second pastry circle onto filling. Trim 1/2-inch beyond edge of pie plate; fold top edge under bottom crust, flute edges. Brush top of pie with milk; sprinkle with sugar. Bake 35 to 40 minutes or until golden brown.

With third pastry circle, cut out 3-inch shapes of the state of Ohio; cut small hole in center of each. Bake for 5 to 8 minutes or until golden brown; cool. To serve pie, place maraschino cherry piece in each hole. Place cutout on toothpick; insert in each piece of pie.

Makes one 9-inch pie

Filling:
1 (20-ounce) bag frozen, unsweetened, pitted tart cherries, thawed (4 cups)
1-1/4 cups sugar
1/4 cup cornstarch
2 tablespoons butter or margarine
1/2 teaspoon almond extract
1/2 teaspoon vanilla extract
1 to 2 drops red food color

Pastry:
3 cups flour
2 tablespoons sugar
1 teaspoon salt
1 cup Crisco solid vegetable shortening
1/2 cup water
1 egg, slightly beaten
1 tablespoon vinegar
1 tablespoon milk
1 tablespoon sugar

Stouffer's Original Dutch Apple Pie

Makes one 9-inch pie

Pastry:
1 cup flour
1/2 teaspoon salt
1/3 cup solid vegetable shortening or
  lard
2-1/2 to 3 tablespoons ice water

Filling:
4 cups peeled, cored and cubed
  Jonathan, Winesap or McIntosh
  apples
1/8 teaspoon ground cinnamon
1-3/4 cups sugar
1/4 cup flour
1/2 teaspoon salt
3 tablespoons milk
6 tablespoons light coffee cream

The Stouffer Food Corporation got its start in 1922 as a stand-up dairy counter run by Abraham E. Stouffer in the Arcade in downtown Cleveland. When customers began asking for dessert, his wife, Lena, would send down her own Dutch Apple Pies. Not ordinary apple pies, but ones made with fresh apples baked with cream and cinnamon sauce.

Stouffer's has probably baked and served two hundred different kinds of pies for customers over the years. The all-time favorite was the very first pie ever served at Stouffer's: Dutch Apple Pie. This is Mother Stouffer's original recipe.

In medium bowl, combine flour and salt; cut in shortening until crumbly. Add water; mix lightly with a fork until dough forms a ball. Cover; chill thoroughly.

Preheat oven to 375 degrees. On lightly floured surface, roll dough to 1/8-inch thickness. Line pie plate, lifting and smoothing dough to remove air bubbles, taking care not to stretch it. Trim 1/2-inch beyond edge of pie plate; fold top edge under; flute edge. Spread apples evenly in pie shell; sprinkle with cinnamon.

In small mixer bowl, combine remaining ingredients; beat at medium speed for 8 to 10 minutes. Pour evenly over apples. Bake 1-1/4 hours or until golden brown. Serve warm.

Campbell's Tomato Soup Cake

For 50 years cooks have been baking Campbell's Tomato Soup Cake; it's become a classic. Cooks like this cake for its moistness and flavor. The cream cheese frosting makes a perfect topping for it.

If you prefer, you may bake the cake in a 13x9-inch pan; baking times remain the same.

Preheat oven to 350 degrees. Sift dry ingredients together into large mixer bowl; add shortening and soup. Beat at low to medium speed for 2 minutes, scraping sides and bottom of bowl constantly. Add eggs and water; beat 2 minutes, scraping bowl frequently. Pour into two greased and floured 9-inch cake pans. Bake 25 to 30 minutes or until wooden pick inserted near center comes out clean. Remove from pans; cool thoroughly.

In small mixer bowl, combine cream cheese and milk; beat until fluffy. Gradually add sugar; beat well. Add vanilla. Fill and frost cake.

Makes one 9-inch layer cake

Cake:
2-1/4 cups sifted cake flour or 2 cups
   sifted all-purpose flour
1-1/3 cups sugar
4 teaspoons baking powder
1 teaspoon baking soda
1-1/2 teaspoons ground allspice
1 teaspoon ground cinnamon
1/2 teaspoon ground cloves
1 (10-3/4-ounce) can condensed
   tomato soup
2 eggs
1/4 cup water

Frosting:
2 (3-ounce) packages cream cheese,
   softened
1 tablespoon milk
1 (1-pound) package confectioners'
   sugar, sifted
1/2 teaspoon vanilla extract

Outstanding in his field—really—is A.W. Livingston of Reynoldsburg (left), the man who tamed the wild tomato and made billions of BLTs possible. In this picture from his 1896 seed catalog, Ohio's tomatic genius (and brother Ebenezer) survey a field of Buckeye State Tomatoes, just one of Livingston's many edible creations. The Livingston Seed Company lives on in Columbus, and so does great grandson A.W. Livingston (although he sold the business and company name years ago).

The Two Universes of Tomatoes

Alexander Livingston and Stanley Berry. The Paragon and Ohio 7814. From these names, all ye need to know of the tomato and the battle for its soul comes forth.

First, Livingston. He spent eighteen years of his life, in the mid-1800s, fooling with the genetics of the garden tomato. His hometown of Reynoldsburg tirelessly champions him as the father of the tomato as you and I know it. The results are with us today: his first truly successful hybrid he dubbed the Paragon, a variety still available and still popular. The Paragon. It is a word used to describe hundred-carat diamonds, perfect pearls, ultimates and epitomes.

Now fast forward a hundred years or so, to a genial and intense plant geneticist at the Agricultural Research and Development Center in Wooster, a man named Stanley Berry. His life's work, like Livingston's, has been in large part tomatic. Like Livingston, Dr. Berry has gotten several varieties out the door, hybrids that these days are planted over thousands of acres of northwest Ohio and the rest of the Western Hemisphere. Of these, his first big hit is known as "Ohio 7814," which is not to be confused with Ohio 7870 or Ohio 7903, or, for that matter, Ohio 3.14159, which is no doubt in the works somewhere. Ohio 7814. It is an *industrial* label, one used to denote something that was engineered. Something high tech.

Alexander Livingston and the Paragon, on the one hand; Stanley Berry and Ohio 7814, on the other. Two gentlemen and their tomatoes, but what a difference. For the tomato embodies a clash of ideals that throughout human history has drawn battle lines through every topic, from the aesthetics of architecture to what should be used to thicken gravy. The tomato reflects a blindness that post-modern literary critics find in us all: our inability to realize that there may not just one ideal, one particular paragon, with all else pale before it. The tomato *difference* exists because there are really two kinds of tomatoes, and only two; many hundreds of varieties of tomatoes, of course, but really two entirely different...events, existences, *universes*. And when one is mistaken for the other, both suffer from the misapprehension. One universe is that of Mr. Livingston. The other is that of Dr. Berry.

The Paragon universe of Livingston and those of like mind is a place where tomatoes are grown by people who may be somewhat dotty about them, connected to the tomato in a kind of spiritual kinship. The tomato grown in this universe is a product of art, science, craft and heart. It is carried into the house in a floppy cap darkened by the sweat of the gardener's brow and served within minutes or hours of picking and within sight of its birthplace. Or it is presented to some worthy soul as a gift, an offering that has overtones of ritual.

These are tomatoes on a first-name basis with the good folk who grew them. They are not for sale except in two circumstances that are themselves ritualistic. The first is at a farm stand by the side of a picturesque country road, preferably in a transaction between a tomato lover in a car and a coffee can with a slot in the lid. Cute children in regional dress may serve as supporting cast. Signs should include at least three variant spellings, at least one of which should cause the tomato buyer at least a dozen miles of contemplation.

Courtesy of Martha Savage

The other commercial theater is the community farmers' market, where growers years ago learned to sell both sizzle and beefsteak. The preferred sales pitch goes something like this: "That (or "That *there*...") is a Rosa Lee tomato, and those are Western Plums; the big one's there are Mary's Choice; they're firmer than the Rosa Lees, but not quite so juicy as the Western Plums." And so on, a patter that lets the buyer know that the "farmer" (who may be an accountant with a large backyard garden and enough sense to wear overalls to market, even if he bought them from J. Crew) is somehow simpatico with tomatoes. That it's not just a job, it's a calling.

A truck gardener at the Athens Farmers' Market, oblivious to his neighbor's incantations of lovely and evocative names, once answered a prospective customer's question of "What are those?" by saying, with evident astonishment, "They're *tomatoes*." He lost a sale but learned a lesson. Now he names them one and all, even if they ARE just tomatoes. "Reubens Red Stars" are what he sells now, a name he made up and had one of his children crayon onto a piece of cardboard. Not only does he sell out, he's able to get a premium. He's thinking about naming the green beans next. This is the world where one lusts to know tomatoes on a first-name basis.

By contrast, the universe of Ohio 7814 is as folksy as the space shuttle and as homespun as a computer. It is the place where the best tomatoes are ones that ripen within hours of each other and fall off the vine, as though by divine intervention, onto a conveyor belt. Operating the belt is someone who not only will sell his tomatoes without bidding them farewell, but will sell them eight months before they're planted to a buyer making choices based on a laboratory analysis and a spreadsheet.

This is the universe of tomatoes by the ton, by the hundreds of tons. It is the universe that created tomatoes to be harvested green and "ripened" by dunking in tanks of ethylene glycol, of tomatoes that grow within tenths of inches of a designated girth and then stop like Peter Pan. It is the universe that produced, with some pride and fanfare, its ultimate creation of a few years ago, the square tomato, one that takes up less space in the packing boxes and reduces overhead.

Calling attention to this last achievement was foolish if the tomato industry thought it was going to win over the tomato lovers who inhabit the Paragon universe. Anyone dotty about tomatoes would have told them that if God had meant for tomatoes to be square, then why did He outfit gardeners with round floppy caps? The square tomato was another instance of big business demonstrating that it just doesn't get it.

Contemporary tomato geneticists have tried to say "Vive la difference," to suggest patiently, as though they were talking to very small children, that certain tomato varieties—Ohio 7814, for example—are more appropriate than others—the Paragon, for example—for certain uses: for canning or sauce or soup or mid-winter salads. But they are preaching to the unconverted, to the never-to-be-converted. "You call that a *tomato?*" is the sort of sneering question asked in restaurants in February and at the cheaper sort of salad bars year round. Implicit within the question is an indictment of the good Dr. Berry and all those like him, those who have made the tomato into something that even the farsighted Mr. Livingston could probably not have imagined.

But Ohio 7814 is just as much a triumph as the Paragon, and was no more meant to replace the garden tomato than a Cleveland town house might be said to replace a Holmes County farmhouse. Ohio 7814 and its brethren are what most recipes other than that for garden salad thrive on; they are canned tomatoes and tomato sauce and tomato puree and crushed tomatoes and tomato juice and tomato paste. They are ketchup and barbecue sauce and spaghetti sauce and hot dog sauce and cream of tomato soup. They are tomatoes in February, tomatoes in ski weekend stew. Without them, in fact, there would be nothing for the Paragons, the Rosa Lees, the Susan's Scarletts, to press against, and thus, no pedestal for homegrown tomatoes to be put upon.

Ohio is a crossroads of the alternative tomato universes. On the one hand, there is the state's Great Northwest, where most of Ohio's 17,000 acres of processing tomatoes are grown, the place of the professional tomato, tomatoes like 7814. On the other hand, there are the tomatoes of Reynoldsburg, home of the Tomato Festival and the home of Alexander Livingston, he of the Paragon. In between there are the home-grown tomatoes of Mount Gilead and the tomatoes of Mount Healthy, the tomatoes of thousands of Ohio backyards and terraces and porches. In the northwest counties, tomatoes are grown by the ton for processing; in every county, tomatoes are grown for the sheer love of the tomato. When the two worlds remain separate, all is well; when the worlds converge, people get testy.

It's a pity, really, especially in a state where the tomato is such a presence. Most people are surprised to learn that Ohio is the second largest producer of processing tomatoes in the nation. Each year Ohio produces nearly a half-million tons of tomatoes, a staggering figure and testament to the *natural* suitability of northwest Ohio for the fruit.

California may produce about twenty times as many processing tomatoes as Ohio, but does it by growing them in a desert with extensive irrigation. Ohio industrial tomatoes prosper because of the natural rainfall, because of the soil, and because of the benevolence of Lake Erie, which makes for a microclimate perfect for raising vegetables. California can boast of volume, but Ohio is the tomato's natural home.

Indeed, the tomato is a force so important in Ohio that the legislature declared tomato juice the official state drink. Heinz operates the largest ketchup factory in the world in Fremont; in Napoleon, Campbell's operates what is thought to be the largest food processing complex anywhere, producing, among other things, an endless stream of tomato soup and V-8 vegetable cocktail. Thanks to people like Alexander Livingston and Stanley Berry, the tomato is a bounteous crop in Ohio—both in the backyard and in the fields of commerce.

And tomatoes are part of the culture in Ohio. One of Ohio's most beloved family businesses, Tony Packo's (of MASH fame), has long used tomatoes in its famous hot dog sauce. Toledo—hometown of the television show's Corporal Klinger and the actor who played him, Jamie Farr—is almost within sight of the tomato fields of northwestern Ohio. Likewise, the Smucker's company of Orrville still makes tomato preserves, a jam-like concoction sweetened with sugar that some tomato lovers swear by. The Henry County Fair each August includes a Tomato Festival, featuring a parade, the selection of Miss Tomato Pretty, and judging of the largest ripe tomato "based solely on weight." At the Reynoldsburg Tomato Festival every September prizes are awarded for inventive tomato use, and vendors offer tomato cookies, tomato pie, tomato fudge, tomato marmalade and fried green tomatoes, which were popular in Reynoldsburg long before anyone thought to put them in a movie. The Columbian House restaurant in Waterville is one of the last places to find tomato pudding, which is indescribable—sweet and tangy but, alas, apparently out of style elsewhere in Ohio.

To describe a love affair with the tomato suggests something of its confused and mythic history, much of which has been debunked. Everyone "knows" that the tomato was long considered poisonous, although it was so regarded only by some people in some places at some times. The real key to this mystery seems to be in the tomato's supposed sensuality—there are references to the "love apple" and its aphrodisiac qualities in European documents of the sixteenth century, impressions that may well have arisen from the tomato's origins in the New World, with its wild red Indians and the like. And most early New World recipe books and cookbooks advised the cooking of tomatoes for many hours to banish the "toxins" within—which may have been a way of removing the aphrodisiac without calling attention to it. After all, why stir up curiosity about something so sensual?

That tomatoes retain their emotive powers even today is apparent. There are few other foods that provoke such deep divisions, such spirit, perhaps because so few foods have such variety and variability: no

Courtesy of Martha Savage

tomatist rests on laurels for even a moment, always envisioning another ruby red horizon in the August sun. To a tomato processor in Ohio's Great Northwest, the perfect tomato in a good year is one that drops through the last slot on a Four Lane Expanding Roll Sizing Machine untouched by paid labor; to a gardener on Cincinnati's Mount Adams who grows tomato plants in tubs on the condominium balcony, the perfect tomato is one that has been coaxed and nurtured into being with the care usually lavished on prodigies headed for the Conservatory. Both tomatoes bring their growers heady pleasures, but they are pleasures of different magnitudes, different universes.

Ohio is not known particularly as a sensual state. But it is an interesting thought, this notion of something so luscious as to be stimulative, all the more interesting in a place where the tomato season is all too short and where so much energy and ingenuity has been applied, over time, to preserving some of its qualities for the long hard winter. Three hours north of that Cincinnati balcony, tomatoes are harvested and packed by the ton in stylized routines that are as businesslike and relentless, as the picking of a single ripe tomato is silent and voluptuous. No other proof is needed that indeed, there are two discrete worlds of tomatoes. In Ohio, they exist side by side.

POSTSCRIPT: *The Reynoldsburg Tomato Festival is held early every September; call 614/TOMATO-1 for information. The Henry County Fair in mid-August also includes a Tomato Festival with a parade and a pageant at which the Tomato Queen is crowned (419/592-9096).*

FACES OF THE LAND

Angel of the
the Black Swamp

A worker, in clothes stained from the field, has come into FLOC's
Toledo office from one of the migrant labor camps that dot the
farmlands of northwest Ohio. His wife and little girl huddle next to him as
he waits, twisting and untwisting his fingers. Soon the family disappears
into the office of FLOC President Baldemar Velasquez; they look more
cheerful when they emerge an hour later. Velasquez walks them to the
door, shaking the man's hand, touching the wife on the shoulder, patting
the little girl on the head.

Another day has begun at the threadbare headquarters of FLOC, the
Farm Labor Organizing Committee, and Velasquez is doing what he does
best: being an angel of mercy. It's an analogy some people find hard to
avoid and others find hard to believe.

For Velasquez is the soft-spoken but tough-minded leader of a labor
union, a disarmingly non-confrontational specialist in the art of confron-
tation. A small man with soft brown eyes and a quiet manner, Velasquez
has been arrested more than 30 times. Asked if he could be termed "a
gentle radical," he shrugs his shoulders, smiles slightly, and says, "Call
me what you will."

Jorge, the man who came to see Velasquez, had brought his family over
a thousand miles to work the cucumber and tomato harvest. But rain cut
the crop and the family didn't even have enough money to get back to
Texas. That's not unusual in the hard world of migrant workers like Jorge;
FLOC says that a typical migrant family of six—with father, mother and
oldest children working—averages $10,000 to $12,000 a year from all
sources, well below the U.S. poverty line. (FLOC also says they have half
as much education as other Americans and life spans 20 years shorter.)

Still, each year thousands come from Florida and Texas for the harvest
in northwest Ohio, a region once so dank and thickly forested that it was
called the Black Swamp. Today, cleared and drained, its rich farmland is
the heart of Ohio's cucumber and tomato country. From here come many
of America's pickles and much of its ketchup. Here, for several weeks late
each summer, the migrants live in tiny cabins and pray it doesn't rain.
"We're talking about hardworking men and women, out here to do a job
that no one else wants to do," says Velasquez. "Even with the decline of
the auto industry, with all those people in Toledo unemployed—they

weren't running out to the pickle fields to get that kind of job. That's a job that nobody [else] wants under any circumstances."

Bent by the weight of centuries of agricultural practice, this stoop labor force toils almost within sight of the gleaming office towers of northwest Ohio. Its members are largely invisible to local folks, but sometimes from a side road, early on a misty morning, you can see their bent-over figures—men, women, and occasionally children—moving like ghosts across the fields. It is to these people—*his* people—that Velasquez has dedicated his life. "That's what I came out of—a family just like that," he says, referring to Jorge's family. Velasquez's parents were migrant workers, and he can remember picking Texas cotton as a child, dragging a bag bigger than he was. ("I started working when I was 6," he recalls. "There was no other alternative, if you wanted to eat.") Later, the family was stranded in northwest Ohio, like Jorge's. They settled in Putnam County, sending Baldemar to a high school where he was the only Hispanic in his senior class.

"You're isolated, you're looked down upon," Velasquez says of the reception northwest Ohio towns can give farm workers of Mexican backgrounds. "In most communities, they just want you to come and do the work and leave. If you overstay your time, they make it very clear you're not wanted." Although he was a good student and a star football player—all while working the crops—Velasquez felt high school classmates kept him at "arm's length. They sort of tolerated you but didn't really consider you part of that inner group. It was probably the athletics that saved me: it was the only place I could take out my anger, my frustrations."

Velasquez's abilities got him into Ohio Northern University and then Bluffton College, where he says he came to understand the prejudices he had faced. "From the time I was little," says Velasquez, "I always thought when I was working out in the field, there has to be some way to do something about these things. Why can't anybody do anything?" In the late sixties, while still in college, he began to do something: he started organizing a union for migrant workers, something that had never been tried before in northwest Ohio. They said it would never work because of the difficulties in organizing scattered field workers, but Velasquez made it work: in 1992 FLOC celebrated its 25th anniversary, with more than 5,000 members enrolled and contracts with some of the biggest names in American food: Campbell, Heinz U.S.A., Vlasic, Aunt Jane Pickles and Green Bay Foods.

It wasn't easy. In the early years, farmers would have Velasquez arrested for trespassing when he approached workers. In 1978, FLOC called a strike; 2,000 workers left the tomato fields and things quickly got nasty for all concerned. FLOC supporters were roughed up, some farmers had to switch to less profitable grain crops, a canning plant in Leipsic closed permanently. More farmers began using mechanical harvesters, ending many migrants' jobs forever. But after eight years—*eight years*—of strike, a boycott of seven years, and a march by FLOC to Campbell Soup headquarters in Camden, New Jersey, the corporation signed a contract

Baldemar Velasquez

with FLOC in 1985. The major pickle producers followed.

One of FLOC's coups has been an unusual three-party negotiating system, bringing to the bargaining table not just the farmers and their workers, but the big processors like Campbell's, who FLOC considers the real power players. Another has been the gradual elimination of share-cropping, under which workers are risk-taking contractors, getting part of the crop as their compensation but none of the usual employee benefits, not even legal protection on such matters as minimum wages, hours, or child labor. Under new FLOC contracts, migrants will be treated like employees are in other industries, albeit at the lowest level. Getting four companies to agree in one year to do this, says Velasquez, "is a miracle, the work of heaven."

Religious allusions rise easily to the lips of FLOC's president, who calls his job "God's work" and decorates his office with a quote from the Bible: *If you want peace, work for justice.* Seared by his own memories, Velasquez uses community building as his theory of union organizing. It begins with recruiting members on a "face-to-face, person-to-person basis, creating individual friendships with people. You develop that rapport with somebody like Jorge and the family, the wives, the children," Velasquez explains. "It's important to listen to Jorge, to learn where his pain is. If you create a nucleus of relationships, then you create a real community that cares about each other. Then, when the call goes out, people respond."

The philosophy even applies to bargaining: "When we look at the opposition, our adversaries, we cannot look at them as unredeemable foes," says Velasquez. "We have to believe we can win them over to our side. I believe what it says in the Scriptures, that what comes out of the mouth comes out of the heart. And if you really believe in your heart that someone can be converted, well, you're not going to call him names." But this kinder, gentler approach masks something harder, as recalcitrant opponents quickly find out: when forced, Velasquez will use nationwide boycotts, letter-writing campaigns, marches and demonstrations with a steely resolve.

For his work, Velasquez has received the National Catholic Bishops' Award, a $265,000 "genius grant" from the MacArthur Foundation (most of which he put in a trust fund that will benefit FLOC), and, in the minds of many followers, angels' wings. Opponents who have felt the sting of his tactics have a darker view. A Putnam County businessman says resentful farmers believe he "dictated terms to them, rather than listening to their offers." But, says Velasquez, "We can see now just the beginnings of honest reconciliation. Many of the farmers that arrested me 10, 15 years ago for being on their farms—now I sit in their kitchens, talking with them about their problems."

Indeed, FLOC's president is sympathetic to the needs of farmers, for he recognizes the need to protect the union's job sites. And he is no soft touch for FLOC members, believing part of his job is getting workers to help themselves, to not always expect FLOC to solve their problems. Jorge, for example, was listened to sympathetically, but given no handout; instead he was given advice on community agencies he could approach himself.

Ultimately, Velasquez is perhaps best seen as an idealistic pragmatist, an angel working in a very tough world. Early one September afternoon it was time for the strategy session Velasquez has many afternoons with his field organizers. First, though, another family had arrived in the office to see him: a young couple with an infant. Talking softly in Spanish, Velasquez shook the man's hand, touched the woman's shoulder.

And, while the meeting waited, Baldemar Velasquez cooed to the baby.

POSTSCRIPT: *More information about FLOC and its work on behalf of migrant laborers is available from the Farm Labor Organizating Committee, 507 South St. Clair Street, Toledo 43602; tel. 419/243-3456.*

RECIPES

Mexican Salsa

Makes about 4 cups

3 medium fresh tomatoes, seeded
  and chopped
1 green pepper, seeded and chopped
1/2 cup chopped onion or green
  onions
1 jalapeno pepper, seeded and finely
  chopped
1 tablespoon lemon or lime juice
2 cloves garlic, finely chopped
1/2 teaspoon chili powder
1/4 teaspoon salt
2 tablespoons chopped fresh cilantro

Salsa recently surpassed ketchup in popularity in the United States. It's just another example of how other cultures have brought exciting new flavors to the American dinner table. Serve this salsa and be grateful to the American of Mexican origin, who not only brought us salsa but may well have picked the tomatoes for it.

In medium bowl, combine all ingredients except cilantro; mix well. Cover; refrigerate. Just before serving, add cilantro. Serve with tortilla chips. *

* To store salsa in refrigerator for more than 2 to 3 days, it should be cooked. Simply place prepared salsa in medium skillet; cook, stirring occasionally for 5 to 8 minutes. Cover; refrigerate.

Tomato Butter

Makes 2 pints

12 medium tomatoes, peeled* and
  cut into quarters
4 cups firmly packed light brown
  sugar
1/2 cup lemon juice
1 to 2 tablespoons ground cinnamon
1 tablespoon grated lemon rind

* To peel tomatoes easily; cover with boiling water, let stand 2 to 3 minutes. Drain: cover with cold water. Drain and peel.

Many early Ohio community cookbooks had recipes for fruit and vegetable butters, but making them is nearly a thing of the past. Fruit and vegetable butters are old-fashioned preserves made with less sugar than traditional jams and jellies. They cook quickly, require frequent stirring and low heat; the mixtures scorches easily. This recipe was adapted from two recipes in cookbooks from the 1920s, and comes from Janet Wood.

In large non-aluminum saucepan, combine all ingredients; bring to a boil. Reduce heat, simmer, uncovered two hours, stirring frequently. Pour mixture into hot, sterilized jars; seal at once. Refrigerate.

Tomato Bisque

In earlier days, it was common practice to home can tomatoes, not only by themselves, but also in the form of concentrated soup base. To make tomato soup, all you had to do was heat the soup base in one pan and an equal amount of milk in another, then combine them. Most older community cookbook in Ohio contain at least one recipe for cream of tomato soup, sometimes called tomato bisque.

In large saucepan, combine broth, canned tomatoes, celery and onion; bring to a boil. Reduce heat; cover and simmer 20 minutes. In blender or food processer, puree mixture in small batches until all mixture is pureed. In same pan, cook fresh tomatoes in butter about 5 minutes; stir in flour. Add half-and-half; over low heat, cook and stir until thickened. Stir in broth mixture and sugar; heat through (do not boil).

Makes about 1-1/2 quarts

2 cups chicken broth or stock
1 (14-1/2-ounce) can whole tomatoes, undrained and broken up
1/2 cup chopped celery
1/2 cup chopped onion
3 medium tomatoes, peeled, seeded and chopped
3 tablespoons butter or margarine
3 tablespoons flour
2 cups half-and-half or light coffee cream
1 tablespoon sugar

BLT Salad with Creamy Herb Dressing

Perhaps most Midwestern way of eating fresh tomatoes in summer is in a Bacon, Lettuce and Tomato Sandwich. After all, it combines that most typical of Ohio vegetables, the tomato, with bacon from that favorite Ohio animal, the hog. This salad offers the same flavors in a new way, and is best served on a front porch during a summer evening. (If you want to get really exotic, add a peeled and sliced avocado.)

In small bowl or jar with tight-fitting lid, combine all ingredients except romaine, tomato, croutons and bacon; shake well. Refrigerate at least 1 hour to blend flavors. Just before serving, in large salad bowl, combine remaining ingredients. Toss with dressing.

Makes 6 to 8 servings

1/4 cup each buttermilk, mayonnaise and sour cream
1 tablespoon chopped fresh parsley or 1 teaspoon dried
1/4 teaspoon basil leaves
1/4 teaspoon oregano leaves
1/4 teaspoon salt
1/8 teaspoon garlic powder
1/8 teaspoon pepper
8 cups (2 medium bunches) torn romaine or leaf lettuce
1 large tomato, sliced
1 cup seasoned croutons
8 slices bacon, cooked and crumbled

Tomato and Green Bean Salad with Lemon Vinaigrette

Makes 6 to 8 servings

1/3 cup vegetable oil
2 tablespoons balsamic vinegar
2 tablespoons lemon juice
1 tablespoon chopped fresh parsley
  or 1 teaspoon dried
2 teaspoons sugar
1 teaspoon grated lemon rind
1 clove garlic, finely chopped
1/2 teaspoon salt
1/8 teaspoon pepper
1 pound fresh green beans, cut into
  2-inch pieces
1/4 cup water
4 medium tomatoes, cut into
  eighths
1/4 cup sliced green onions
Romaine or leaf lettuce

Good friend and terrific cook Nelson Mapel prepared this salad for us one summer evening years ago. The combination of vegetables and vinaigrette was memorable. Beans were one of the main crops of the Native American settlers of Ohio. It is thought beans were brought here from the Southwest sometime during the Hopewell Indian period, which began about 350 B.C. and ended about A.D. 500.

In small bowl or jar with tight fitting lid, combine oil, vinegar, juice, parsley, sugar, rind, garlic, salt and pepper. Refrigerate at least 1 hour to blend flavors. In 12x7-inch glass baking dish, combine beans and water; cover loosely with plastic wrap, place in microwave oven. Cook on 100% power (high) 6 to 8 minutes or until crisp-tender, stirring after half the cooking time. (Or, in medium saucepan, combine beans and water; bring to a boil. Reduce heat; cover and simmer 6 to 8 minutes.) Rinse under cold water; chill. Just before serving, in large salad bowl, combine beans, tomatoes and green onions; toss with vinaigrette. Serve on lettuce.

Marinated Tomato Slices

Makes 6 servings

6 medium tomatoes, sliced crosswise
  into 1/2-inch slices
2/3 cup vegetable oil
1/4 cup white wine vinegar
1/4 cup sliced green onions
2 tablespoons chopped fresh parsley
1 teaspoon chopped fresh marjoram
  leaves, or 1/2 teaspoon dried
1 clove garlic, finely chopped
1/2 teaspoon salt
1/4 teaspoon pepper

The tomato was unknown to early Ohioans, but by the mid 1840s it had come into general use in all but the country districts. There it was still thought to be poisonous and useful only as an ornament. Fresh tomatoes still make good ornaments, but they make even better salads. This easy marinated tomato salad is perfect for when having company for a summer barbecue.

In shallow serving dish, arrange tomatoes. In small bowl or jar with tight-fitting lid, combine remaining ingredients; shake well. Pour over tomatoes. Cover and refrigerate 2 to 3 hours, occasionally spooning dressing over tomatoes.

Herb-Topped Tomatoes

The Shakers, who had four communities in Ohio at one time, were great users and producers of herbs. In fact, they were pioneers in marketing them, pointing out in advertising that herbs "stimulate appetitie, they give character to food and add charm and variety to ordinary dishes." The Shakers used herbs to flavor many different foods, and no doubt would have appreciated this recipe.

Preheat oven to 400 degrees. Salt and pepper insides of tomatoes; turn upside down on paper towels to drain. In small bowl, combine remaining ingredients except oil. Add oil gradually, tossing crumbs with fork. Divide crumb mixture evenly among tomato halves, mounding slightly; place in 12x7-inch baking dish. Bake uncovered, 20 minutes or until lightly browned.

Makes 4 to 8 servings

*4 medium tomatoes, halved cross-
  wise and seeded
Salt
Pepper
1/2 cup fresh bread crumbs, made
  from firm textured bread
1 tablespoon chopped fresh parsley
1/2 teaspoon fines herbes*
1/4 teaspoon garlic powder
2 tablespoons olive oil*

* *Fines herbes* is a commercial herb mixture of equal parts parsley, tarragon, chives and chervil. It is available in the dried herb and spice section of your grocery store.

Scalloped Tomato Casserole

The Centennial Buckeye Cookbook, was published by the women of the First Congregational Church, Marysville, in 1876. Editor Estelle Wilcox (1849-1943) set out to publish a book by women who were "good book-makers and good bread makers." The book sold over 6,000 copies the first year printed. In 1877, Estelle and her husband bought the copyright to the book and published a second edition, entitled *Buckeye Cookery and Practical Housekeeping*. Dedicated to "those plucky housewives who master their work instead of allowing it to master them," it became a best-seller and was re-published over 30 times. The 1880 edition contains a recipe for "Escaloped Tomatoes," so the history of this dish goes back more than 100 years. The recipe has more ingredients, but it is nice to know Ohio families have been enjoying scalloped tomatoes for such a long time.

Preheat oven to 350 degrees. In large skillet, cook bacon until crisp; drain off all but 2 tablespoons drippings. Add celery and onion; cook until tender. Add remaining ingredients except butter and cheese; mix well. Turn into lightly greased 1-1/2 quart baking dish. Dot with butter and sprinkle with cheese. Bake 30 minutes or until bubbly.

Makes 6 servings

*6 slices bacon, diced
1/2 cup chopped celery
1/2 cup chopped onion
1 (28-ounce) can tomatoes,
  undrained and broken up
4 slices firm textured bread, torn
  into pieces
1 tablespoon brown sugar
1/2 teaspoon salt
1/2 teaspoon summer savory leaves
1/4 teaspoon pepper
2 tablespoons butter or margarine
2 tablespoons grated Parmesan
  cheese*

Tomato Pudding

Makes 4 to 6 servings

4 cups (about 8 slices) bread cubes
1/2 cup butter or margarine, melted
1 (15-ounce) can tomato puree
1/2 to 1 cup firmly packed light
  brown sugar
1 tablespoon lemon juice
1/2 teaspoon salt
1/8 teaspoon pepper

The Columbian House in Waterville (3 North River Road, 419/878-3006) is famous for its Tomato Pudding. The exact recipe is a secret, but this is a very close approximation. (Thanks to Mary Alice Powell, food editor of The Blade, Toledo, for her help.) Tomato Pudding is a vegetable side dish that can also be served as a dessert.

The Columbian House has a long history in Waterville. The first section of the building was constructed in 1828 by John Pray, the founder of Waterville. The inn was used as an important stagecoach stop between Dayton and Detroit. The Inn was acquired in 1943 by the late Ethel Arnold of Findlay, who continued the efforts to restore the structure. She reopened it as a restaurant in 1948. During her ownership, the Columbian House was added to the National Register of Historic Places. Upon her death in 1971, her son George and his wife, Jacqueline, expanded the restaurant operation. They carry on the food heritage of the restaurant by still preparing many of the dishes for which Ethel Arnold was famous.

Preheat oven to 350 degrees. Arrange bread in lightly greased 1-quart baking dish; pour butter over bread. In medium saucepan, combine remaining ingredients; bring to a boil. Reduce heat, cover and simmer 5 minutes. Pour over bread cubes; do not stir. Bake 35 to 40 minutes or until top is puffed and dark brown.

Hartmut Handke's Oven-Roasted Tomatoes

Makes 6 to 8 servings

1/4 cup olive oil
1 teaspoon each chopped fresh basil,
  oregano and thyme leaves
2 cloves garlic, finely chopped
1 teaspoon finely chopped shallots
1/2 teaspoon salt
1/4 teaspoon pepper
2 pounds (about 20) fresh plum
  tomatoes, sliced lengthwise

Chef Hartmut Handke is one of fewer than 50 American Culinary Federation Certified Master Chefs in the United States. The opening of his own restaurant, Handke's Cuisine (520 South Front Street, German Village, 614/621-2500), marked his return to Columbus after serving as executive chef at the Greenbrier Resort in West Virginia. Over 35 years of cooking in Germany, Switzerland, Holland, the Bahamas, Jamaica, Eluthera and Antigua has given him experience on a global scale. As member of two U.S. Culinary "Olympic Teams" in 1984 and 1988, Chef Handke helped American chefs win world champion status. In 1992, Chef Handke won the American Culinary Federation National Chef Professionalism Award.

Preheat oven to 250 degrees. In medium bowl, combine all ingredients except tomatoes; mix well. Add tomatoes; stir until lightly coated. Lay tomatoes in a single layer on broiler pan, or on cooking rack placed on 15x10-inch jellyroll pan. Bake for 2 hours. Cool.

Fresh Tomato Pasta Sauce

This recipe was created one summer evening when pantry supplies were low but fresh tomatoes abundant. It was an instant success. It can be served as a side dish or as a light pasta meal. You can enjoy it while thinking of pasta's American history. That Man for All Seasons, Thomas Jefferson, wrote a recipe for pasta and designed a machine for shaping it into macaroni. A hundred years later, Estelle Woods Wilcox included a recipe for Macaroni with Tomatoes in the 1880 edition of that best-seller, *Buckeye Cookery and Practical Housekeeping.*

In large skillet, cook garlic in oil until golden brown. Add tomatoes, basil and salt; bring to a boil. Reduce heat; simmer uncovered 5 to 10 minutes or until some of the liquid has evaporated. In large bowl, toss hot pasta with tomato mixture and cheeses; serve immediately.

Makes 4 to 6 servings

2 cloves garlic, finely chopped
2 tablespoons olive oil
3 medium tomatoes, seeded and chopped
2 tablespoons chopped fresh basil leaves or 1-1/2 teaspoons dried
1/4 teaspoon salt
1 cup (4 ounces) shredded Mozzarella cheese
1/4 cup grated Parmesan cheese
8 ounces pasta (any shape desired), cooked and drained

Christophers Marinara Sauce

Christophers is a restaurant specializing in American fine dining from atop The Vern Riffe Center in downtown Columbus (77 South High Street, 614/224-4100). Chef Roland Fellows is constantly developing recipes that utilize Ohio products and freshly grown local produce. He says that, although modern technology has made foods available from around the world, their best produce seems to come from employees' gardens. This wonderful marinara sauce can be frozen in batches for use at a later time.

In large kettle, cook carrot, onion and garlic in oil until tender. Add remaining ingredients except salt and tomato juice; bring to a boil. Reduce heat; cover and simmer one hour, stirring occasionally. Remove bay leaf; cool slightly. In blender or food processor, puree mixture in small batches until all mixture is pureed. Salt to taste. If mixture is too thick, add tomato juice as needed.

Makes about 8 cups

1 medium carrot, finely chopped
1 medium onion, finely chopped
8 cloves garlic, finely chopped
6 tablespoons olive oil
1 (28-ounce) can whole tomatoes, undrained and broken up
1-1/2 teaspoons basil leaves
1 teaspoon each oregano leaves, paprika, pepper and sugar
1/2 teaspoon thyme leaves
1 bay leaf
Salt
Canned tomato juice

Fried Green Tomatoes

Makes 4 servings

1 cup yellow cornmeal
1/2 cup flour
1/4 teaspoon salt
1/8 teaspoon pepper
6 green tomatoes, sliced crosswise
  into 1/2-inch slices
Vegetable oil
2 tablespoons brown sugar

Fried green tomatoes have always been thought of as a down home dish. The 1992 movie by that name caused a surge in their popularity. Fried green tomatoes are great served at brunch, but go equally well as a side dish at lunch or dinner. Or you can enjoy them at the Reynoldsburg Tomato Festival, held each September.

In shallow dish, combine cornmeal, flour, salt and pepper. Coat both sides of tomatoes with mixture, pressing firmly so mixture adheres evenly. In large skillet, pour oil to a depth of about 1/4-inch; add tomatoes to hot oil without crowding. Sprinkle lightly with sugar. Fry 2 minutes on each side or until golden brown; sprinkle with sugar again after tomatoes are turned. Remove from skillet; drain on paper towels.

Neva's Dilled Green Tomatoes

Makes 6 quarts

6 teaspoons dill seed
6 cloves garlic, whole
6 medium jalapeño peppers, whole
6 pounds (approximately 18) medium green tomatoes, quartered
8 cups water
4 cups cider vinegar
1 cup salt
2 teaspoons powdered alum

Shirley Failor of Toledo (mother-in-law of the co-author) has been making this recipe for 30 years. She got from her friend Neva and still has the original copy, written on a receipt from Bob's Shell Service in Holland, where Neva's husband was manager.

In each of 6, sterilized 1-quart canning jars, place 1 teaspoon dill seed, 1 clove garlic and 1 jalapeño pepper. Divide tomatoes evenly among the jars. In large saucepan, combine water, vinegar, salt and alum; bring to a boil. Boil 5 minutes. Pour in each jar, making sure to cover tomatoes. Seal at once. Store in cool spot.

Cindy's Fire and Ice Pasta

Cindy Kirkland, born and raised in Mount Sterling, earned her bachelor's degree in home economics from Ohio State University. She and her husband, Al, and sons Courtney and Cory live in Dublin. Cindy likes to add special touches to her dinners, such as a colorful ribbon tied around the wine glasses. The effect of "fire" in this unique dish is achieved with hot pepper flakes and the "ice" with vodka.

In large skillet, cook onion and garlic in butter and oil until tender. Add tomatoes, ham, basil and red pepper; cook, uncovered, 40 minutes or until slightly thickened. Add whipping cream, vodka and 1/4 cup cheese; heat through. Serve over pasta; top with remaining cheese. Add salt and pepper to taste.

Makes 6 to 8 servings

1/2 cup chopped onion
3 cloves garlic, finely chopped
2 tablespoons butter or margarine
2 tablespoons olive oil or vegetable oil
2 (28-ounce) cans plum tomatoes, undrained and broken up
1 cup (2 ounces) sliced Tasso ham or proscuitto, cut in strips
2 teaspoons basil leaves
1/2 teaspoon crushed red pepper flakes
1/3 cup whipping cream
1/4 cup vodka
1/2 cup grated Parmesan cheese
1 (16-ounce) box Penne pasta (or any shape desired), cooked and drained
Salt
Pepper

Green Tomato Pie

Reynoldsburg is home to annual Reynoldsburg Tomato Festival, which began in 1965 and is held in early September. The ladies group of Knights of Columbus 5253 sells tomato foods. This one is very popular.

In large colander, drain tomatoes for 30 minutes. In large saucepan, combine all ingredients, except butter and pastry. Bring to a boil; cook and stir until thickened. Cool 30 minutes.
Preheat oven to 425 degrees. Divide pastry dough in half; on lightly floured surface, roll each half out to 1/8-inch thickness. Line pie plate; trim edges even with plate. Turn tomato filling into pastry lined plate; dot with butter. Moisten edges of pastry in pie plate; lift second pastry circle onto filling. Trim 1/2-inch beyond edge of pie plate; fold top edge under bottom crust, flute edges. With sharp knife, slit top pastry in several spots for steam vents. Bake 15 minutes. Reduce oven temperature to 325 degrees; bake 40 to 45 minutes until golden brown.

Makes one 9-inch pie

4 cups thinly sliced green tomatoes, cut into quarters
1-3/4 cups sugar
3/4 cup raisins
1/4 cup flour
3 tablespoons lemon juice
1 tablespoon grated lemon rind
1/4 teaspoon ground cinnamon
1/4 teaspoon salt
1/8 teaspoon ground ginger
2 tablespoons butter or margarine
Pastry for 2-crust pie

Since 1874, the Ohio State Fair has resided comfortably in Columbus, but from 1850 through 1873 it changed sites annually, to share the wealth with all regions. In 1854 the opportunity to host the fair fell to Newark, giving it the chance to share ITS wealth of prehistoric Indian mounds. Fairgrounds were set up inside the Great Circle Mound, a 15- to 20-foot embankment covering 20 acres. An crowd estimated at 50,000 to 75,000 came, saw and were edified.

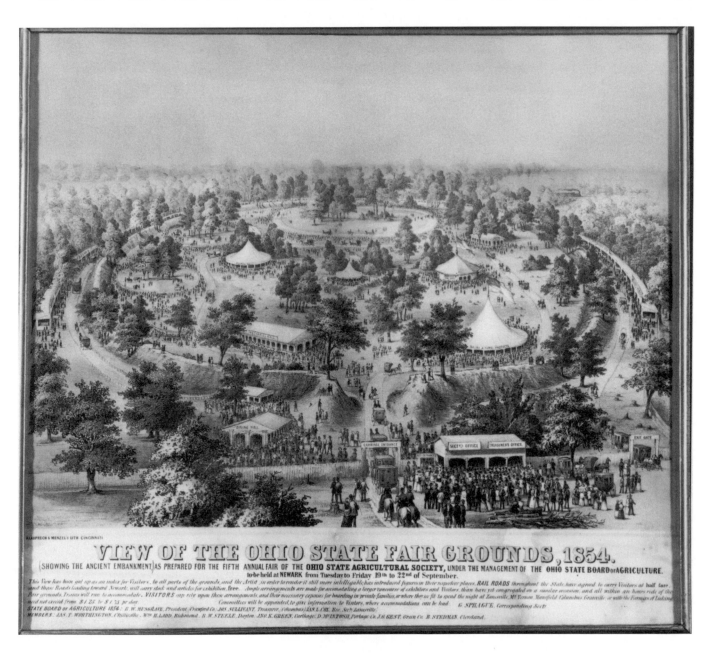

VIEW OF THE OHIO STATE FAIR GROUNDS, 1854.
[SHOWING THE ANCIENT EMBANKMENT] AS PREPARED FOR THE FIFTH ANNUAL FAIR OF THE **OHIO STATE AGRICULTURAL SOCIETY**, UNDER THE MANAGEMENT OF THE **OHIO STATE BOARD** OF **AGRICULTURE**.
to be held at NEWARK from Tuesday to Friday 19th to 22nd of September.

The Fairest
State of All

Almost every evening each fall you'll find Jack Baker roaming his corn fields near Arcanum in the gently rolling land of west-central Ohio. He's looking for perfect ears, ones with plump, round kernels neatly aligned in even-numbered rows (an odd number signals a genetic defect). Shucking an ear, rejecting it, moving on until he finds one he likes enough to pick, Baker keeps up the hunt for weeks. He doesn't stop until he has hundreds of specially selected ears carefully tucked away in a section of his barn called the "fair room."

Back in the farmhouse, meanwhile, his wife Diane is making jams and jellies: apple, quince, rhubarb, peach—20 or more kinds. The best she'll put aside, to be stored in a cool place and not touched until next August. Then she'll rally her two sons, ages 7 and 8, and in a whirlwind of activity begin mixing, stirring, baking: zucchini bread, banana bread, angel food cakes (white and chocolate), cornbread, gingerbread, chocolate chip cookies, and a popular treat called snickerdoodles.

In late August, all of this bounty—hundreds of examples of Jack's corn, as well as soybeans, buckwheat and spelt, plus the jams, jellies, cakes, breads and cookies—will be loaded into the Baker family vehicles and taken to Greenville, the county seat. It's time once more for the Great Darke County Fair, and the battling Bakers are back, ready to take on all comers in the farm and home products competitions.

The Bakers, who regularly lug home armloads of ribbons and rosettes, may be unusually successful, but they among tens of thousands of Ohioans for whom the annual agricultural fair is one of the highlights of the year.

Simply put, Ohio is fair country. Other states may have more fairs of all kinds, but they are apt to count parking lot carnivals with only a few cows standing around to dress things up. Ohio believes it has more authentic *agricultural* fairs, the genuine article with lots of hopeful 4-H youngsters and their parents showing cows and hogs and pumpkins and baked goods. The state has 94 such fairs sanctioned by its Department of Agriculture, plus an uncounted number of smaller, unaffiliated ones. In every one of Ohio's 88 counties there is at least one state-sanctioned fair and in some there are two. And on top of that, there's the Big Daddy of them all: the Ohio State Fair in Columbus.

Almost every year the Ohio State Fair has one of the largest atten-

dances of any state fair in the nation. It isn't just attendance that gives
Ohio's event its heavyweight status: it also claims the biggest all-breed
horse show, plus the largest shows of barrow (market) hogs, dairy cows,
dairy goats, rabbits, sheep, and llamas (yes, llamas). All in all, the State
Fair alone displays more than 20,000 animals and offers 18,000 exhibits;
35,000 youth get involved with its competitions and exhibits. Some of
these youngsters can walk away with substantial rewards, too: the annual
Junior Fair's "Sale of Champions" auctions off their prizewinning cattle,
hog and other livestock projects, with buyers like the Kroger Company
paying hundreds or thousands of dollars per animal. The "Sale of Champions" is so important that Ohio's governor has been known to delay
attending his party's presidential convention to preside over it instead.

From June through October, all of this is re-enacted on a smaller scale
at sites across Ohio. There's something mythic about these country fairs.
In the American imagination, fair time is when the farmer and his wife set
aside their work for a few days. He hoses down the prize pig, she gathers
up her best pickles, and Junior currycombs the heifer he's spent all year
raising. With the pig, pickles and heifer sitting in back of the old pickup
truck, the family sets off together for the fair's glittering mix of sounds
and smells; there they will cross paths with their city cousins, who have
come to gawk at the animals, and everybody will learn something. All
that may *seem* mythic, but in Ohio, images like those are not very far
from reality.

And that's why fairs are serious business in this state. According to
Mark List, deputy state director of agriculture, Ohio fairs are not just
carnivals (although they have plenty of the usual glitz, too), they are
educational events, officially certified as such by the Internal Revenue
Service. List calls them opportunities to educate farmers and their wives
on the best in agriculture and home economics, to show city folk what
farming is all about, and to give youth a chance to demonstrate what they
have learned during a year's worth of 4-H or other youth group activity.
The last is deemed especially important. Although the first agricultural
exhibitions in Ohio started out in the 1820s for adults only, the modern
junior fair—a fair-within-a-fair largely run by the kids themselves—is a
major part of every state-sanctioned fair. Anyone who thinks America's
young people are headed for hell in a hand basket may change their mind
after visiting one of these events: they'll find plenty of kids looking as if
they stepped right out of a Norman Rockwell painting as they wash their
pigs, brush their rabbits, shear their sheep, and, in time-honored fair
tradition, bed down at night in the stalls.

Part of what makes all this possible are the volunteers: thousands of
them who get together every year in every county to work on these
nonprofit events, doing something really big for their community. They
are fair buffs, community boosters, retired farmers, people who like to
work with kids. Divided into task forces, with jobs ranging from organizing the baked goods competition to hiring the country music, they
remind you of the senior prom committee, all grown up and a lot less

giggly. Volunteering at the fair is a time-honored tradition in Ohio.

And part of it, according to Al Rhonemus of Aberdeen, president of the Ohio Fair Managers Association, is Ohio state government's long tradition of supporting fairs. In 1846 the legislature passed an "act for the encouragement of agriculture" to help the county agricultural societies. That financial aid, though small, continues to this day; so does the practice of the state making sure that fairs stay clean, educational and committed to agriculture. You can see how serious Ohio is about this when you look at its rule book for fairs: the latest edition has 93 pages specifying everything from health standards for show animals to guidelines for prizes in the junior fair. Family values prevail here: the book solemnly intones that it is illegal in Ohio to keep a house of ill fame "within two miles of the place at which an agricultural fair is being held." There will be no untoward temptation of OUR farmers.

Ohioans love their fairs. But for pure enthusiasm, not too many can match dairy farmer Dale Perry, who tends 200 head near Athens in the southeastern part of the state. In high season, Perry and his wife go to two or three fairs each week. "Last year, we went to 32 in Ohio," says Perry; "this year we're shooting for 35." One year the Perrys were able to hit three fairs in one day—no easy feat, since the state won't allow neighboring counties to schedule at competing times.

Why does he do it? "Well, that's the way you learn," explains Perry, who has served 20 years on the board of the Athens County Fair. But like others who work on these events, mostly Perry just likes fair people and feels a kinship with them. He doesn't even look at the cows first when visiting a fair. Instead, he heads to the office to schmooze with friends in the business. "I have yet to find a bad fair person," he says. "Everybody you meet will just sit down and talk with you."

Over the years, Perry estimates, he has attended about half the fairs in Ohio. Attending every one of the 95 sanctioned fairs in the state is a distant dream, however. "I've got to stop milking cows first," he says.

Ohio offers more than fairs, however.

The land of the country agricultural fair, Ohio is also a land of harvest festivals, the sole purpose of which is to celebrate food. An informal survey reveals dozens of such affairs, honoring everything from apples to zucchini. From April through October, Ohioans are busy glorifying the food they produce, often in ways that would surprise you.

While fairs and festivals are both about food, serious eaters know the difference. Fairs are agricultural expositions, with the Ohio Department of Agriculture placing great stock in how educational all this is for farmers, city folk, and youth. You can look at the cattle, the corn, and the home-made pies, but you can't eat them. The food instead is mostly midway grub, so unless your taste runs to elephant ears and corn dogs, fairs are—with the occasional exception of an indigenous food tent—mostly about food in the abstract.

At harvest festivals, on the other hand, *eating* food, glorious *native* food, and doing it extravagantly is the whole point. Festivals are where

The Ohio Farmer, June 19, 1920

you can pig out and feel you are exploring local culture at the same time. And festivals are a place to get in touch spiritually with ancestors who, from ancient Greek and Roman times, have gathered to celebrate the gathering of the crops.

Of course, rib burn-offs, chili cook-offs and chicken barbecues abound in Ohio during warm weather, but they are not what we are talking about here. Nor do we mean those festivals which may nominally salute a local food, but are really just carnivals offering the same midway grub found at the fairs. Instead, the best Ohio food festivals are authentic celebrations of the harvest, offering food produced in the region or at least spiritually connected to it. Such events have several earmarks: (1) the honored food itself is offered in abundance and often in great variety, in forms that can range from creative to bizarre; (2) a queen is selected, reflecting the ancient custom of Druids and others, of crowning a maiden; and (3) there are competitions involving the honored food, such as making, eating or playing with it.

Food festival season builds slowly in Ohio. In April, winter-weary Buckeyes greet the new festival season with the Geauga County Maple Festival in Chardon, held since 1926 in the heart of Ohio's maple country, just east of Cleveland. A working sugar house is set up in the town square and sweet smells fill the air. Professional foresters judge the handiwork of local maple producers. Maple-flavored cotton candy joins the more traditional syrup and candy on sale. May brings the Old-Fashioned Ice Cream Festival in Utica, an ice cream producing center, giving Ohioans a head start on the big ice-cream eating season ahead.

June brings a flurry of strawberry festivals, with the biggest in the nation held the first weekend in June in Troy, just north of Dayton. The largest strawberry fields east of the Mississippi are located here. At the festival, more than 10,000 quarts of berries are served to an average of 150,000 visitors each year. Races using beds decorated with strawberry motifs, a strawberry pie-eating contest, and a parade featuring the strawberry queen are all sideshows to the main feature: the strawberry in its myriad forms. You can, of course, buy just plain strawberries. But the festival also offers strawberry shortcake, strawberry cheesecake, strawberry jams, strawberry-lemon cooler, strawberry fudge, strawberry yogurt and ice cream, strawberry pies and tarts, strawberry pizza, strawberry milk shakes, strawberry soda, strawberry cotton candy, strawberry fruit cups, strawberry slush, strawberry meringues, strawberry punch, strawberry chocolates...and even strawberry pretzels. The biggest seller? Strawberry donuts.

July brings the Lorain International Festival, which deserves a special mention even though it is not a harvest festival. The Lorain event celebrates the rich ethnic stew that characterizes the industrial belt encompassing greater Cleveland and the Mahoning Valley. Among the week's worth of cultural events is a food fair with the community's 55 ethnic groups offering their special dishes.

Assorted fruit and vegetable festivals occur during the summer, with the zucchini coming into its own as Labor Day approaches. The prolific zucchini has become notorious for its generosity to those who dare plant it; there have been reports in Ohio of "Zucchini Nights," during which desperate gardeners, working under the cover of darkness, have unloaded their harvests on neighbors' porches. Similar motives may be behind the Obetz Zucchini Fest. No matter: delicious zucchini bread and muffins are readily consumed at this annual event held the weekend before Labor Day. A Miss Zucchini and her court preside over zucchini relay races, a zucchini baking competition, and a contest with prizes for biggest, smallest, most unique and best dressed zucchini.

The really big harvest festival season begins in September, and serious eaters bend to their task. In Millersport, more than 100,000 ears are consumed at the Sweet Corn festival. As that event is winding down, the Milan Melon festival—featuring muskmelon ice cream and watermelon sherbet—is getting underway. About the same time comes the Tomato Festival in Reynoldsburg, where grazers can enjoy green tomato pie, tomato fudge, and tomato-laced bakery, all washed down with free tomato juice. Those looking for new thrills should try the soybean spitting contest at the American Soya Festival in Amanda. The wondrous apple in all its forms—apple butter, cider, sauce, pie, and so on—is offered by the Jackson County Apple Festival. Other apple and apple butter festivals abound in October during the fall, while October is highlighted by the Circleville Pumpkin Show. This squash and pumpkin extravaganza, which as been going on for more than 80 years, features the world's largest pumpkin pie. Inspired by this monster, you can then dine on pumpkin waffles, pumpkin chili, pumpkin ice cream, pumpkin taffy....you get the idea.

Fairs, then, teach us something about food production in Ohio; festivals give us a chance to taste it. Anyone who wants to capture the flavor of Ohio should plan to go to both.

POSTSCRIPT: *An annual listing of Ohio agricultural fairs can be obtained by calling the Office of Fairs of the Ohio Department of Agriculture: 614/866-6361.*

A list of festivals belonging to the Ohio Festivals and Events Association can be obtained by calling 800/BUCKEYE, the state's travel information line. Additional festivals are listed in the Ohio "Calendar of Events" available at the same number.

FACES OF THE LAND

The Man Who Loves Fairs

In politics the biggest job of all is the Presidency of the United States; in religion, the Papacy is tops. And among agricultural expositions...it just might be the managership of the Ohio State Fair.

Now, Mark List is not a pretentious man and never aspired to the White House, even if he did serve five years on the Grove City council. The Papacy wasn't a real live possibility either. And as for being head of one of the biggest and best-known agricultural expositions of them all...forget it. Unbelievable.

Well, one out of three isn't bad. In late August 1992, the former farm boy from Pickaway County found himself at the helm of fairdom's Big Enchilada. With almost no notice he had been named acting manager of a state fair with a big name, and not a few headaches.

Fortunately, List kept his sense of humor: "This job is like cleaning up after a cat," he said one day in the fair manager's office on the fair grounds in Columbus. "You keep discovering buried messes." Not everyone could have smiled under the circumstances. List was inheriting the fallout from a controversial predecessor who had spent the eight months of his tenure in one uproar after another. Fairs are important to Ohioans, so, shortly after the '92 fair had closed its 17-day run, the Ohio Expositions Commission fired the previous manager, to no one's very great surprise. List found himself occupying the front office, trying to learn whether the fair had made or lost money from its stormiest season.

It turned out to have lost money, but nobody doubted the fair would bounce back, so List went to work unraveling what he had inherited. A quietly genial man, List is the kind of person who gets things done, the son of a workaholic farmer who has no hobby but his job. And, for most of his life, List's job just happens, in one way or another, to have involved fairs.

At the time of his appointment to the temporary position at the State Fair, List was one of two deputy directors of the Ohio Department of Agriculture, responsible for—among many other things—the Office of Fairs. The Office of Fairs regulates the state's 94 county and independent agricultural fairs (but not the Ohio State Fair). It makes sure they are "operated under guidelines of [an] educational, agricultural and...moral nature."

Before that, List had been executive secretary of the Ohio Fair Managers Association for eight years, advancing the interests of all of Ohio's state-sanctioned fairs. One of List's projects involved taking fair officials on busman's holidays to fairs in other states, learning how they did things elsewhere and in the process learning how good Ohio fairs are. After seeing the competition in 20 other states, List says, "I would have to have someone prove to me that's there any state that has the quality of our fairs."

List is especially proud of the so-called "junior fairs," the fairs-within-fairs built into all of Ohio's agricultural expositions. Junior fairs are where the year-long livestock, sewing, craft and service projects of 160,000 4-H and other youth culminate; they are overseen by boards composed of the youngsters themselves. "Someone had the foresight long ago to give these youngsters responsibility," List explains. "They have their own officers, they have a budget, they hire the judges, they secure the sponsors for the trophies, they're there during the fair to make sure all the events take place. We even have a junior fair board at the State Fair—to my knowledge, it's only state fair in the nation with a junior fair board. So far as youth involvement goes, there isn't any state like Ohio."

List's affection for fairs goes back a long way. He brought home his first ribbon after showing a calf when he was 10—winning it felt "fabulous," he recalls—and at age 15 he won a county tractor rodeo. That led to the state fair tractor rodeo, where he came in second to a youth who went on later to win the national championship. Over the years List was able to festoon his bedroom with many other prize ribbons; along the way he served on the junior fair board in his county.

With that much experience in fair competition, List was able to bring some new thinking to his job as 4-H agent in the early 1970s. He was one of the first to expand the judging of youngsters' 4-H projects by also interviewing them, asking them, for example, to explain HOW they made the apron they had submitted, what materials and needles they had used, and so on. The "interview-judging" process is now used in all categories of junior fair competition throughout the state; it's one of the factors reinforcing the educational role of the fairs and qualifying them with the IRS as tax-exempt.

Mark List

List had planned a life of farm work, but his parents insisted he try college. After graduating from Ohio State University with a degree in agronomy he held a variety of jobs, among them selling animal feed for a grain company, being secretary-treasurer of the Ohio Agricultural Council, and serving as education and business coordinator for the Ohio Florists' Association.

But through most of his life, List has worked with fairs, cared about fairs, savored fairs—and been recognized for it. In 1983 the Ohio Fair Managers Association presented him with its Lifetime Pass Award. It was the right award for List: in his lifetime he has attended about 80 different fairs in the state.

But wasn't that just part of his job? Going to a fair is never work, replies List; "I've never been on a fairgrounds and felt like it was just a job."

That may help explain something astonishing: early on, List decided he would not be a candidate for the permanent appointment as state fair manager, although he was urged at high levels to do so. Instead, he returned his post at the Department of Agriculture in late January 1993, the search process for a new fair manager having been completed with the hiring of someone else.

Managing the State Fair is like dancing with a gorilla, the way List explained it: it's so huge that it concentrates your attention powerfully. There's no time for anything or anybody else. Worst of all, it's a little like becoming President of the United States: being manager of an event that big sets you apart and cuts you off from other people. And knowing people—*fair* people, that special breed of community volunteers who form an Ohio fraternity all their own—is what List likes most about fairs. Through years of fair work, List has friends in every corner of the state, friends with whom he can sit down with as an equal anywhere and talk farming and fair business. The manager of the Ohio State Fair can't do that.

On the other hand, because his role at the Department of Agriculture includes supervision of the Office of Fairs, List can have easy contact with fairs and fair boards around the state. And that may be why he has no outside hobbies: "My work is my hobby," he says. "Fair work is fun, it's a ball."

"I love fairs," says Mark List...too much to become head of one of the biggest in the world.

RECIPES

Grand Champion Pumpkin Pie

Boosters like to call the Circleville Pumpkin Show "The Greatest Free Show on Earth." It has taken place every year since 1903 except one during World War I and two during World War II. It is said to attract over 400,000 visitors and features every type of pumpkin product imaginable (and some that are hard to imagine). The "World's Largest Pumpkin Pie" is baked annually for the Pumpkin Show by Lindsey's Bake Shop, but you'll have to go there to find out what happens to it when the festival ends.

The food contests are popular, and include categories for baked goods, jams and jellies, relishes, canned goods and several kinds of pie. The recipe that follows has won in different categories over the years. In 1992, Cathy Morehead of Kingston won the Grand Champion Award with it for a second time. Through trial and error, she developed the crunchy topping on this pie. The recipe makes two pies, for as Cathy says, "One just isn't enough!"

In medium bowl, combine flour and salt for pastry; cut in shortening until crumbly. Add water; stir until dough forms a ball. Divide in half. On lightly floured surface, roll each half out to 1/8-inch thickness. Line pie plates; trim pastry 1/2-inch beyond edge of pie plate; fold under, flute edge.

Preheat oven to 375 degrees. In large bowl, combine brown sugar, flour, pumpkin pie spice and salt. Add pumpkin, milk and eggs; mix well. Pour filling into pastry lined plates. Bake 40 minutes.

In small bowl, combine topping ingredients; mix until crumbly. Sprinkle evenly over top of pies. Bake an additional 10 minutes or until knife inserted near center comes out clean. Cool; serve with whipped cream if desired.

Makes two 9-inch pies

Pastry:
2 cups flour
1 teaspoon salt
3/4 cup lard or solid vegetable shortening
5 tablespoons cold water

Filling:
2 cups firmly packed light brown sugar
2 tablespoons flour
2 tablespoons pumpkin pie spice
1 teaspoon salt
1 (29-ounce) can pumpkin or 4 cups home-canned pumpkin
2 (12-ounce) cans evaporated milk
2 eggs, slightly beaten

Topping:
1 cup chopped pecans
1/4 cup firmly packed light brown sugar
2 tablespoons butter or margarine, softened

Strawberry Coffeecake

Makes one 8-inch cake

Filling:
2 cups sliced fresh strawberries
1/4 cup sugar
1 tablespoon cornstarch

Cake:
2-1/4 cups flour
3/4 cup sugar
3/4 cup unsalted butter
1/2 teaspoon baking powder
1/2 teaspoon baking soda
3/4 cup buttermilk
1 egg, slightly beaten

I tasted this coffee cake while judging the "Coffee Cake, non-yeast" category at the 1992 Ohio State Fair and decided it belonged in this book. Its originator, Susie Kopf, lives in Westerville and hopes to have her own cake-decorating and specialty food business someday. She has been entering Ohio State Fair food competitions for over 10 years, and usually enters several categories. This recipe is one she put together for the competition.

Preheat oven to 350 degrees. In medium saucepan, combine filling ingredients; cook and stir until thickened. Remove from heat. In large bowl, combine flour and sugar; cut in butter until crumbly. Reserve 1/2 cup of mixture. Add baking powder and baking soda to remaining mixture. In small bowl, combine buttermilk and egg. Add to dry ingredients, stirring until just moistened. Turn 2/3 of batter into greased 8-inch square baking pan; top with strawberry filling. Drop remaining batter by tablespoonsful on top of strawberry filling: sprinkle with reserved crumb mixture. Bake for 35 to 40 minutes or until golden brown. Cool 15 minutes.

Marilyn's Yeast Rolls

Makes about 36

1 cup milk
1/2 cup sugar
1/2 cup solid vegetable shortening
1 teaspoon salt
2 packages active dry yeast
1/2 cup warm water (105-115 degrees)
1-1/2 teaspoons sugar
6 cups flour*
3 eggs, slightly beaten

* Whole wheat flour may be substituted for part of the white flour.

Marilyn Hartley won First Place and Best of Show ribbons for these yeast rolls at the Franklin County Fair. Recently someone who had met her some time before at a potluck told her, "I remember you; you are the lady who baked those delicious rolls !" Marilyn and her husband, Russ, and children Lauren and R.J. live in Hilliard. She has an extensive herb garden, and loves to cook with fresh herbs. Marilyn is a member of "Herb Thyme," a local group of herb enthusiasts.

In medium saucepan, heat milk; add 1/2 cup sugar, shortening and salt. Cool to lukewarm. In large bowl, sprinkle yeast over water: add sugar, stir to dissolve. Add milk mixture, flour and eggs: mix well. (Chopped fresh herbs may be added to dough. Use 1 tablespoon herbs of your choice.) In large, greased bowl, place dough. Set bowl in warm place; let rise until doubled in bulk. Punch down dough; shape into rolls. Place close together on two lightly greased 15x10-inch jelly roll pans. Cover: let rise until doubled in bulk. Bake at 350 degrees 10 to 15 minutes or until lightly browned. Brush with melted butter if desired.

Snickerdoodles

Snickerdoodles are popular entries in county fair baking competitions across the state. Most recipes for them are very similar. They all instruct you to roll the cookie dough in a cinnamon-sugar mixture before baking, so when done, the cookies have a mottled appearance. This is a great cookie to make when the pantry is low, as the ingredients are all basic items.

Preheat oven to 350 degrees. In large mixer bowl, combine butter, shortening and 1-1/2 cups sugar; beat well. Add eggs; beat well. In medium bowl, combine flour, cream of tartar, baking soda and salt; add gradually to sugar mixture, stirring well by hand.

In small bowl, combine 2 tablespoons sugar and cinnamon; mix well. Shape dough into 1-inch balls; roll each in cinnamon sugar mixture. Place 2 inches apart on ungreased cookie sheets. Bake 8 to 10 minutes or until edges are lightly browned. (Cookies will puff up in oven, then flatten out.) Let stand 1 to 2 minutes; remove from cookie sheets. Cool. Store tightly covered.

Makes about 5 dozen

1/2 cup butter or margarine
1/2 cup solid vegetable shortening
1-1/2 cups sugar
2 eggs
3 cups flour
2 teaspoons cream of tartar
1 teaspoon baking soda
1/4 teaspoon salt
2 tablespoons sugar
2 teaspoons ground cinnamon

Sheila's Banana Bread

Banana bread is of the most popular entries in baking contests across the state, and it is difficult to find an Ohio community cookbook that does not include at least one recipe for it. My friend Sheila VanZile, who was raised in Orrville, gave me this recipe several years ago and I have been making it ever since. It is slightly sweeter than some, so even children who previously stuck their noses up at the thought of banana bread before like it. Be sure to use overripe bananas as they impart a stronger banana flavor.

Preheat oven to 350 degrees. In medium bowl, combine flour, baking powder, baking soda and salt. In large bowl, combine butter and sugar; beat well. Add eggs; beat well. Add dry ingredients alternately with bananas; stir well. Add nuts. Turn into greased and floured 9x5-inch loaf pan. Bake 45 to 50 minutes or until wooden pick inserted near center comes out clean. Cool 5 minutes; remove from pan, cool completely. Store tightly wrapped in refrigerator.

Makes one 9x5-inch loaf

2 cups flour
1/2 teaspoon baking powder
1/2 teaspoon baking soda
1/2 teaspoon salt
1/2 cup butter or margarine
1 cup sugar
2 eggs
1 cup mashed overripe bananas
1/2 cup chopped nuts

Historical Society Rose Geranium Cake

Makes one 10-inch cake

1 (14.5- or 16-ounce) package angel
   food cake mix
1/4 teaspoon rose flavoring*
Rose geranium leaves, clean and dry
1 to 2 teaspoons ground cardamom
1 cup (1/2 pint) whipping cream,
   whipped, or 1 (8-ounce) container
   frozen non-dairy whipped topping,
   thawed

* Rose flavoring is usually available at cake decorating
  stores. If unavailable, substitute 1/2 teaspoon rosewater
  and couple drops red food coloring.

Outsiders may think of Midwestern food as plain and bland, but, in reality, herbs have been used for seasoning foods for many generations in Ohio. The Herb Festival held annually the third Saturday in May in Old Gahanna is one example of the importance of herbs. Sponsored by the Gahanna Historical Society, all proceeds go to preservation of three historic buildings in Gahanna. One of the highlights of the festival is the sampling of their famous Rose Geranium Cake.

Rose geranium is a variety of sweet scented geraniums, or Pelargoniums, and is NOT the annual geraniums we grow in our yards. (Please do NOT use those leaves in the following recipe.) Dried rose geranium leaves are also used in potpourri.

Preheat oven to 350 degrees. Lay rose geranium leaves upside down in bottom of greased 10-inch tube pan. Prepare cake mix according to package directions, adding rose flavoring to batter; bake. Cool as directed: remove from pan, keeping leaves in place.

In medium bowl, fold cardamom into whipped cream. To serve, slice cake through leaves with serrated or electric knife, or cake divider. Top each slice with whipped cream.

Zucchini-Oatmeal Bread

Makes two 9x5-inch loaves

2 cups flour
1 cup oats
1/2 cup sugar
1/2 cup firmly packed light brown
   sugar
1 teaspoon baking powder
1 teaspoon baking soda
3/4 teaspoon ground cinnamon
1/2 teaspoon salt
3/4 cup vegetable oil
3 eggs
1 teaspoon vanilla extract
3 cups grated zucchini
1 cup chopped nuts

The Obetz Zucchini Festival, held annually since 1985, is observed the weekend before Labor Day. Over 30,000 people attended in 1992, and 2,000 loaves of zucchini bread and 3,000 zucchini burgers were sold. Recipes for zucchini bread abound. Although this recipe is not the one baked in Obetz, it is reminiscent of it. It is the favorite zucchini recipe of Evelyn Oldham, of Mount Victory. Although she and her husband no longer actively work their land, Evelyn has fond memories of the wonderful lunches she would make and take to her husband and sons out working in the fields.

Preheat oven to 350 degrees. In large bowl, combine flour, sugars, baking powder, baking soda, cinnamon and salt. In medium bowl, combine oil, eggs and vanilla; add to dry ingredients, stirring until just moistened. Add zucchini and nuts. Turn into two greased and floured 9x5-inch loaf pans. Bake 50 to 55 minutes or until wooden pick inserted near center comes out clean. Cool 5 minutes; remove from pans and cool completely. Store tightly wrapped in refrigerator.

Sauerkraut Pie

The Ohio Sauerkraut Festival in Waynesville began in 1970 after a prominent Waynesville businessman, the late Albert "Cap" Stubbs, had the idea. "Why sauerkraut?" he was asked. "Why not?" he replied.

Today the festival attracts over 200,000 people and is overseen by the Chamber of Commerce. All food booths are run by community organizations. Their products include cabbage rolls, sauerkraut balls, sauerkraut bread, sauerkraut cookies, sauerkraut pizza, sauerkraut donuts, sauerkraut fudge, and yes...Sauerkraut Pie! If you try this pie, you will discover that the sauerkraut tastes remarkably like coconut.

Preheat oven to 375 degrees. In medium bowl, beat eggs. Add milk, sugar, flour, butter and vanilla; mix well. Add sauerkraut and lemon rind. Pour into pastry shell. Bake 40 to 45 minutes or until golden brown. (If pie does not brown sufficiently, place under broiler until golden brown.)

Makes on 9-inch pie

2 eggs
1 cup milk
1 cup sugar
3 tablespoons flour
1 tablespoon melted butter or margarine
1/2 teaspoon vanilla extract
1/2 cup sauerkraut, rinsed, drained and chopped
1 teaspoon grated lemon rind
1 (9-inch) unbaked pastry shell

Buckeyes

The state tree of Ohio is *Aesculus glabra* or horse chestnut, known as the buckeye. Ohioans are nicknamed Buckeyes, and so is the Ohio State University football team. And if there were an official state candy, it would be...the Buckeye.

Recipes for Buckeyes vary, but this one is the favorite of Sue Dawson. Sue is a home economist and food editor of the Columbus Dispatch. She and Dispatch food writer Karin Welzel have made the paper a major source of recipes for central Ohioans.

In large mixer bowl, combine sugar, peanut butter and butter; beat well. Roll mixture into 3/4-inch balls and place on waxed paper.

In top of double boiler, over hot water, melt chocolate morsels and paraffin. Stick a toothpick into each peanut butter ball; dip in warm chocolate so all but tip of ball is covered. Let excess chocolate drip back into pan. Place on waxed paper; remove toothpick. Repeat until all balls have been dipped. With fingers, pinch toothpick holes closed; smooth top. Refrigerate.

Makes about 3 pounds candy

1 (16-ounce) box confectioners' sugar
1 (18-ounce) jar creamy peanut butter
1/2 cup butter or margarine, softened
1 (12-ounce) package semisweet chocolate morsels
1 (1-inch) square paraffin wax

An Afterword

She's a Beauty

Yes, boys and girls, there really is an Elsie the Cow. I've met her, and she's even prettier than her pictures on milk cartons and TV. Elsie always wears a daisy chain around her neck, so you can tell her from the other cows. If you ever see a cow with daisies around her neck, that's Elsie.

Elsie is the most famous cow in America, but she isn't stuck-up at all. She is very friendly to everyone, and calm and gentle, too. If you were to meet Elsie, you could walk right up and pat her, and she'd like that. (Watch out for her nose, though: it's usually very wet.)

Elsie lives in Ohio. Her home is on the farm of Scott and Belinda Jenks, in the southwest part of the state. Unlike most cows, though, Elsie travels a lot, meeting people and making friends wherever she goes. Mrs. Jenks says, "That cow gets around more than I do," and then she laughs. Mrs. Jenks likes Elsie a lot. You would, too.

The rest of this message is for adults only.

Elsie is a road cow. Like a lot of adults who used to work at home, she has a professional career now: public relations for Borden, Inc. She makes up to 300 appearances a year, appearing at company-sponsored events, fairs, hospitals and in parades.

Elsie is like Lassie: a role is filled over the years by, uh, various individuals. Notice that we do not say "animal." Company guidelines for Elsie warn, "Elsie is a personality, not an animal." That's why you won't find her in the animal area of state or local fairs. Instead, she's usually out front with the Big Names.

Elsie can show up in the darndest places: cocktail parties for key Borden customers, for example. Or New Orleans' Mardi Gras (complete with mask). Or on the children's floors of big hospitals. She gets there by riding the elevator, just like everyone else. (We know what you're wondering, but were too polite to ask. Elsie's handlers carry buckets. Cows give off signals when they're about to go, and, with the speed and grace of the great Olympians, the handlers intercept those deliveries before they even hit the floor. Startled onlookers have broken into applause.)

Cows are picked for the Elsie role according to their gentleness and good looks—not too hard a task with Jerseys, who are sweet babes by nature. The babelicious Elsie is fawn-colored and officially weighs 950 pounds; unofficially, she's chubbier than your average barn cow. Her schedule is managed by Borden's Lewis Rayburn, and her travels, via a custom-designed trailer dubbed the Cowdillac, are handled by teams of "Borden cowboys," usually college students earning tuition money.

Elsie gets lots of attention from the Jenkses, because the farm primarily grows corn and soybeans and Elsie and her helper cows are the only livestock on the premises. There is one retired cow, an old trouper put out to pasture. There's also an ingenue, who is studying for the role, and there is Elsie herself, plus two cows who are understudies, so to speak.

The original Elsie appeared in 1936, one of several cows in Borden medical advertisements. She existed only in the ad department's imagination until 1939, when public interest prompted the company to pick a real cow. An instant hit with the public, Elsie has since had many adventures. She was in the 1940 Hollywood movie *Little Men*, married a bull named Elmer (of glue bottle fame), had children Beauregard and Beulah, sold $10-million in War Bonds during World War II, was a mystery guest on TV's "What's My Line?", led the Rose Bowl parade, and received an honorary Ph.D. in Bovinity from Ohio State University.

Elsie the Cow

People always smile when they see Elsie. That's one reason why she has been on the road most of those years, even though her role in mass media has waxed and waned. Realizing in the early 1990s that she had become one of the best-loved advertising symbols in America, Borden decided to bring her back to prominence.

A wise move. People not only like cows, they love them. They see them as symbols of nature's bounty and even of motherhood. After all, cows provide the food with which we all start life. Cows are gentle creatures, too, and yet we know they will defend their young. (After all, what do you think those horns are for?)

A cow has an ineffable loveliness, too. Just why may be hard to understood at first, for the creature seems designed by someone with a sense of humor: a cow's all awkward angles, flapping ears and jiggling faucets. But she has the larger grace and glory of nature about her. It's what prompts people, like one fan of Elsie, to breathe in awe, "She's a beauty!"

Some Indian tribes adopted animals as their spiritual protectors, and the animals became their symbols. The cow should be Ohio's—not just because this is one of the biggest dairy states (which it is), but because the cow is so emblematic of it. Like the cow, this unpretentious state has many gifts, and it offers them gently to us all. It is a bountiful land of corn and tomatoes and apples and pork and many other good things that we can wash down with a glass of fine Ohio wine (or milk, of course).

Ohio is a land of good and gentle people, too—not only our Amish friends, but Germans, Italians, Latinos, Poles, Hungarians, Scots, native Americans, people of color...hardworking, friendly middle Americans who are not glamorous, but something better. Ohio is not glamorous, but it is something better, too. Like the cow, it is beautiful.

So, Ohioans, here's to Elsie, the Ohio road cow. She's bounteous. She's beautiful. And she's ours.

Going Home

It's supper time in Ohio farm country, sometime between 1910 and 1915, and two boys and their dog are heading home. That's their house up ahead, where Ma will have the table groaning with food grown right there on the farm. Farm life was not always easy then, but there was a sweet innocence to it...when the century and these children were young.

Index

A

Akron 77, 122
Alta's Hearty Vegetable Soup 40
Amanda 195
Amish 7-8, 23, 30-35
Anselmo, Nate 68, 72-74
Antonoplos, Anastasia 81
Apple Butter 104
Apple Cashew Pasta 99
Apple Pie Bars 128
Apple-Stuffed Pork Loin with Raspberry
    Sauce 98
Apple-Pumpkin Streusel Muffins 105
Apples 86-91
Appleseed, Johnny 8, 87-95
Athens 174
Aunt Ruth's Concord Grape Pie 151
Autumn Harvest Soup 97

B

Baker family 191
Baking Powder Biscuits 131
Bartlett, Molly 115-119, 124
Bash, Winston 158-159
Bayberry Inn 103
Beam Road Berry Farm 129
Beef and Roasted Vegetable Kabobs 62
Berry, Stanley 173
Beside the Point's Split Pea Soup 122
Biddie's German Apple Cake 100
Bison Stew 12
Black Forest Sauerkraut Balls 78
BLT Salad with Creamy Herb Dressing 183
Bluestone, Susie 24
Bob Evans 18, 49, 154
Bob Evans Farms Hearty Meat Loaf 165
Borden, Inc. 4, 76, 153, 167, 204-205
Bosley, Parker 10-13
Boursin Cheese 121
Bowling Green 9, 83, 129
Bradac, George 69, 70
Breaded Pork Chops and Tomato Gravy 59
Bromfield, Louis 109
Bruns, Pat 102
Brunswick 89
Bryan 156
Buckeye Lake 100
Buckeyes 203
Budget, The 31, 45
Butler, Bill & Jane 136, 149
Buxton Inn 98

C

Campbell Soup Co. 156-157
Campbell's Tomato Soup Cake 171
Caponata 75
Carpenter, Sandra 76

Carpenter, Tom 6, 20-22
Celestial Crusts (Bozi Milosti) 80
Chalet Debonné 137
Chalet Debonné Famous Shrimp Dip 142
Chapis, Ken & Lyn 129
Cheerios 154, 164
Cheerios Toasted Party Mix 164
Cheesy Corn Bread 25
Chef Tom's Honey Apple Chops 166
Chicken Fricassee with Tomato Dumplings
    63
Chikwich Sandwich 63
Chili 80
Chilled Melon Soup 124
Chiquita Brans 154
Chocolate Angel Pie 128
Christophers Marinara Sauce 187
Cincinnati 9, 49-53, 67, 71, 78, 80, 133,
    152
Cincinnati Chili 80
Cindy's Fire and Ice Pasta 189
Circleville 7, 195, 199
Cleveland 15, 24, 67-74, 79
Clinton County 52
Columbian House 186
Columbus 9, 15, 67, 71, 155
Conneaut 138
Cookin' with Maudie Ho Ho Cake 45
Cordial, Diane 101, 168
Corn 14-22
Corn Bread Sausage Stuffing 27
Corn Chowder 23
Corn Pone 130
Corn Pudding 27
Corn and Pasta Salad 24
Corn Spoon Bread 24
Cranberry-Apple Crisp 100

D

Darke County 17, 52, 191
Dawson, Sue 203
Dayton 92
Debevc family 137, 142
Delia's Guacamole 83
Deppner, Dave 92-95
Der Dutchman Date Nut Pudding 43
DeWine, Mike & Fran 96, 99
Di's Dutch Apple Pie 101
Di's Ohio Sour Cherry Pie 169
Dunn, Lawrence 104

E

Elsie the Cow 153, 204-205
Enshayan, Kamyar 110-111
Erickson, Rick & Billie 158
Esterer, Arnie 138-141, 146
Evans, Chuck & Karen 163
Eyssen family 90-91

F

Failor, Shirley 188

Farm Bureau 112, 114
Farm Labor Organizing Committee
    178-181
Findlay Market 67, 71
Firelands Braised Beef Noir 150
Firelands Winery 137, 150
Fisher's Fresh Herbs 120
Fluffy Rice and Chicken 41
Food Industries Center 158-159
Fowler's Mill 158
Fratelli Spaghetti Sauce 76
Fraundorfer, George 78
Fresh Country Fried Corn 29
Fresh Peach Cobbler 103
Fresh Tomato Pasta Sauce 187
Freshwater Farms Rainbow Trout with
    Orange-Basil Sauce 130
Fried Green Tomatoes 188

G

Gahanna 202
Geauga County 104, 194
General Mills 154
Geneva 123, 135
Gentile, Roger 134
George Voinovich's Favorite Pork Chops
    96
Gerber, Dave 54-56
Gerlosky, Wes 135-136, 151
German Potato Pancakes 78
Glaus family 147
Glazed Raspberry Pie 129
Glory Foods 160-162
Golden Lamb 44
Graham Cracker Pudding 46
Grand Champion Pumpkin Pie 199
Grandma Failor's Cranberry Relish 105
Great Grandma Porter's Applesauce Cake 129
Green Tomato Pie 189
Grilled Lamb Markko 146

H

Handke, Harmut 186
Harpersfield Chicken 151
Harpersfield Organic Garden 123
Harpersfield Vineyard 135-136
Hartley, Marilyn 121, 122, 200
Hartmut Handke's Oven-Roasted Tomatoes
    186
Heartland Corn Bread 25
Heinz Super Burger Sauce 164
Heinz 155
Henry County Fair 176
Herb Butter 122
Herb-Topped Tomatoes 185
Heritage Grilled Breast of Chicken and
    Sauce 64
Historical Society Rose Geranium Cake 202
Hogs 48-56
Holmes County 31
Homestead Grilled Mushrooms 123

Honey-Mustard Marinated Pork Tenderloins 57
Hot Cider Punch 96

I

Ianuci's Italian Ristorante 75

J

J.M. Smucker Co. 154
Jackson County Apple Festival 128, 195
Janet's Smoked Pork Chops with Apples and Onions 59
Jindra, Lou 134, 143
Johnny Marzetti 165
Johnson, Tom 144
Johnstown, Dean 123

K

Kahn's 152
Karen's Favorite Chicken Bake 64
Katie's Peanut Butter Pie 46
Kirkland, Cindy 189
Knox County 91
Kolaczki 79
Kopf, Susie 200
Krema Prima Peanut Butter Pie 168
Kroger's 155, 166

L

Langan, Karen & Mark 125
Lazarus-Style Cheesecake 168
Leniwe Pierogi 79
Lennie's Fried Okra 83
Leu, Bob 69-70
Licking County 88
List, Mark 192, 196-198
Livingston, Alexander 172-173
Logsdon, Gene 109
Longworth, Nicholas 133
Lonz Winery 132, 137, 144
Lorain 194
Lynd, Mitch 88-89

M

Magic Cookie Bars 167
Maisonette, The 13
Mansfield 128
Mantey Vineyard 137
Mapel, Nelson 184
Mapleside Farms 89-91
Marietta 157
Marilyn's Yeast Rolls 200
Marinated Tomato Slices 184
Markko Vineyard 138-141, 146
Marzetti's 155
Matzo Balls 84
Matzo Ball Soup 84
Meier's 143, 146, 148
Meier's Sparkling Catawba Punch 143
Mercer County 52, 102
Mexican Salsa 182
Miamisburg 92

Mike DeWine's Favorite Apple Dumplings 99
Milan Melon Festival 124
Milan Inn Corn Sticks 26
Miles, Jim 129
Millersport 195
Mon Ami Winery 148
Montezuma Deluxe Nachos 163
Moore, Carla 108
Moore, Carol 122
Moravian Sugar Cake 82
Morehead, Cathy 199
Mount Vernon 9, 91
Mr. Coffee 154
Mulberry Creek Farm 125
Mullet, Alta 40, 41

N

Napoleon 156
National Pork Producers Council 52
Neidert, Elizabeth 77
Neva's Dilled Green Tomatoes 188
Newark 190
Nix, Lennie V. 83
North Market 67, 71
North Ridgeville Corn Festival 130

O

Obetz 195, 202
Ohio Agricultural Research & Development Center 173
Ohio Apple Maple Chutney 97
Ohio Cream Sherry Pound Cake 148
Ohio Department of Agriculture 108, 143, 191, 193, 196-198
Ohio Ecological Food & Farm Assn. 110, 114
Ohio Egg Marketing Program 25
Ohio Fair Managers Assn. 193, 196
Ohio Field Greens with Sprouts and Orange Segments 121
Ohio Magazine 13
Ohio Pork Producers Council 52
Ohio Shaker Lemon Pie 43
Ohio State Fair 190-192, 196-198, 200
Ohio State University 54, 111, 113, 158-159, 197
Ohio State University Extension 52, 54, 112
Ohio Turnpike 9
Old-Fashioned Corn Relish 23
One-Day Root Beer 47
Orrville 154
Orzech, Carol & Jim 79

P

Packard, Frannie 99
Palmer, Karen 128
Paramount Distillers 144, 148, 150
Pareve Noodle Kugel 84
Parker's 10-13
Pastichio 81

Peach Mountain Muffins 103
Peanut Butter Cookies 47
Peerless Mill Inn Corn Fritters 26
Penuche Icing 129
Percheron Horse Society of America 14
Perkins, Freddie & Bunny 126
Perry, Dale 193
Pettinelli family 76
Plain People's Lemonade 47
Pomeroy 131
Porcupine Meatballs 61
Pork 48-53
Port Clinton 86
Portage Hills Chinese Chicken and Peanuts 147
Potatoes Supreme 41
Preble County Barbecued Pork Chops 57
Preble County Pork Festival 49
Procter & Gamble 50-51, 155
Pullins, Mike 113

Q

Quail Hollow 97
Quilter, Tom & Mary 6, 135

R

Red Door Tavern 77
Red Cabbage 76
Reynoldsburg 176, 177, 189, 195
Rhonemus, Al 193
Rhubarb Crunch Cake 104
Rhubarb Pie 102
Richland County 109
Rider's Inn Lake Erie Walleye 127
Rios, Tim 97
Roasted Corn with Seasoned Butters 29
Rosemary Scalloped Potatoes 125
Rosencrans, Joyce 80
Rossi Pasta 157
Rossi Pasta with Peas, Onions and Eggs 167
Rothschild Berry Farm 157
Rothschild Pork Chops with Raspberry Sauce 58

S

Salisbury Steak 60
Sandusky 125
Sara's Amish Dressing 40
Sauces and Salsas, Ltd. 163
Sauerkraut Pie 203
Sausage and Kale Soup 123
Sauteed Zucchini with Walnuts 125
Savory Pork Chop Bake 58
Scalloped Tomato Casserole 185
Schmierkase Pie 77
Schuchter, Ken 145
Sevilla's Custard Pie 45
Sevilla's Oatmeal Cake 44
Shaker Corned Beef and Cabbage 42
Shaker Heights 42
Shakers 34, 185
Shamrock Vineyard 6, 135, 142

Shamrock White Sangria 142
Sheila's Banana Bread 201
Shorter, Toni 160-161
Silver Creek Farm 115-119, 124
Simmons, Lorine 105
Sister Lizzie's Sugar Cream Pie 44
Smith Dave & Carol 130
Smith, George R. 31-33
Smucker's 154
Smucker's Apricot Chicken 166
Snickerdoodles 201
Southern Peach Pork 60
Sowash, Rick 8, 87
Soybeans 20
Spaghetti Squash with Garlic and
    Parmesan 124
Spangler Candy Co. 156
Spatzle 42
Spray Farm 111
Stevens, Andrew 114
Stewart, Linda 123
Stouffer's 155
Stouffer's Original Dutch Apple Pie 170
Straub, Adele 125
Strawberry Coffeecake 200
Strawberry Rosé Crepes 148
Stuffed Nasturtiums 120
Succotash 28
Sugarcreek 31
Summer Vegetable Medley 28
Sunnyside Farms 121
Sunnyside Farms Roast Leg of Lamb Dijon
    126
Swank, Bill 112-113
Swartzentruber, David 31, 35, 36-39
Swartzentruber, Sevilla 36-39, 44, 45
Swiss Steak 61

T
T. Marzetti Co. 164, 165
Thomas, Dave 154
3 Islands Madeira 137
3 Islands Madeira Cheesy Chowder 144
Toledo 83, 85, 178
Tomato Bisque 183
Tomato Butter 182
Tomato & Green Bean Salad with Lemon
    Vinaigrette 184
Tomato Pudding 186
Tomato-Onion Sauce 85
Tomatoes 172-177
Tony Packo's Hungarian Stuffed Cabbage
    85
Tony Packo's 176
Trees for the Future 94-95
Troy 194
Turkey Cutlets in Catawba Cream Sauce
    143
Tweeten, Luther 111-114

U
Urbana 130, 157

V
Valley Vineyards Pork Ragout 145
VanZile, Sheila 201
Vargas, Delia 83
Veal Romano 65
Velasquez, Baldemar 178-181
Vernon, Russ 122
Vince, Maxine and Judy's Spaghetti Sauce
    76
Voinovich, George & Janet 96

W
Wadsworth 126
Waldorf Slaw Salad 164
Wale, Ruth 151
Walleye White Walleye 146
Walnut and Poppy Seed Kuchen 77
Waynesville 203
Weinstein, Paula 84
Weiss, the Rev. Carol 80
Weiss, Mrs. Louis 124
Welzel, Karin 203
Wendy's Pesto 120
Wendy's Hamburgers 154
West Side Market 10, 66-71
West Point Market 122
Wheat 20
Wherley, Carrie 82
White Castle Systems 155
Whitefeather Farm 126
Williams, Bill 160-162
Wine 132-137
Wm. Graystone Wine Omelet 149
Wm. Graystone Winery 136
Wood, Janet 104
Wooster 173

Y
Yannacey, Mike 75
Yoder, Katie 46, 47
Yoder, Sara 40
Youngquist, Ruth 77
YZ Enterprises 158

Z
Zaliouk, Yuval 158
Zay, Gary & Kathy 121, 126
Zesty Barbecue Beef Sandwiches 62
Zoar 34, 42
Zucchini-Oatmeal Bread 202

We made this book.

Right:

Story author **James Hope** of Bowling Green grew up in New England and moved to Ohio in 1976. He teaches journalism at Bowling Green State University, where he shares an office and many ideas with Dr. James H. Bissland. Recipe author **Susan Failor** of Dublin graduated cum laude in home economics from Michigan State University, but has lived in Ohio for many years. She is a professional home economist and consultant to major food companies.

Bottom row, left to right:

Paul Patton of Maple Heights, cover painter, is a retired elementary school principal. He grew up in Rix Mills and often paints his memories of it. **Janet Wood** of London, consulting editor for recipes, was raised on a farm in Van Wert County. She works for an insurance company, collects cookbooks, and cooks. **Barbara Vogel** of Columbus, the book's photographer, is a portrait and art photographer who grew up in Granville. She has received many awards, and teaches photography. **Gene Hite** (front) and **Dean Kette**, designers of the book, are the principals of Design Communication, Inc., of Upper Arlington.

Typesetter:
UniGraphics, Bowling Green State University. Nancy Lee Nelson, production manager.

Printer:
Thomson-Shore, Inc., Dexter, Michigan. Diane Nourse, customer representative.

Cover Separations:
SFC Graphics, Inc., Toledo. Kim Cribb, customer service.

Assistant Editor:
Andrew J. Bissland, Bowling Green.

Communications and Marketing Consultant:
Jo Ellen Helmlinger, Columbus.

Production Consultant:
Will Underwood, Kent.

Photographic Processing:
The Image Source, Toledo.

Colophon: *Using text written in WordPerfect 5.1 on MS-DOS computers, Uni-Graphics composed the text of this book in Clearface on a Varityper 4300P PostScript imagesetter. The book is printed on 60-lb. Glatfelter natural booktext.*

Sources of Pictures Not Otherwise Credited:
Page 2: Bowling Green State University Center for Archival Collections; page 14: Ohio State University Archives; page 30: Cleveland Public Library Photograph Collection; page 48: National Agricultural Library (top) and Ohio Pork Producers Council (bottom); page 66: Cleveland Public Library Photograph Collection; page 86: Bowling Green State University Center for Archival Collections; page 106: Ohio Historical Society; page 132: Bowling Green State University Center for Archival Collections; page 152: Ohio Historical Society; page 172: Reynoldsburg-Truro Historical Society; page 190: Ohio Historical Society; page 206: Western Reserve Historical Society.

Books of Interest from Gabriel's Horn

BOUNTIFUL OHIO, by James Hope and Susan Failor (1993). A celebration of the food and people of the state where America's Heartland begins. This 224-page book offers 163 down-home recipes, plus lore about Ohioans and their bountiful state. Generously illustrated with pictures both old and new. *Softcover:* $21.95 postpaid; *hardcover:* $32.95; *signed and numbered limited first edition, first printing* (while supplies last): $62.95 postpaid.

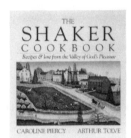

THE SHAKER COOKBOOK, by Caroline Piercy and Arthur Tolve (1984). The latest revision of a classic, this 192-page book is filled with delicious, authentic recipes updated for modern convenience. And there's abundant historical lore and many drawings of Shaker artifacts. *Softcover:* $14.95 postpaid.

INTRODUCING THE SHAKERS, by Diana Van Kolken (1985). The first pocket guide that concisely answers all the most commonly asked questions about the Shakers...and provides a directory of interesting sites as well, all in 64 pages. *Softcover:* $5.50 postpaid.

SISTER JENNIE'S SHAKER DESSERTS, by Arthur Tolve and James Bissland (1983). A collectors' item, this 48-page book contains the treasured dessert recipes of Sister Jennie M. Wells—both in her own writing AND in modern versions tested and edited for today's cooks. *Softcover:* $5.50 postpaid.

Call 800/235-4676 or write: Gabriel's Horn, Dept. B, P.O. Box 141, Bowling Green, OH 43402

- -

Please try your local store first. If not available, you may order directly from the publisher.

All prices include shipping and handling. Satisfaction guaranteed; books may be returned for a full refund.

(Order form may be photocopied)

Mail form and payment to:

Gabriel's Horn Publishing Co.
Department B
P.O. Box 141
Bowling Green, OH 43402

Quantity	Title and Edition	Price each	Total
_____	BOUNTIFUL OHIO (soft)	$21.95	_____
_____	BOUNTIFUL OHIO (hard)	32.95	_____
_____	BOUNTIFUL OHIO (limited)	62.95	_____
_____	THE SHAKER COOKBOOK	14.95	_____
_____	SISTER JENNIE'S DESSERTS	5.50	_____
_____	INTRODUCING THE SHAKERS	5.50	_____
Y or N	UPS instead of mail		$1.00
	Ohio orders add 6% tax		_____

TOTAL AMOUNT ENCLOSED _____

(Orders sent by mail unless UPS requested at $1 extra per total order)

Name _____

Address _____

City _____ State _____ ZIP _____

We're looking for MORE good food! *Can you help?*

At Gabriel's Horn, we're cooking up more books about Ohio. But we can't do it without you. Please write and tell us about **(1)** the best Ohio eating places you know, *ones worth traveling for;* **(2)** the best Ohio food growers, makers or sellers, big or small, *who are "something special;"* **(3)** the best Ohio recipes *you are willing to share.* And if you have comments about this book, or ideas for others, we'd like them, too. (Please don't use cards for ordering books.) Thank you! *James Hope and Susan Failor.*

Gabriel's Horn Publishing Co., P.O. Box 141, Bowling Green, OH 43402.

Here are my OHIO favorites:
1. Ohio eating places worth traveling for.
2. Ohio food growers, makers or sellers, big or small, who are "something special."
3. Best Ohio recipes to share (titles only. We'll send our recipe forms).
4. Also, if you wish, comments about this book...
5. And ideas for other books.

Please print:
Name ....
Address ....
City .... State .... ZIP ....

Here are my OHIO favorites:
1. Ohio eating places worth traveling for.
2. Ohio food growers, makers or sellers, big or small, who are "something special."
3. Best Ohio recipes to share (titles only. We'll send our recipe forms).
4. Also, if you wish, comments about this book...
5. And ideas for other books.

Please print:
Name ....
Address ....
City .... State .... ZIP ....

We're looking for MORE good food! *Can you help?*

At Gabriel's Horn, we're cooking up more books about Ohio. But we can't do it without you. Please write and tell us about **(1)** the best Ohio eating places you know, *ones worth traveling for;* **(2)** the best Ohio food growers, makers or sellers, big or small, *who are "something special;"* **(3)** the best Ohio recipes *you are willing to share.* And if you have comments about this book, or ideas for others, we'd like them, too. (Please don't use cards for ordering books.) Thank you! *James Hope and Susan Failor.*

Gabriel's Horn Publishing Co., P.O. Box 141, Bowling Green, OH 43402.